D0991612

THE
WOMEN'S ATLAS
OF THE
UNITED STATES

REVISED EDITION

Timothy H. Fast & Cathy Carroll Fast

Facts On File®

AN INFOBASE HOLDINGS COMPANY

THE WOMEN'S ATLAS OF THE UNITED STATES, Revised Edition

Facts On File, Inc.
460 Park Avenue South
New York NY 10016

Library of Congress Cataloging-in-Publication Data
Fast, Timothy.
The women's atlas of the United States / by Timothy H. Fast &
Cathy Carroll Fast. — Rev. ed.
p.   cm.
Includes bibliographical references and index.
Contents: Demographics — Education — Employment —
Family — Health — Crime — Politics.
ISBN 0–8160–2970–9
1. Women—United States—Maps.   2. Women—United
States—Economic conditions.   3. Women—United States—
Social conditions.   4. Sex distribution (Demography)—
United States—Maps.   I. Fast, Cathy Carroll.   II. Facts on
File, Inc.   III. Title.
G1201.E1G5   1995   <G&M>
305.4'0973'022—dc20   94–29084
                                                                      CIP
                                                                      MAP

Facts On File books are available at special discounts when purchased in bulk quantities for businesses, associations, institutions or sales promotions. Please call our Special Sales Department in New York at 212/683-2244 or 800/322-8755.

Text Design : Jo Stein
Jacket Design: Semadar Megged

Manufactured by Toppan Printing Co.
Printed in China

10 9 8 7 6 5 4 3 2 1

This book is printed on acid-free paper.

To our children, Laura and Adam,
who saw to it that we never forgot
what is really important in life.

ACKNOWLEDGMENTS

Of those who provided assistance and support during this project, we would like to thank:

Our co-workers at ICF Kaiser, Inc., in Richland, Washington, who encouraged us and tolerated our distraction during this project.

For research assistance, Julius Fast, and librarians at the following libraries: the Law Library of the Attorney General of Washington, Olympia, Washington; Whitman College, Walla Walla, Washington; and the State Library of Washington, Olympia, Washington.

Our thanks also for the support of our families on the east coast and particularly to our west coast family, Lee and Lorraine D'Alessandro, for opening their home and hearts to us.

CONTENTS

Washington
Montana
North Dakota
Minnesota
Oregon
Idaho
South Dakota
Wisconsin
Michigan
Wyoming
Iowa
Nebraska
Nevada
Utah
Colorado
California
Illinois
Indiana
Ohio
Kansas
Missouri
Kentucky
Arizona
New Mexico
Oklahoma
Arkansas
Tennessee
Texas
Mississippi
Alabama
Georgia
Louisiana
Florida
Alaska
Hawaii
New Hampshire
Vermont
Maine
Massachusetts
New York
Rhode Island
Connecticut
Pennsylvania
New Jersey
Delaware
Maryland
West Virginia
Virginia
North Carolina
South Carolina

MAJOR CITIES

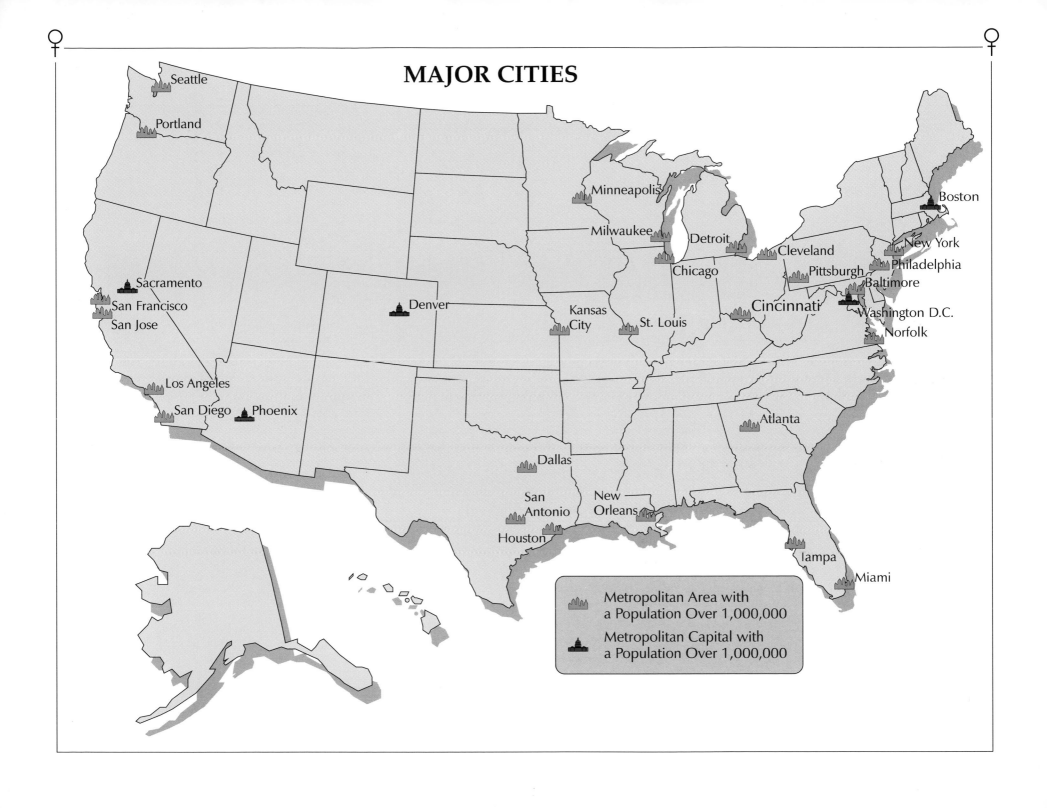

GEOGRAPHIC REGIONS*

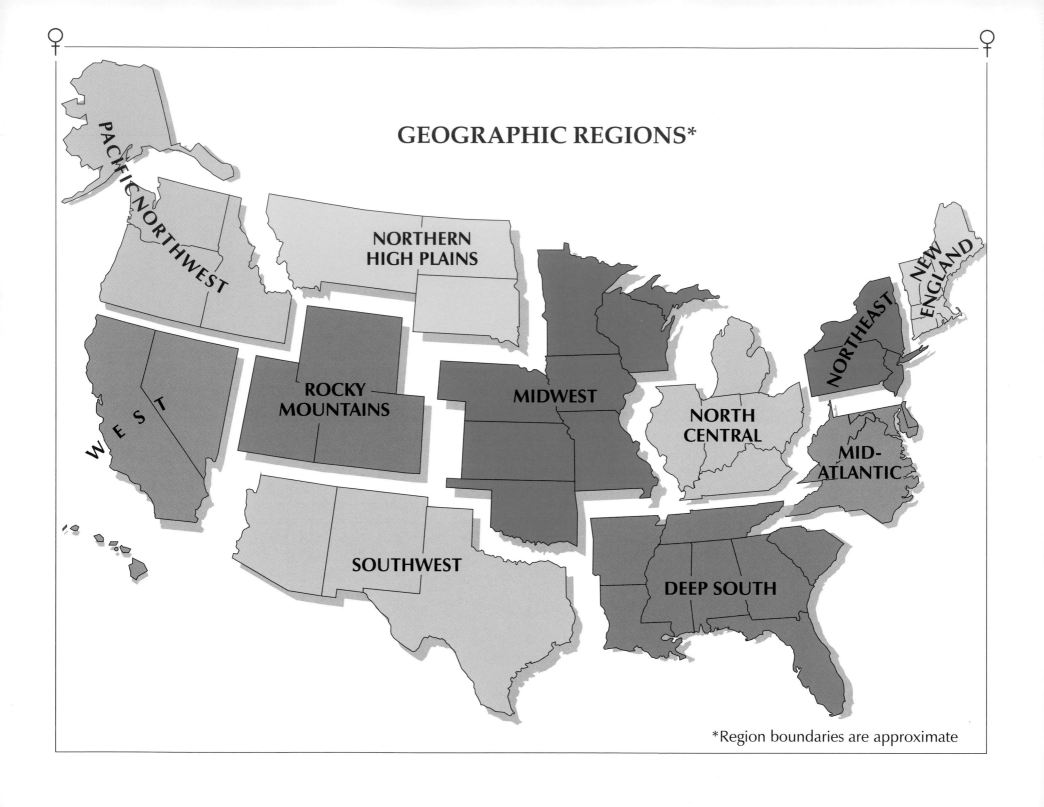

PACIFIC NORTHWEST

NORTHERN HIGH PLAINS

NEW ENGLAND

NORTHEAST

WEST

ROCKY MOUNTAINS

MIDWEST

NORTH CENTRAL

MID-ATLANTIC

SOUTHWEST

DEEP SOUTH

*Region boundaries are approximate

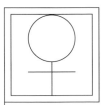 # INTRODUCTION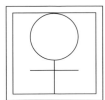

A decade ago, when we wrote the previous edition of this atlas, the new conservatism was in full swing. Ronald Reagan had just begun his second term in office and many of the rights that woman had fought for were being challenged. The Reagan administration saw a marked decrease in funding for family planning clinics, shelters for abused women, federally funded day-care centers and other providers of services to women and children. It also mounted the attack on *Roe v. Wade* culminating in the 1989 Supreme Court decision in *Webster v. Reproductive Health Services*—the most serious threat to a woman's right to choose an abortion.

The 1990s have brought some drastic changes, particularly in the political arena. In 1992, women won more seats in federal, state and local elections than at any time in history. A record six women now sit in the United States Senate, one of which is the first African-American woman to be elected senator.

The passage of the Family Leave Bill early in the Clinton administration is a small step in the right direction toward helping American families cope with the prolonged illness of a family member or the need to be at home with a new baby.

This is a time when women face new and greater challenges. We have included topics in this atlas that were not so prominent when the first atlas was published. Ten years ago, AIDS among women was so rare that it was not even mentioned. Now it is a reality and a concern to all women. Women are also meeting new challenges in the workplace, balancing work and motherhood. More mothers are employed than ever before, making the availability of safe and affordable day care of paramount importance. Homelessness among women is a greater problem today than ten years ago.

The falling of the Berlin Wall, the reunification of Germany and the breakup of the Soviet Union—all seemed impossible in 1985. War in the Persian Gulf brought women closer to combat than ever before. These and other events have both directly and indirectly changed women's lives. A new edition of the *Women's Atlas of the United States* was needed to examine issues of importance to women today and to see how these issues have changed over the past ten years.

This atlas explores events involving women and their lives geographically. It will tell you that the Northern High Plains has the greatest percentage of women with post-graduate degrees as compared to men. You will also learn that women residing in the northern Midwest have the longest life expectancy while those in the Deep South have the shortest. Although the atlas will supply specific information on the geography of women, our hope is that it will also open the door to further study of the issues examined here. Why do women in Alaska have such a low incidence of heart disease? Why do state legislatures in the West have more women legislators than in the East? You will discover that there are regional differences in attitudes about women. Change has come more slowly to some states than to others. Differences between women and men may be more marked in some regions than in others. Examination of the maps will give you a picture of the diversity that exists.

We have included topics in the atlas that we believe are of importance to women. Education, employment, family, health, crime and politics represent areas of great concern to women and changes in these areas can have the greatest impact on women's futures. In addition, we have included a section on the demographics of women to use as a foundation for a basic geography of women.

You, of course, should formulate your own questions about the geography of women. How do the topics we examine differ for women and for men? How does your home state fit into the nation as a whole? Do your state and its neighbors combine to form a regional pattern? A common theory among geographers is that the differences among regions increase as they get further apart. Likewise, areas that are close tend to be more homogeneous. In instances when the theory doesn't hold, it máy be interesting to explore the reasons why.

We hope that these statistics will not be viewed merely as indicators of the degree to which women have "caught up" or not "caught up" with men. We hope, rather, that they will be viewed as indicators of women's participation in areas that significantly affect their lives. Are women's voices being heard in a partic-

ular region? What is the level of opportunity available to women in a particular state? Are women participating more as doctors, teachers or politicians in some regions than in others? These maps show the differing levels of participation by women from state to state and the ground yet to be made up before true equality is attained.

The preparation of this atlas differed greatly from the previous edition. The past ten years have seen an explosion in computer technology. While the maps of the previous atlas were prepared by hand, the maps for this edition were created entirely on a computer. This allowed a more interactive design process in which we could introduce a greater variety of map styles and charts.

DECIPHERING MAPS

Many of us have limited map reading skills. Unfortunately, public schools in the United States have never stressed geographic or cartographic skills as a part of a basic education. As a result, many people find maps both intimidating and confusing. Maps, like charts and diagrams, present information in a visual format. But unlike those other graphic forms, maps have the unique ability to associate information with a place. Through the use of symbols and color, maps can show where something is located, as well as qualitative or quantitative information about it.

Thematic mapping involves designing a map that depicts the spatial distribution of a particular set of data. This is opposed to the kind of map that most of us are familiar with, those used for navigational or location purposes. If you glance through the sections of this atlas, you will discover six basic types of thematic maps that depict different kinds of geographic information. Since many people are unfamiliar with different styles of map presentation, a brief discussion on how to read the maps is in order.

Choropleth Maps

This is the most common thematic map type used in the atlas and one of the easiest to read. In a choropleth map, information is ranked from the highest to the lowest values and then divided into several groups or classes of values. Each data class is represented on the map by a different color. The colors are arranged from light to dark or through logical progression of hues (for example: yellow to orange to red) to parallel the progression of low to high values.

Typically the data will be divided into no more than six classes. The average person cannot easily distinguish more than seven shades of a color when they are distributed throughout a map. Because most choropleth maps use classed data, the choice of how that data is divided will influence the appearance of the map. For the majority of the choropleth maps the data have been classed into round numbers (for example: 10, 20, 100, 250, etc.).

When looking at a choropleth map you need not limit yourself to knowing the values of individual states. It is equally important to observe any broad regional patterns that may exist by looking at clusters of states that share the same color. For example, a strong east–west distribution can be seen in the "Suicide" (Health section) map. A north–south distribution can be seen in the "Volunteer Work" (Employment section)

map. Examples of regional patterns can be observed in the "Secondary School Teachers" (Education section) and "Women in Nursing Homes" (Health section).

Two-Variable Choropleth Maps

Information from two related choropleth maps can be combined to form a single map known as a two-variable choropleth map. The process of reading this type of map is similar to that for a regular choropleth map, but requires working in two dimensions instead of one. The "Marriage vs. Divorce" (Family section) can be used as an example. In this map there are two variables, or types of information, being compared: marriage rates and divorce rates. By consulting the legend we see that it is divided into nine sections with each section representing one of the possible combinations of the two variables. In the example of "Marriage vs. Divorce" all of the colors in the legend are different variations of green, a mixture of blue and yellow. In this example, marriage rates are represented by shades of blue:

- •Above Average Rates = Dark Blue
- •Average Rates = Blue
- •Below Average Rates = Light Blue

Divorce rates are represented by shades of yellow:

- •Above Average Rates = Dark Yellow
- •Average Rates = Yellow
- •Below Average Rates = Light Yellow

Therefore, the color of each section of the legend is formed by the mixture of the blues and yellows representing marriage and divorce rates respectively. The table below outlines the mixtures of the colors in the legend.

MARRIAGE RATE	MARRIAGE COLOR	DIVORCE RATE	DIVORCE COLOR	COMBINATION COLOR
Above Average	Dark Blue	Above Average	Dark Yellow	Dark Green
Above Average	Dark Blue	Average	Yellow	Blue-Green
Above Average	Dark Blue	Below Average	Light Yellow	Dark Blue-Green
Average	Blue	Above Average	Dark Yellow	Med. Yellow-Green
Average	Blue	Average	Yellow	Green
Average	Blue	Below Average	Light Yellow	Med. Blue-Green
Below Average	Light Blue	Above Average	Dark Yellow	Dark Yellow-Green
Below Average	Light Blue	Average	Yellow	Yellow-Green
Below Average	Light Blue	Below Average	Light Yellow	Light Green

Other examples of two variable choropleth maps are:

"Place of Abortion vs. State of Residence" (Health section)

"Democratic and Republican Committees" (Politics section)

Symbol and Graduated Symbol Maps

Sometimes instead of using color to classify state data, we can use different symbols or different sizes of a symbol placed within each state to represent its data value. Important to note is that the symbol does not reflect an actual location within the state, as with the dot map discussed below, but rather represents the state as a whole. An example of a symbol map is "Women Cabinet Appointees" (Politics section) while "Death from Heart Disease" (Health section) is an example of a graduated symbol map. In several cases we have combined both choropleth and symbol mapping techniques on the same map. An example is "Teenage Marriage and Age of Consent" where the percentage of teenage marriages is represented by shading and the age of consent is represented by graduated symbols.

Pie Chart Maps

Pie chart maps are a special kind of symbol map. Most of us are familiar with pie charts from their use in diagrams or charts. A circle is divided into wedges each representing a percentage of the total "pie." On a pie chart map, each state has a pie chart containing information specific to that state. In the table below are sample pie charts divided into several selected percentages to give you an idea of how much each percentage divides the pie.

Representative Pie Wedges

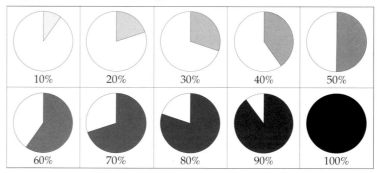

Dot Maps and Graduated Circle Maps

Dot maps are very simple to read. An example of a dot map is "Women's Studies Programs" (Education section). In this map, each dot represents the location of a college or university that offers a women's studies program. The dot size may also be varied to represent different magnitudes of data. Circles are used to represent the larger magnitudes. The actual location of the variable is at the center of the circle. The map "Women's Correctional Institutions" (Crime section) is an example of a graduated circle map.

Cartograms

The cartogram is one of the most dramatic map styles. It can, however, be somewhat confusing at first. In a cartogram, the area of the state is proportional to the data being mapped. An example of a cartogram is the "Most Populus Sex" (Demographics section) map. Since the sizes of the states must be adjusted to match the relative size of the data, their shapes may be distorted to preserve the topological relationships with neighboring states.

In addition to understanding different mapping techniques, it is equally important to have the ability to tell one geographic region, state or city from another. For those of you unfamiliar with some states' locations, we have included a map labeling all the states as a guide. Note that Alaska and Hawaii are located in the lower left-hand corner. Hawaii, of course, is far south and west in the Pacific and Alaska is on the northwestern border of Canada. Actual locations cannot be shown because of their great distances from the continental United States. Also keep in mind that the scale at which Alaska is drawn is much smaller than that of the other states.

It is also helpful to know the locations of large urban areas. To familiarize you with the location of the major cities of the United States, we have included a map showing the location of 31 of the largest metropolitan areas with populations greater than 1,000,000 as of 1990.

Finally, you will discover that we refer to various portions of the country by regional geographic names. Regions such as the Midwest, Deep South and Southwest are not well defined. In fact, geographers often disagree as to what areas are included in a given region. The Midwest provides an excellent example. Depending on where people come from and their experience in travel, definitions of the Midwest will vary to a great extent. At one extreme, the Midwest has been defined as an area contained entirely within Ohio, Indiana and Illinois, and at the other, it is viewed as a region covering 14 states from Ohio to Colorado and from North Dakota to Texas.

To give you an approximate idea of our definition of these different regions, a map has been included that identifies 11 geographic regions in the United States. Please be aware that the boundaries between any two areas are never exact and that the regional map is to serve only as a guide to the text. Also note that data for the District of Columbia have been combined with that of Maryland in most cases.

A WORD ABOUT DATA

One of the most important data handling techniques is that of standardization. In many cases, mapping data in raw form is not very useful. If we did, then most of the maps in the atlas would simply reflect the population distribution of the United States. That is, states with larger populations would consistently show a greater value than the more sparsely populated states. To prevent this problem, we have standardized most of the data to eliminate differences based on population size.

One way to standardize data is to express it as a rate, or as the number of occurrences for a specified number of units. As an example, City A with a population of 5,000 might have 100 deaths from cancer, whereas City B, population 8,000, might have 120 deaths. Even though City B has a higher actual number of cancer deaths, data standardization using a rate will show that City A actually has a higher incidence of cancer mortality *relative* to its population. If we establish our unit as 1,000 persons, we can see that City A had 20 deaths for every 1,000 persons, whereas City B had only 15.

Percentages are a special kind of rate. The base population of each state, whatever its actual size, is considered to be 100%. The data are then expressed as a proportion of that amount. For example, 50% of secondary school teachers in one state might be women, as compared to 20% in another. It no longer matters that the total number of teachers differs from state to state. We are interested in relative proportions.

In addition to standardizing the data, we have tried to collect data from the same time period. The data for the majority of the maps are from 1990. For those maps whose information is for years other than 1990, the date is noted on the map. As much as possible data were standardized against the base populations from the same time period. For maps where data was from a year other than 1990, we had to use 1990 population figures, because female/male state-by-state population estimates for other years were not available.

If you acquaint yourself with the sources of our data, you will note that most are from government agencies. One of the most massive data collection efforts is that undertaken by the United States Bureau of the Census every ten years. The 1990 census contains a wealth of information about education, employment, income, family structure and ethnic origin for the whole country and municipal levels. Census information and information from many other government agencies are available to the public at many libraries, or directly from the agency concerned.

The accuracy of statistics can legitimately be called into question. Thus, we thought it would be useful to offer some cautions in regard to the 1990 Census data. While the Bureau of the Census conducts one of the most efficient and professional data collection operations of this magnitude in the world, 100% accuracy is impossible to achieve. The concerns mentioned in regard to census data are applicable to any set of statistical information from any source.

Census statistics are based on either complete count or sample data. With complete count data, the base population includes all relevant persons in a given area. For example, if we wanted to know the percentage of women in Seattle who had a high school diploma, we would do a survey in which we personally asked each and every women in Seattle about the status of her high school education. The percentage of high school graduates would be based on the complete population. Such a survey, however, would be very time consuming because of the large number of women who would be questioned. An alternative strategy would be to sample just 1,000 women. Perhaps 730 of these women had high school diplomas. We would then infer, on the basis of our sample population, that approximately 73% of all Seattle women were high school graduates.

It is imperative that the sample population be representative. An accurate cross section must be taken of all the women in the city. If we were not careful to se-lect a representative sample, our data might be very misleading. Perhaps we selected our 1,000 women from a very disadvantaged section of the city. Their level of educational attainment would not necessarily be an accurate representation of the educational level for women in the city as a whole. Even complete count data, while preferable to the sample variety, is often not 100% accurate if large numbers of people are in-volved. For example, it is particularly easy to under-count low income people, people in remote areas or people who do not speak English.

Statisticians at the Census Bureau have worked hard to devise techniques and sampling procedures that minimize sampling errors as much as possible. You should remember, though, that figures derived from sample data are very carefully designed estimates. The Census contains technical appendices that yield infor-mation on possible sampling errors.

Another potential source of error in any survey lies in the persons answering questioners. Sometimes peo-ple make a mistake, sometimes they have not remem-bered correctly, sometimes, particularly when sensitive issues are discussed, they simply lie.

Familiarize yourself with the mapping techniques, carefully examine the legend and find examples of each category on the map. Look at individual states and see where they fit in the legend. Finally look at the country as a whole and try to get a feeling for any re-gional patterns that may emerge. Enjoy your explo-ration of the geography of women!

DEMOGRAPHICS

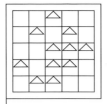
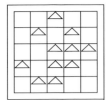

"We want to unite our . . . sisters into a solid whole, so that they can call to each other."[1]

—Ch'iu Chin (1874–1907)

This atlas focuses on issues common to women. To create the maps identifying these issues it is necessary to find the "average" American woman. To discover the "average" American woman we must look at all women and their lives. Among other variables, their race, age, education and place of residence must be compared with one another, thus creating a portrait of the average woman.

Who is the average American woman? She differs in each state. These differences contribute to regional variations. For example, the average age of women in Pennsylvania is 38. Compare this with the average age in Texas of 32. These state averages combine with their neighbors to reach predictable regional averages. Pennsylvania combines with New York and New Jersey for an average age in the Northeast region of 37, while Texas joins with New Mexico and Arizona for a Southwest regional average of 33. What we will try to do is to compare these regional differences and try to explain why they occur.

It is important to know what makes up the population being examined. In 1980, one in 340, or 0.29%, of women died from heart disease in the United States. Restricting the population to women over 40 would give a different percentage. Examining the data in this manner reveals that a higher percentage of women over 40 die of heart disease than other age groups. Leaving the 40+ age group in the data makes it appear that more young women are dying of heart disease than is actually the case. The 40+ rate of deaths from heart disease "weights" the average, concealing important differences in the base population. It follows that the more homogeneous the base population, the more accurately the statistic will predict the experiences of any one individual.

By looking at nationwide variations in age, ethic origin and place of residence we are able to see regional patterns in areas such as health, education, crime, etc. The maps in this section are basic breakdowns of age, sex, location, etc., and should be viewed in tandem with those in later sections.

While this atlas focuses on the issues and experiences women have in common, it is important not to lose sight of the important differences among them. The problems faced by a woman of a particular ethnic, racial or age group may supersede purely feminist concerns. For example, the growing population of senior citizens may find that the problems of living on a fixed income, dealing with the health care system or coping with the loss of a spouse outweigh any sex-related or engendered problems.

America has a rich ethnic and racial diversity. Immigrants have brought with them languages, values, customs and traditions unique to their cultures and struggled to adapt to mainstream America. Thus we have the concept of America as a melting pot, a blending of cultures. But for some this "melting" process has been difficult, with language and cultural barriers too great to overcome. In this atlas we have focused on five groups: Native Americans, Asians, Hispanics, African Americans, and Whites, each making a unique contribution to America's rich cultural heritage.

The Europeans began coming to this continent in the 16th century searching for economic opportunity and religious freedom. Soon after the Europeans began to arrive, Native Americans began to see their population decline and their culture destroyed. In the 17th, 18th and 19th centuries, African Americans were brought here as slaves for these same Europeans. The expanding industrialization of the 1800s and the famines in Ireland brought immigrants from that country followed by those from Asia as a source of cheap labor. The His-panic influx, which can be of any racial origin, fol-lowed—fleeing oppressive regimes and in search of greater economic opportunity. Today, most immigrants come for one of those reasons.

In order to organize data in a meaningful way, we must divide women into age groups or structures. Here, we have divided women into four age groups based on common concerns.

Childhood (0–14)
The Childbearing Years (15–44)
The Middle Years (45–64)
The Elderly (65+)

The concerns of each age group differ. The formative childhood years (0 to 14) are critical. These are the years when both positive and negative influences have the most impact. Poverty, with its poor nutrition, inadequate health care and substandard housing does the most damage here, while a nurturing environment gives this age group the basic tools it needs to become productive citizens.

Ages 15 to 44 mark the beginning of adult life. These are typically the years when women pursue higher education, select a partner, begin a career and have children.

The middle years, ages 45 to 64, are usually years of great change. Very few women are still having children in this group. Those that have reared families are facing the "empty nest" and must change the focus of their lives from childrearing to other areas. Many choose to begin new careers or to reevaluate and change the directions of their current careers.

The elderly, age 65 and over, are one of the faster growing segments of the population. This age group has historically been associated with retirement and,

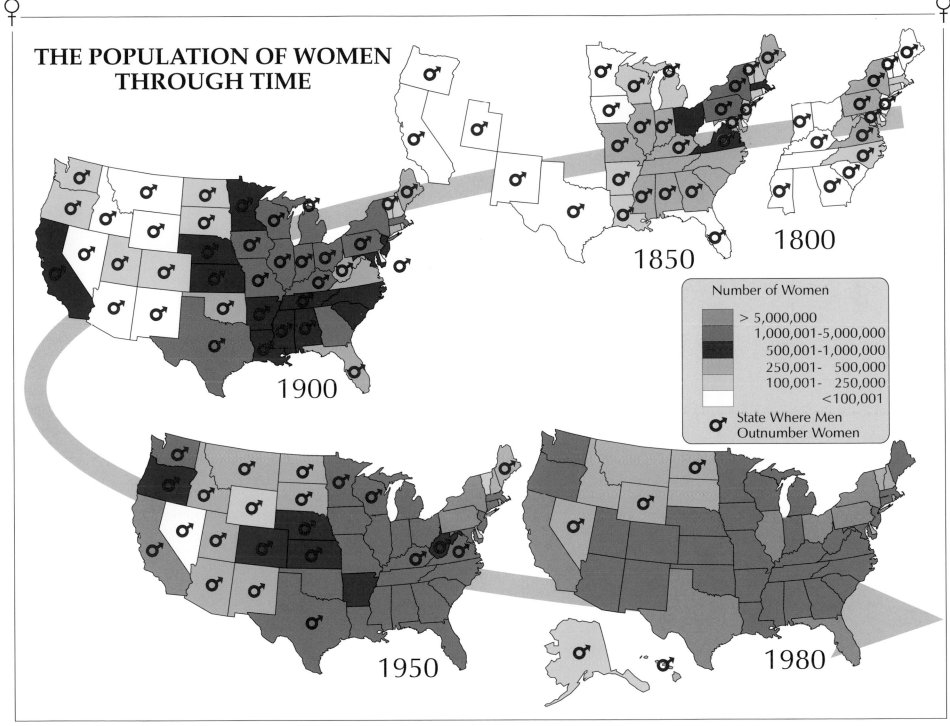

THE POPULATION OF WOMEN THROUGH TIME

1800

1850

1900

1950

1980

Number of Women

> 5,000,000
1,000,001-5,000,000
500,001-1,000,000
250,001- 500,000
100,001- 250,000
<100,001

State Where Men Outnumber Women

11

though many still choose to retire at 65, many others continue working well past traditional retirement age. Members of this group are healthier, are living longer than ever, are increasing their activity and are raising their political voice.

Over time the age structures for a state or region will change. The attitudes and priorities of the preceding generation will affect the age structure of the area. Even climate, religion and the economy can influence age structure. A relatively large percentage of children in a region can be the result of several different factors. For religious or cultural reasons, the previous generation could have favored large families, as is the case in largely Mormon Utah. Or factors such as a growing economy and the return of men home from war can have the same result as is evidenced in the "baby boom" following World War II. The warm climate and reasonable cost of living have changed Florida's age structure as senior citizens continue to flock there, making it among the states having the highest average age for women.

At times it has been necessary to compensate for variations in age structure by restricting our base population to a specific age group. For example, maps showing the percentage of women who are married use a base population of women over the age of 15 instead of a base population of all females. Similarly, the base population on maps dealing with reproductive issues such as birth rates and abortion rates is limited to women in their childbearing years.

In seeking out the "average" woman, we must also examine residential location. Even within a state or region, there is a vast difference between urban and rural environments. For example, New York City residents and farmers in upstate New York probably have vastly different life and environmental experiences. Perhaps women in rural areas have a higher life expectancy than their urban counterparts. Thus, knowing which states are predominantly rural, urban or have an even mixture of both environments becomes important.

The maps that follow will allow you to explore these differences in more detail.

THE MOST POPULOUS SEX

In the United States as a whole, women outnumber men. However, this is a relatively recent development. Our opening map, "The Population of Women Through Time," shows that up until 1950, men outnumbered women in all but a handful of states. In 1950 nearly half of the states had men in the majority and slightly more than half had women in the majority. Since 1950 the tide has turned dramatically and by 1980 only five states had a male majority population. By 1990 that number had dropped even further. The trend of women outnumbering men can be seen as starting in 1900 along the east coast and progressively expanding westward to the present distribution where only four states, California, Nevada, Hawaii and Alaska, have men in the majority. States with men in the majority are shown in purple on the second map, "The Most Populous Sex." This map is a cartogram with the size of each state proportional to the number of women living there in 1990. Viewed in this manner, the northeastern states appear disproportionately large, while many of the western states are reduced to slivers.

The third map, "Women vs. Men," provides more detailed information about the ratio of women to men.

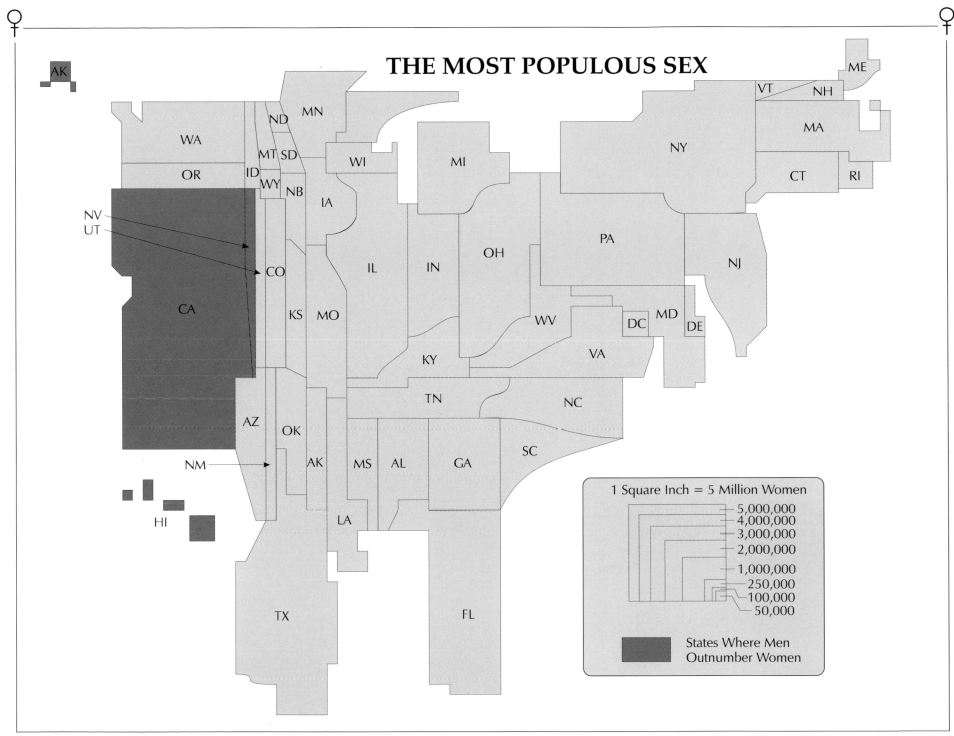

THE MOST POPULOUS SEX

1 Square Inch = 5 Million Women

5,000,000
4,000,000
3,000,000
2,000,000
1,000,000
250,000
100,000
50,000

States Where Men
Outnumber Women

13

WOMEN VS. MEN

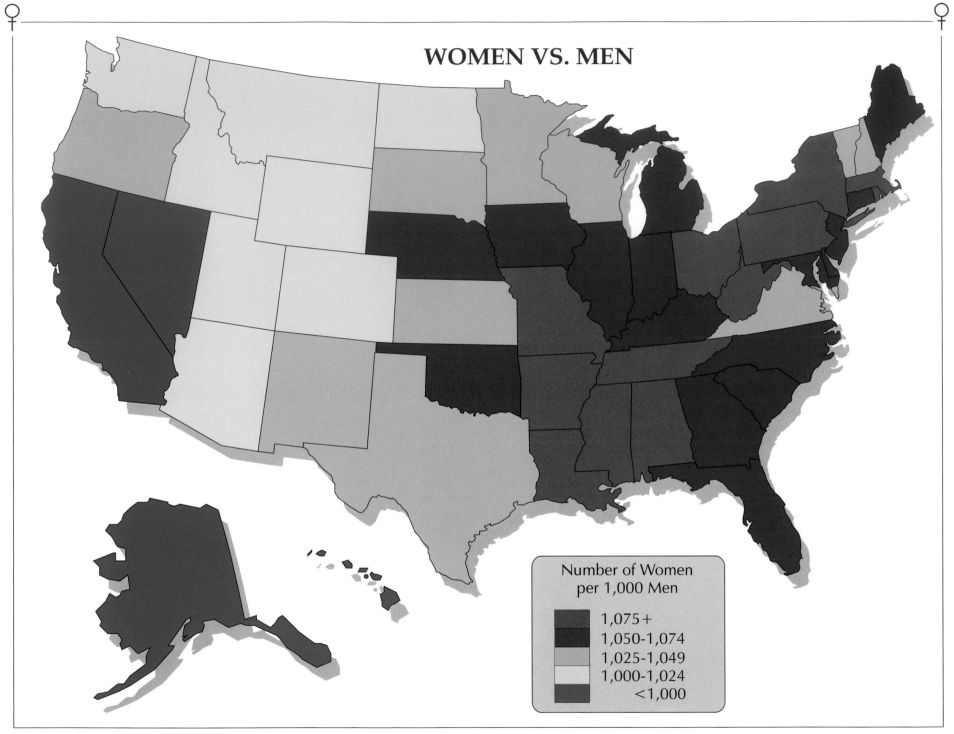

Number of Women
per 1,000 Men

1,075+
1,050-1,074
1,025-1,049
1,000-1,024
<1,000

14

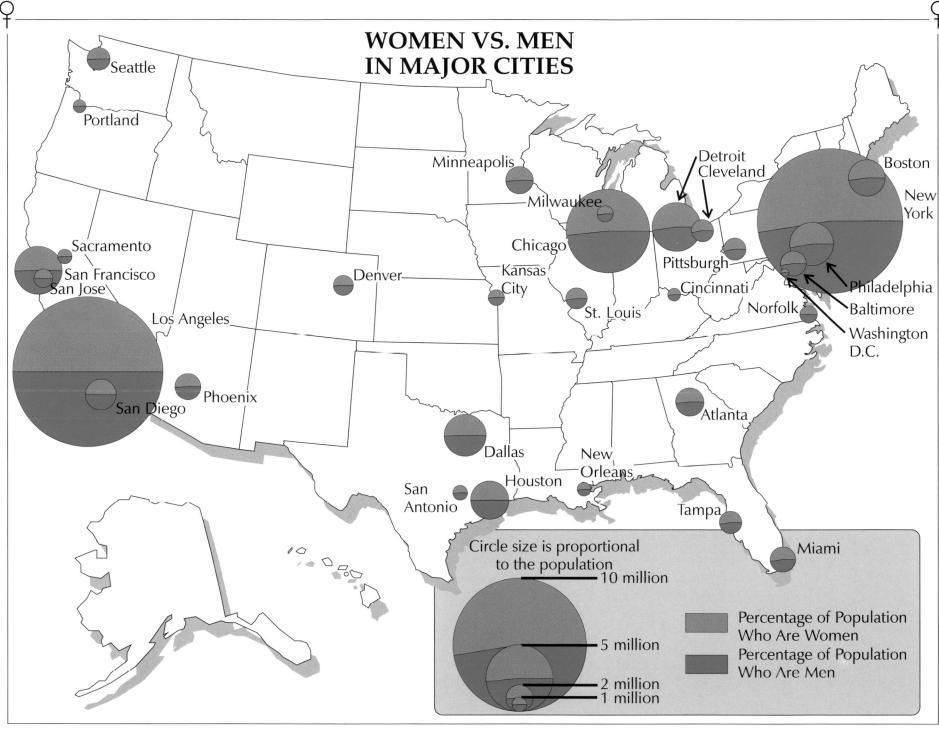

WOMEN VS. MEN
IN MAJOR CITIES

Seattle

Portland

Minneapolis

Milwaukee

Detroit
Cleveland

Boston

New
York

Chicago

Pittsburgh

Sacramento

San Francisco
San Jose

Denver

Kansas
City

Cincinnati

Philadelphia

Baltimore

Los Angeles

St. Louis

Norfolk

Washington
D.C.

San Diego

Phoenix

Atlanta

Dallas

New
Orleans

San
Antonio

Houston

Tampa

Miami

Circle size is proportional
to the population

10 million

5 million

2 million
1 million

Percentage of Population
Who Are Women

Percentage of Population
Who Are Men

15

The proportions range from a low of 898 women per 1,000 men in Alaska to a high of 1,091 women to 1,000 men in Mississippi. In general, the eastern states have a higher female to male ratio than the western states. The map, "Women vs. Men in Major Cities," uses proportionally sized circles to show percentages of women vs. men in major United States cities. In viewing the urban distribution of women vs. men, the same east–west division of the population of women vs. men emerges.

WOMEN AS MINORITIES

This section opens with a pie chart map entitled "Women Minorities (Non-Hispanic)." This map includes African Americans, Asians and Native Americans. A fourth category, Other, includes all remaining minorities. Hispanic women are shown on a separate map, "Hispanic Women," because a woman of Hispanic origin can be of any race. Here, and in many of the maps that follow, the northeastern states have been enlarged to facilitate viewing of the data.

Native American women make up the smallest of the four racial groups. They are more populous in the rural West and in nine states outnumber any other non-Hispanic minority. In Hawaii and 34 states located in the Deep South and Mid-Atlantic regions, Native American women make up less than 1% of all women. In ten states Native Americans are between 1% and 5% of the female population. And in six states, Alaska, Arizona, Montana, New Mexico, Oklahoma and South Dakota, the female Native American population is greater than 5%, with Alaska topping the list at 16%. Higher Native American populations in the West result from the large number of reservations in this part of the country. Alaska owes its large Native American population to the fact that, until the discovery of gold and oil, the state held little of economic interest. What farmland and rangeland the state could offer were dwarfed by the vast expanses of the West and Midwest, thus, Alaska's native populations were not pushed aside in the name of progress as happened in the lower 48 states.

The population of female Asian Americans (included here are Japanese, Chinese, Filipino, Korean, Asian Indian and Vietnamese) has increased significantly in the past ten years. In 1980 they constituted less than 1% of the female population in 36 states. By 1990 that number had decreased to 22. In Hawaii, 64% of women are of Asian descent. The coastal areas of the United States have the highest concentrations of Asians and in major cities on the West coast they are the largest non-Hispanic minority. California is the only state on the mainland where their proportion was more than 5%. The lowest populations of Asian women are found in states running in a roughly diagonal strip from Montana to South Carolina where trade with the Asia-Pacific rim is less of a factor.

African-American women make up the largest racial minority, composing 12% of the total female population. However, in 16 states they were outnumbered by one or both of the other minority groups. In Alaska, Idaho, Maine, Montana, North Dakota and South Dakota both Asian Americans and Native Americans have larger female populations than do African Americans. In general, African-American women are in the minority in the western United States and in northern

WOMEN MINORITIES
(NON-HISPANIC)

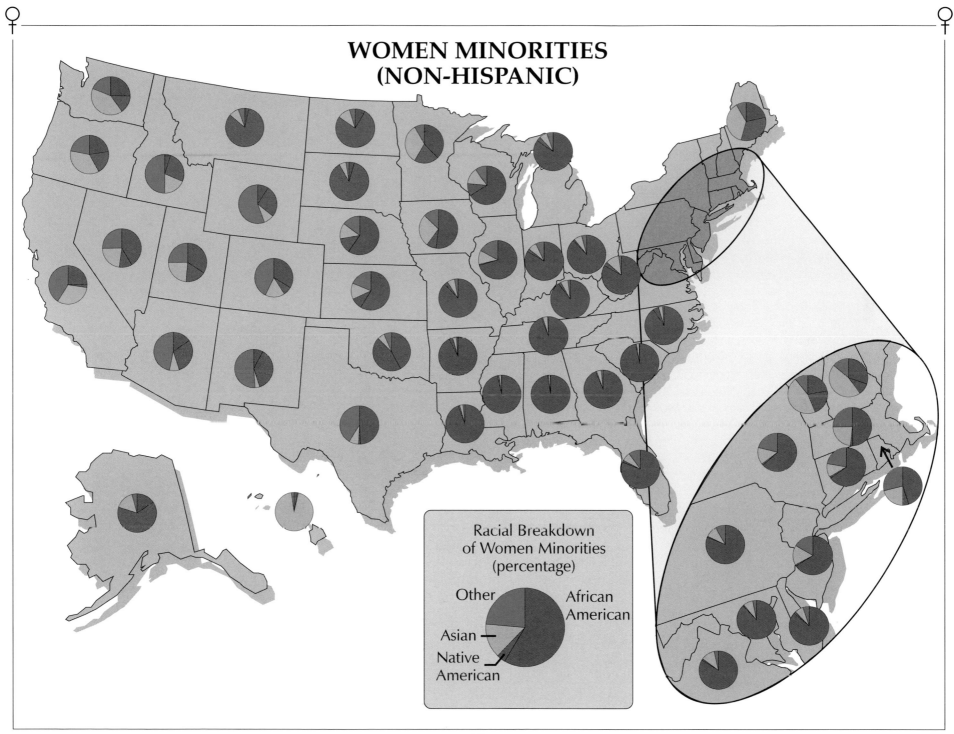

Racial Breakdown
of Women Minorities
(percentage)

Other

African
American

Asian —

Native
American

New England. They constitute less that 1% of the total female population in only eight states, as compared with 36 for Asian women and 35 for Native Americans. They make up more than 10% of the female population in 19 states and in five Deep South states, Alabama, Georgia, Louisiana, Mississippi and South Carolina, and one Mid-Atlantic state, Maryland, African-American women account for more that 25% of the total female population. The largest concentrations of African-American women are in the Deep South, due to the large slave population of pre–Civil War America. After the Civil War, many African Americans migrated to the industrialized urban areas of the Northeast and North Central regions to seek greater economic opportunities.

Women of Hispanic origin, who can be of any racial group, constitute more than 10% of the female population in seven states (see map, "Hispanic Women"). Four of these states, Arizona, California, New Mexico and Texas, border Mexico. These, along with Colorado, are states with an enduring Mexican heritage, while Florida's Hispanic population is largely Cuban. New York's Hispanics have various cultural origins, among them Puerto Rican, Mexican and Cuban, with more than 93% of the state's Hispanic population residing in New York City.

Women who describe themselves as White are the majority in all but one state, Hawaii, where they are only 32% of the total population (see map, "White Women"). In three states, Maine, New Hampshire and Vermont, more than 98% of the female population is White. In eight states scattered throughout the United States, less than 5% of the female population belonged to a racial minority.

Focusing on major cities, we see a somewhat different picture than if we look only at data for the states.

Minority populations tend to be concentrated in major cities. For example, only 2%, or 45,981, of Minnesota's female population is African American. Of that number, more than 95% reside in Minneapolis with the remaining 5% scattered throughout the state. The map, "Women Minorities in Major Cities," shows that in major cities throughout the central and eastern United States, African-American women make up the largest minority group. In fact, in 14 states more than half of the state's African-American and Asian women reside in major cities. Hispanic women residing in major cities of eight different states account for more than 50% of the total Hispanic female population in those states (see map, "Hispanic Women in Major Cities"). Urban Native American females, however, make up half of the total female Native American population in only three states. This suggests that Native Americans, unlike other minority groups, tend to live in rural rather than urban areas.

POPULATION PYRAMIDS THROUGH THE AGES

The population pyramids compare the numbers of women and men in five-year-age increments. Our first group, "Population Pyramids Through Time," reveals how the balance of men and women changed from 1850 through 1980. In 1850 the numbers of women and men appear virtually equal across all age groups. From 1900 on, the numbers of women and men are about equal from birth to the 25–29 year old age groups. From this age group until about age 45, women

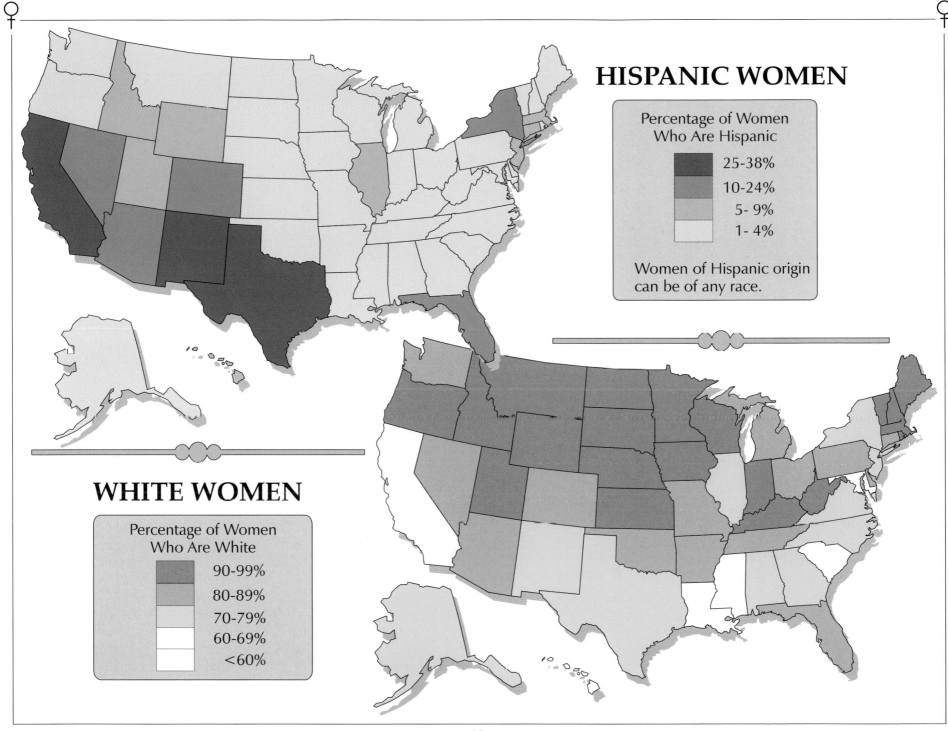

HISPANIC WOMEN

Percentage of Women
Who Are Hispanic

25-38%
10-24%
5- 9%
1- 4%

Women of Hispanic origin
can be of any race.

WHITE WOMEN

Percentage of Women
Who Are White

90-99%
80-89%
70-79%
60-69%
<60%

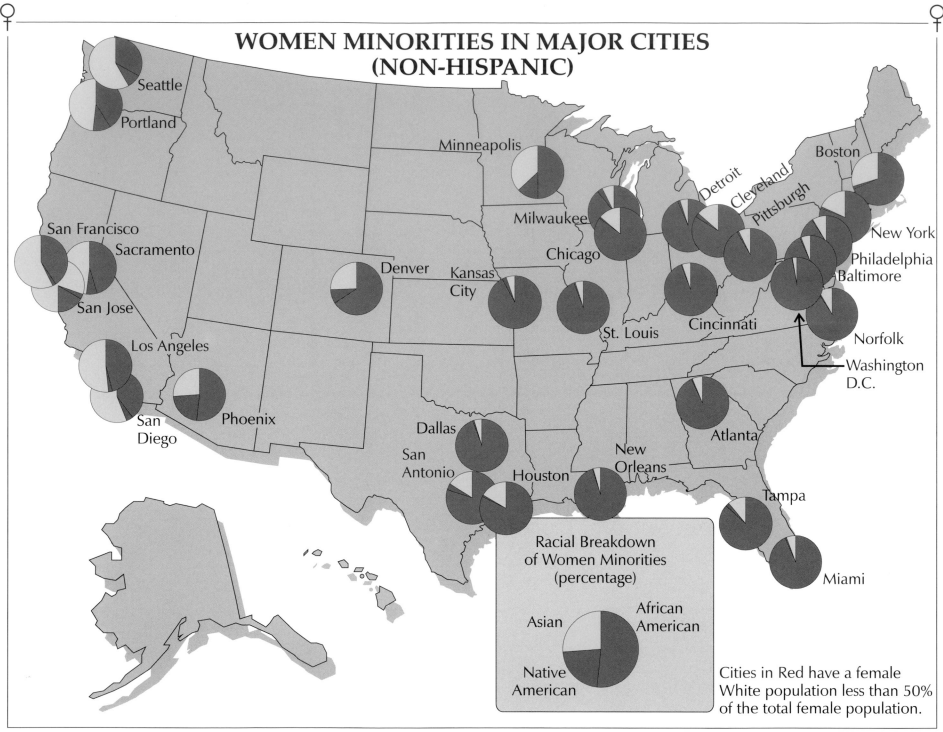

WOMEN MINORITIES IN MAJOR CITIES
(NON-HISPANIC)

Seattle
Portland

San Francisco
Sacramento
San Jose

Los Angeles

San Diego

Phoenix

Minneapolis

Milwaukee

Chicago

Denver

Kansas City

St. Louis

Dallas

San Antonio

Houston

New Orleans

Detroit
Cleveland
Pittsburgh

Boston

New York

Philadelphia
Baltimore

Cincinnati

Norfolk

Washington D.C.

Atlanta

Tampa

Miami

Racial Breakdown of Women Minorities (percentage)

Asian

African American

Native American

Cities in Red have a female White population less than 50% of the total female population.

20

HISPANIC WOMEN IN MAJOR CITIES

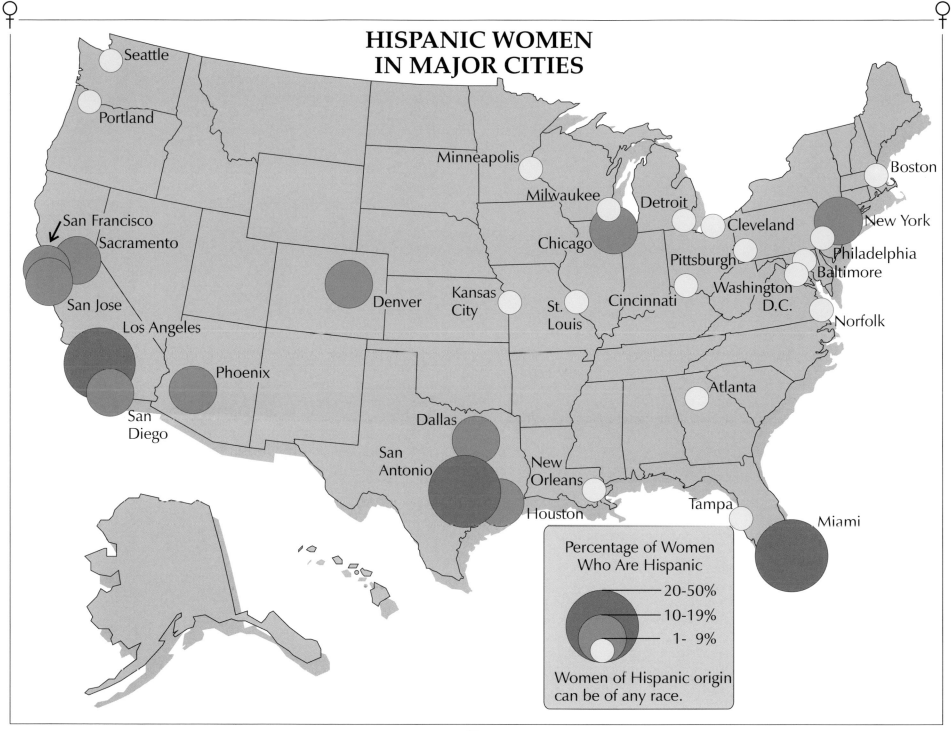

Seattle
Portland
Minneapolis
Milwaukee
Detroit
Boston
San Francisco
Sacramento
Chicago
Cleveland
New York
Pittsburgh
Philadelphia
Baltimore
San Jose
Washington D.C.
Los Angeles
Denver
Kansas City
St. Louis
Cincinnati
Norfolk
Phoenix
San Diego
Atlanta
Dallas
San Antonio
New Orleans
Houston
Tampa
Miami

Percentage of Women Who Are Hispanic

20-50%

10-19%

1- 9%

Women of Hispanic origin can be of any race.

slightly outnumber men. At age 45 the difference becomes greater as the number of women vs. men increases steadily. If we look back to an earlier map, "The Population of Women Through Time," we see that in most states through 1950 the total population of men was greater than women. While, at first, this information appears to contradict the population pyramids, the maps are accurate. In actuality, the population of men was only slightly higher and occurred almost exclusively between ages 0 to 25. Since there are more people in these younger age groups than in the older groups, even a slightly higher male population in the younger group can outweigh the higher female population of the older age groups.

In 1980 continuing through 1990 a dramatic increase in the elderly population occurred, as seen in both the historical population pyramids and the 1990 population pyramid. This trend contributed to the population of women outnumbering men because women have a greater life expectancy. The post-war baby boom can be observed in the 0–4 age group of 1950, the 15–24 age groups in 1980 and the 25–34 age groups in 1990.

THE AGES OF WOMEN

We have used four maps, "Childhood," "Childbearing Years," The Middle Years," and "The Elderly," to show the variations in age structure for women from state to state. These maps are composed of states that are shaded according to the percentage of women in particular age groups. This enables us to compare one state with another for each age group. The "Childhood" map reveals that the percentage of women under the

age of 15 varied from a low of 18% in Massachusetts and Rhode Island to a high of 30% in Utah. In four states, Alaska, Idaho, Utah and Wyoming, children made up more than one-quarter of the female population.

The distribution is not surprising. Utah is predominantly Mormon with large families being the norm. Larger families are also typical of rural populations and so it is not unusual to see the states, Alaska, Idaho, New Mexico and Wyoming with large "childhood" populations. Higher percentages of children generally occur in the West, while the eastern states, with three exceptions (Georgia, South Carolina and Vermont), have the lowest percentages.

The proportion of women who are of reproductive age will influence many demographic events, including birth rates, fertility ratios, single parent family ratios and the ratio of women to men in the labor force. Women in this age group were more numerous than in any other, the result of the post-war baby boom of the 1950s. The highest percentage of females—54%—in this age group is found in Louisiana. The lowest rate of 42% is shared by Iowa and South Dakota. Low percentages appear in a noticeable band from Montana to Arkansas and also in two eastern states, Pennsylvania and West Virginia. These mostly rural states possess very few of the nation's major cities and also have among the lowest percentages of children. In some of these rural farm areas, women of reproductive age have moved away either alone or with their families to seek better economic opportunities elsewhere.

On the map, "The Middle Years," we see that the majority (33) of states have between 18% and 20% of their female populations in this age group. This age group had the narrowest range of percentages from state to state with a difference of only eight percentage points

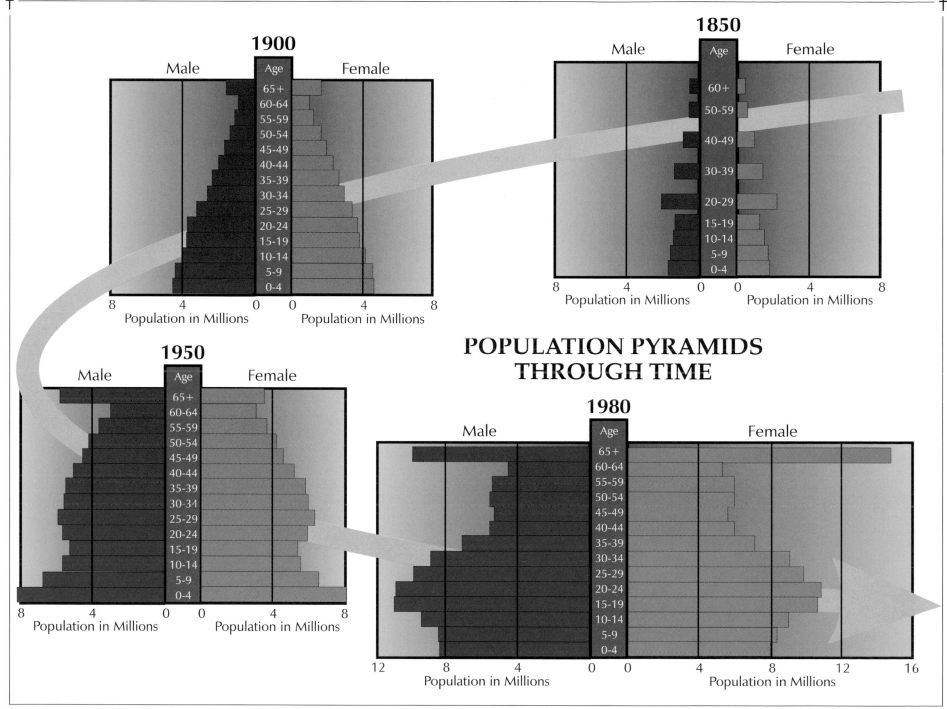

POPULATION PYRAMIDS THROUGH TIME

1900

Male — Female

Age
65+
60-64
55-59
50-54
45-49
40-44
35-39
30-34
25-29
20-24
15-19
10-14
5-9
0-4

8 4 0   0 4 8
Population in Millions   Population in Millions

1850

Male — Female

Age
60+
50-59
40-49
30-39
20-29
15-19
10-14
5-9
0-4

8 4 0   0 4 8
Population in Millions   Population in Millions

1950

Male — Female

Age
65+
60-64
55-59
50-54
45-49
40-44
35-39
30-34
25-29
20-24
15-19
10-14
5-9
0-4

8 4 0   0 4 8
Population in Millions   Population in Millions

1980

Male — Female

Age
65+
60-64
55-59
50-54
45-49
40-44
35-39
30-34
25-29
20-24
15-19
10-14
5-9
0-4

12 8 4 0   0 4 8 12 16
Population in Millions   Population in Millions

POPULATION PYRAMID
1990

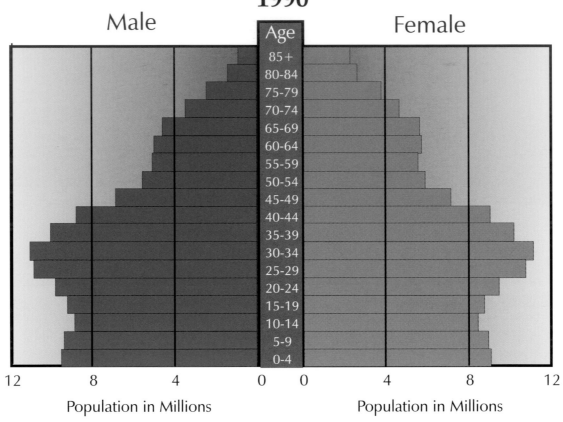

Male

Female

Age
85+
80-84
75-79
70-74
65-69
60-64
55-59
50-54
45-49
40-44
35-39
30-34
25-29
20-24
15-19
10-14
5-9
0-4

12   8   4   0   0   4   8   12

Population in Millions   Population in Millions

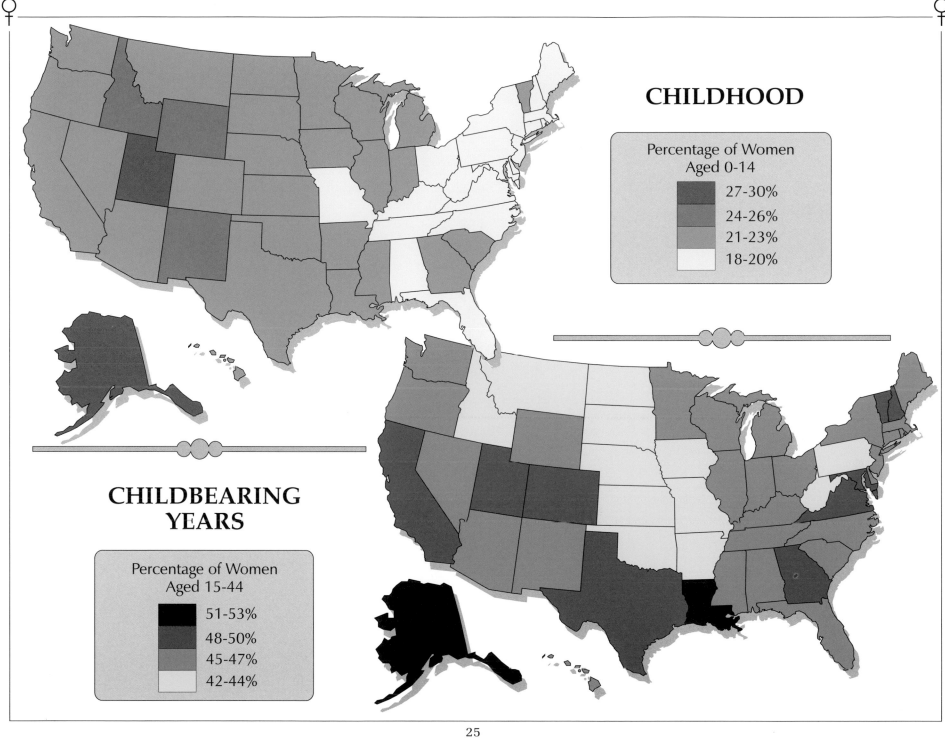

CHILDHOOD

Percentage of Women
Aged 0-14

27-30%

24-26%

21-23%

18-20%

CHILDBEARING YEARS

Percentage of Women
Aged 15-44

51-53%

48-50%

45-47%

42-44%

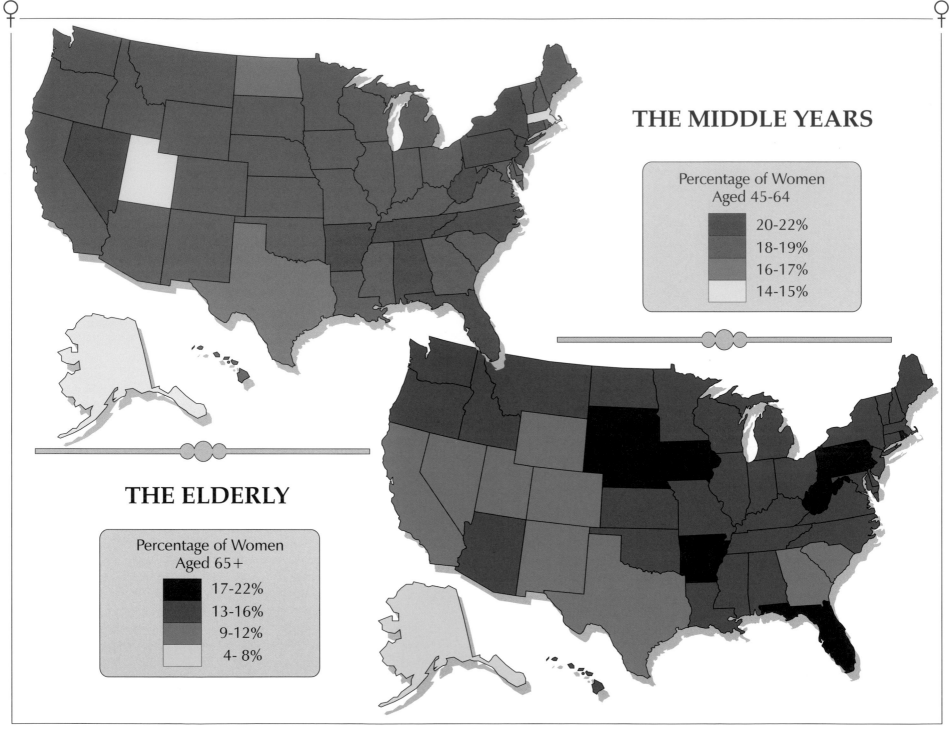

THE MIDDLE YEARS

Percentage of Women
Aged 45-64

20-22%
18-19%
16-17%
14-15%

THE ELDERLY

Percentage of Women
Aged 65+

17-22%
13-16%
9-12%
4- 8%

26

between the lowest and highest values, those of Massachusetts at 14% and Florida at 22%. Only three regions, the Northeast, the North Central and the Midwest, had values consistent throughout the region. The Northeast had a particularly high proportion of women in this age group, greater than one in five.

In 1980, 19% of Florida's female population was over 65 years of age. It was the only state that would have been in the highest percentage group (17–20%) of the 1990 map, "The Elderly." By 1990, Florida's elderly population had grown to 22%. Seven other states are now in this group. Florida is almost four percentage points higher than the next in line, Iowa. This seems to confirm Florida's reputation as a retirement haven. Its hospitable climate combined with no state income tax attracts more and more of the elderly. In recent years, Arizona has also been identified as a retirement haven and thus stands out in the Southwest as an area with a larger-than-average elderly population. Alaska's harsh climate and its high cost of living keep the elderly population of Alaska at only 5%, five points lower than the next lower state, Utah.

The graph, "Median Age Through Time," compares the median ages of women and men from 1800 to 1990. Median refers to the middle value in a distribution below and above which fall an equal number of quantities. For example the median value of the set of numbers 14, 19, 20, 29, and 36 is 20. The median ages of women and men have more than doubled in the past 200 years. Between 1900 and 1950, the median age of women surpassed that of men. This is in part due to advances in health care that caused a significant drop in the deaths of women during pregnancy and in childbirth. The difference in median age was never more than a year until 1990 when women were 2.4 years older than men. Again this can be attributed to advances in health care.

Now that we have shown how women's median age is increasing over time, we will look at it on a state level in two separate maps. The map, "Median Age Women vs. Men," compares the median age of women to that of men on a state by state basis. Not surprisingly, the states where the median age of women is more than three years older than the median age of men are also states with a high percentage of elderly women. Conversely, Alaska, the state with the lowest median age of women compared to men, also has among the highest proportion of female children. This distribution reflects the trend that the older the median population, the greater the differences of the median ages between women and men.

Only in Alaska is the median age of women lower than that of men and only by one-tenth of a year. In all other states, the median age of women is higher than men, reflecting women's greater life expectancy.

The second "Median Age" map displays the median age of women in each state. As is consistent with the previous map, the highest median ages tend to be in the Northeast and Florida, while Alaska and Utah have the lowest median ages.

URBAN VS. RURAL

The United States Census Bureau defines "urban" as comprising all territory, population and housing units in urbanized areas and in places of 2,500 or more persons outside urbanized areas.[2] An urbanized area comprises one or more central places and the adjacent

MEDIAN AGE THROUGH TIME

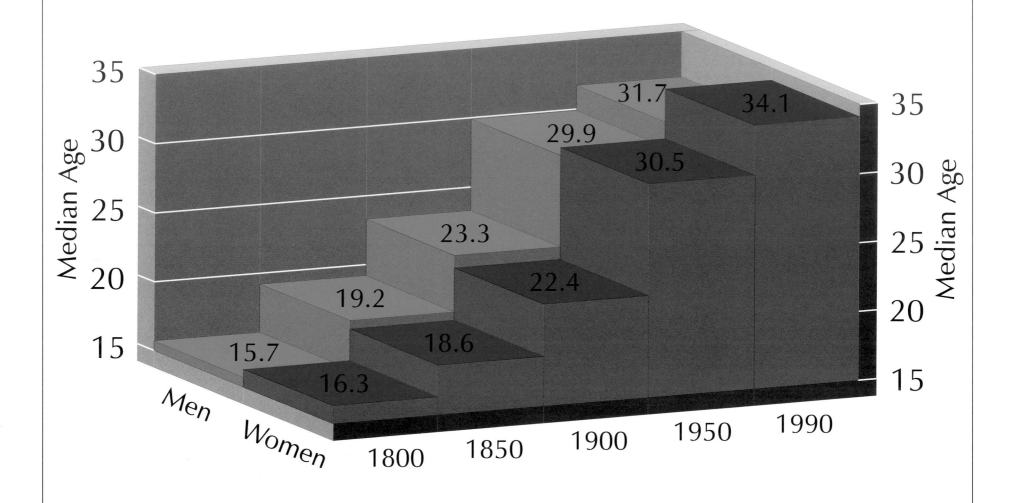

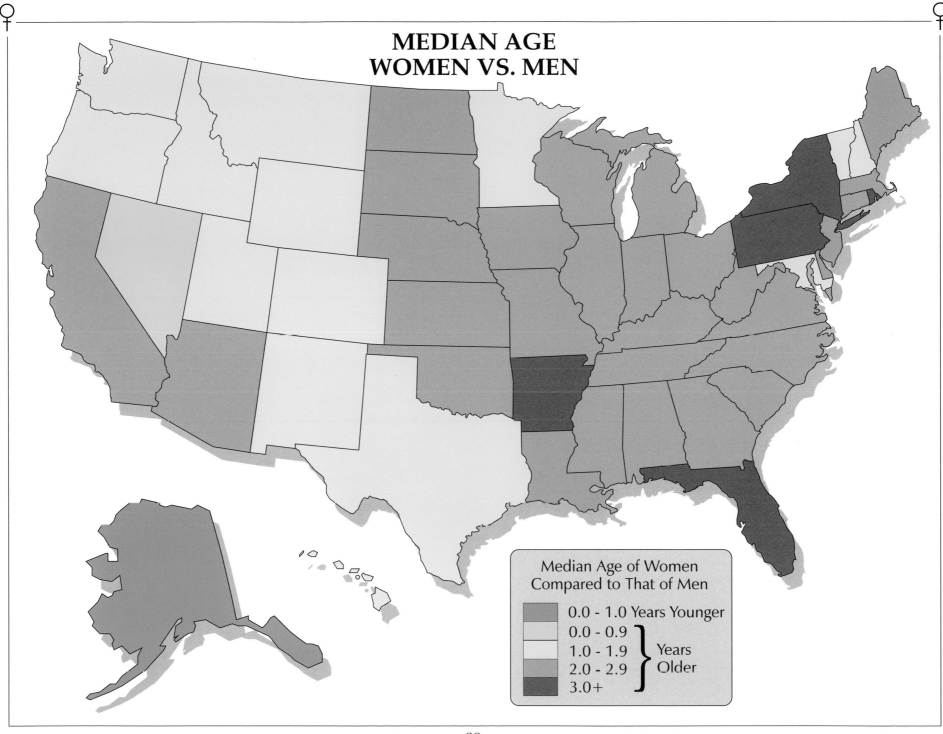

MEDIAN AGE
WOMEN VS. MEN

Median Age of Women Compared to That of Men

- 0.0 - 1.0 Years Younger
- 0.0 - 0.9 } Years Older
- 1.0 - 1.9 } Years Older
- 2.0 - 2.9 } Years Older
- 3.0+ } Years Older

MEDIAN AGE

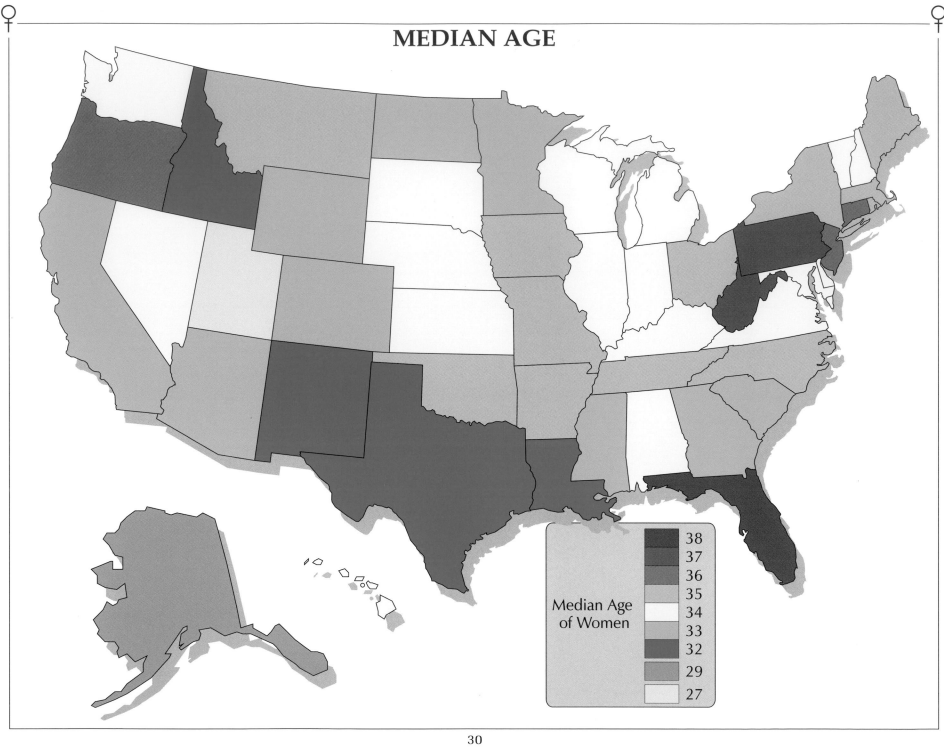

Median Age
of Women

38
37
36
35
34
33
32
29
27

densely settled surrounding territory that together have a minimum of 50,000 persons.[3]

The "Urban vs. Rural" map shows the percentage of women living in urban versus rural areas. California at 93% and New Jersey at 90% have the highest percentages of women in urban areas. In only four states, Mississippi, West Virginia, Vermont and Maine, do rural-dwelling women outnumber their urban counterparts. These four states are less industrialized than many states and generally have no large cities. Vermont and West Virginia have particularly low percentages of urban dwellers. About two-thirds of the women in these states live in rural areas. Looking at the values on a regional basis, we find that the West, the Southwest and the Northeast all have high percentages of urban women. The Northern High Plains and the Deep South, with the exception of Florida, have high percentages of rural women.

Now that we have looked at such demographic issues as race, age and place of residence and seen how women fit into these categories, let's examine the issues affecting all women. The maps that follow will graphically demonstrate the effect of education, employment, health, crime and politics on women.

URBAN VS. RURAL

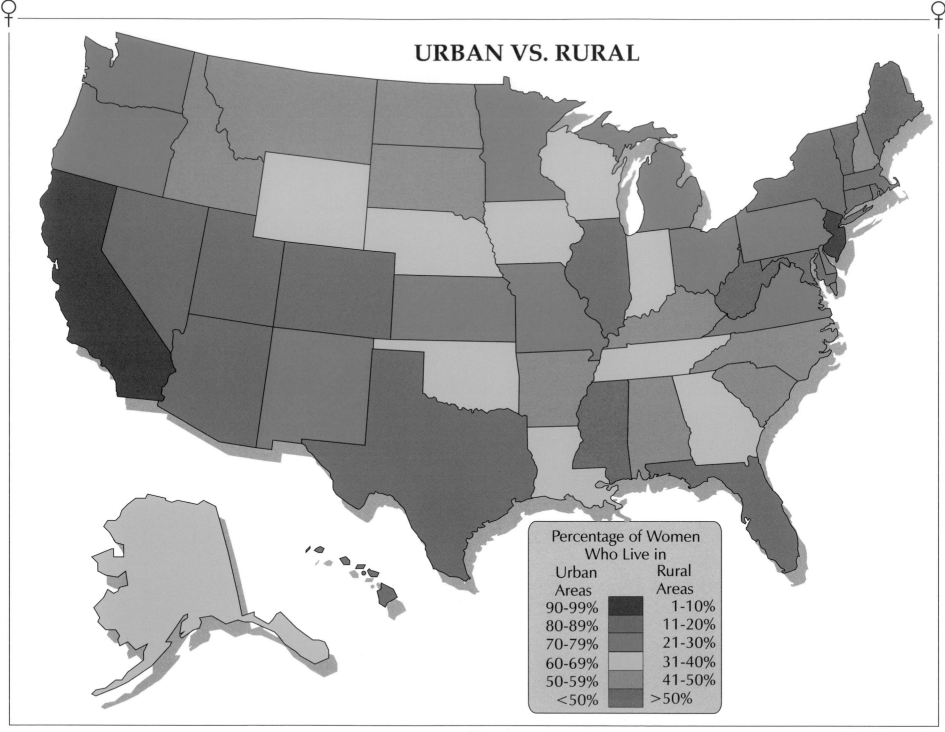

Percentage of Women
Who Live in

Urban Areas		Rural Areas
90-99%		1-10%
80-89%		11-20%
70-79%		21-30%
60-69%		31-40%
50-59%		41-50%
<50%		>50%

EDUCATION

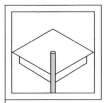
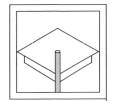

"It is a rare privilege to watch the birth, growth and first feeble struggles of a living mind…"[1]

—Annie Sullivan

Historically, education has been the prerogative of the wealthy. Until recently, it was available only to those who could afford the expense of private schools or tutors. Education was the almost exclusive province of young men; women's access to education was severely limited. Throughout history, however, some women have advocated equal opportunities for women and men. In 1792, Mary Wollstonecraft, in *A Vindication of the Rights of Women*, challenged the idea that women exist only to please men and proposed that women should receive the same treatment as men in education, work and politics. Two hundred years later, women are still struggling to attain these goals. Working against women are the social pressures exerted by tradition, market forces and the vested interests of certain professions to limit access to instruction and thus the numbers of individuals, especially women, in certain professions.

Although the first secondary school in colonial America, the Boston Latin School, was founded in 1635, it was not until 200 years later that liberal Massachusetts lawmakers created a state board of education and a truly public school system.[2] But even then a girl's chances of attending school past the elementary level were slight. Throughout the mid-19th century, women's educational opportunities continued to be hampered by the taboos of the time, particularly that an educated woman was unfeminine and unattractive to men and that education beyond the most basic reading and math skills was unnecessary for a woman's primary role as wife and mother. Even if a girl received instruction beyond elementary school, her schooling usually did not include college preparatory work as it did for boys. Higher education for girls most commonly meant attendance at a "female academy." These were run almost exclusively for the daughters of the wealthy and emphasized such areas as music, drawing, needlework and French. The female academy was often little more than a "finishing school" to prepare young women for their future roles as wives and mothers.

At the beginning of the 19th century, women faced three major problems in their quest for higher learning. First, few or no opportunities existed for college preparatory training; second, colleges did not admit women as students; and third, no opportunities existed for advanced or professional training. Even if a woman succeeded in overcoming these obstacles, she faced even tougher ones when she attempted to engage in her profession. Also a factor was the belief that training women for a profession and allowing them to practice it would take away the sometimes scarce employment opportunities for men.

By the 1830s, this situation slowly began to change. As America advanced industrially and more women went to work in factories, their horizons expanded beyond their traditional roles. Later in the century the typewriter, the telegraph and the telephone created a new kind of employment, the clerical worker, with positions filled almost exclusively by women. Once in the workplace, women began to better understand the opportunities that higher education provided for men and wanted these opportunities for themselves. Recognizing this need, two Ohio colleges opened their doors to women, Oberlin in 1833, and Antioch 20 years later. However, it wasn't until 1861 that a truly first-rate women's college, Vassar, was founded, starting a movement that sought to make colleges for women comparable to those for men.

The final educational barriers to cross were at the graduate and professional levels. These began to fall after 1850 when women were admitted to graduate and professional schools, primarily in the fields of medicine and law. However, significant numbers of women did not enter these professions until the establishment of medical and law schools exclusively for women.

The debate concerning higher education for women predominantly centered on two issues. The first was the question of whether or not women should attend college at all. The majority of the arguments against it, presented by both men and women, were based on the assumption that all women would eventually be married. Those against educating women believed that a woman, because she would have a husband, was unlikely to become the breadwinner of a family. Also, her future social and economic status would not depend on her professional occupation or earning capacity, but on that of her husband. Finally, they believed that because a young woman would eventually get married and leave her profession in favor of being a wife and mother, the investment of time, money, and energy for her education was unwarranted. Indeed, too much education might actually cause a woman to become discontented with her role as wife and mother and venture into the workplace, providing a powerful source of competition for jobs. Others argued that the rigors of education would damage the delicate female constitution, mentally, physically and emotionally. Clearly, education for women would upset the status quo.

The second issue was the debate about the merits of a coeducational versus a single sex institution. The main argument in favor of coeducational institutions was that it was cheaper to admit women to men's colleges than to build separate facilities for women. In addition, having the sexes working together in the classroom imitated the interaction between women and men in society and the interaction itself would be educational. Also, the presence of women might exercise a civilizing effect on the male students.

The opposition felt that the moral character and virtue of the female students would be at risk and that the delicate nature of young women would be compromised by contact with high-spirited young men. Some thought there was a lack of decorum in allowing young women and men to associate so freely with each other, particularly in clinical settings such as medical school.

The debate concerning coed colleges is still alive today. However, shrinking enrollments have caused many women's colleges to admit men as students. Others have simply had to close. The number of women's colleges in the United States fell from 300 in 1960 to fewer than 100 in 1990. Some colleges admit women only, but share facilities with nearby men's colleges; Barnard and Columbia are good examples of this.

Although the trend seems to be going toward coed institutions, there is evidence that women's colleges offer distinct advantages over coed schools. Studies show that graduates of women's colleges tend to be higher achievers than women who attend coed schools. Some educators believe that women perform better in women's institutions because of the absence of "intellectual sexism" that exists in coeducational institutions.

Psychologists Lisa Serbin and K. Daniel O'Leary have discovered that, beginning at the preschool level, teachers give boys more attention, praise them more often and are at least twice as likely to have extended conversations with them.[3] Other studies have established that this kind of treatment exists at virtually all educational levels.

Attendance at a women's college is one way for a woman to circumvent these biases. Some educators believe that these colleges better prepare women for the challenges of modern society and encourage them to take a more active role. Recent studies by Myra and David Sadker further examine the gender bias in classrooms. After a 1992 appearance by the Sadkers on the evening news show, *Dateline*, in which they showed videos of gender bias in action, enrollment in women's colleges rose 14%.[4] While many see this trend as advantageous for women, a resulting change in the number of women-only institutions is unlikely.

While the number of women's colleges may be declining, the number of institutions offering women's studies programs is rising. Most colleges and universities are dominated at both the instructional and administrative levels by men. The addition of women's studies programs establishes the importance of women's experiences, values and perspectives, both in the academic world and outside, and teaches an alternative to the male perspective put forth by predominantly male educators.

Male bias in the educational setting is evident in various areas of research, particularly the "people-oriented" disciplines of sociology, history, psychology and anthropology, where much of the foundation work was laid initially by men. The research efforts of many scholars have been permeated by personal bias and stereotypical views about the place of women in society. This bias exists particularly in medical research where research efforts and money tend to focus on men. For example, even though heart disease is the number one killer among women, until very recently, all of the major studies of heart disease had been done only on men.

In fact, men dominate the educational system as a whole. While women make up a sizable percentage of teachers up through the high school level, men are disproportionately represented at the administrative level where the majority of educational policy is determined. The higher one looks in the administrative hierarchy, the fewer women one sees. Women's participation as educators at all levels is of vital importance to ensure that female values and perspectives are given equal consideration as those of men.

Women generally take primary responsibility for family and child care. Their need to focus on these responsibilities is one of the reasons women are sometimes willing to remain in less demanding positions than their male counterparts. Such responsibilities also prevent many women from completing their education. The increasing number of part-time study programs has enabled many women (and men) with the responsibilities of family and full-time jobs to continue their education, either completing a first degree, working on a graduate degree, or simply expanding their knowledge in particular areas of interest.

The maps that follow illustrate a number of important issues concerning women and education.

LITERACY

Ours is a nation that prides itself on its literacy rates, but what quickly becomes apparent is that we are in danger of becoming a society of functionally illiterate citizens. The first two maps (Literacy) in this section concern literacy rates of fourth grade female students in selected states.

In 1992, a sampling of fourth grade students in selected states was given reading proficiency tests ranking their skills as Basic, Proficient or Advanced. The skill levels were judged as follows: When reading literary text appropriate for fourth graders, students performing at the Basic level should be able to tell what the story is generally about and be able to connect aspects of the story to their own experiences. Proficient level students should have Basic level skills and in addition should be able to summarize the story, draw conclusions about the characters or plot, and recognize relationships such as cause and effect. Advanced level students should have both Basic and Proficient level skills and be able to make generalizations about the point of the story and extend its meaning by integrating personal experiences and other readings with the ideas suggested by the text. They should also be able to identify literary devices such as figurative language. Comprehension of informational text was tested as well.[5] The survey revealed that only between 2% and 7% of female fourth graders were reading at or above an advanced reading achievement level. In all but six of the selected states, more that 30% of fourth grade girls were reading below the most basic reading achievement level. And in California, Hawaii, Louisiana and Mississippi half of all students were reading below the basic level. Nearly three-quarters of fourth grade students in the District of Columbia fell below the basic reading achievement level. Regionally, scores were lowest in the Deep South and California and highest in New England and portions of the Northeast. In all areas of the country, girls outperformed boys.

While the flaws in such proficiency exams have been widely discussed, it would be safe to say that even with a relatively large margin for error, these statistics are frightening. Assuming that the education received by the nation's fourth graders is indicative of other

LITERACY
(In Selected States)

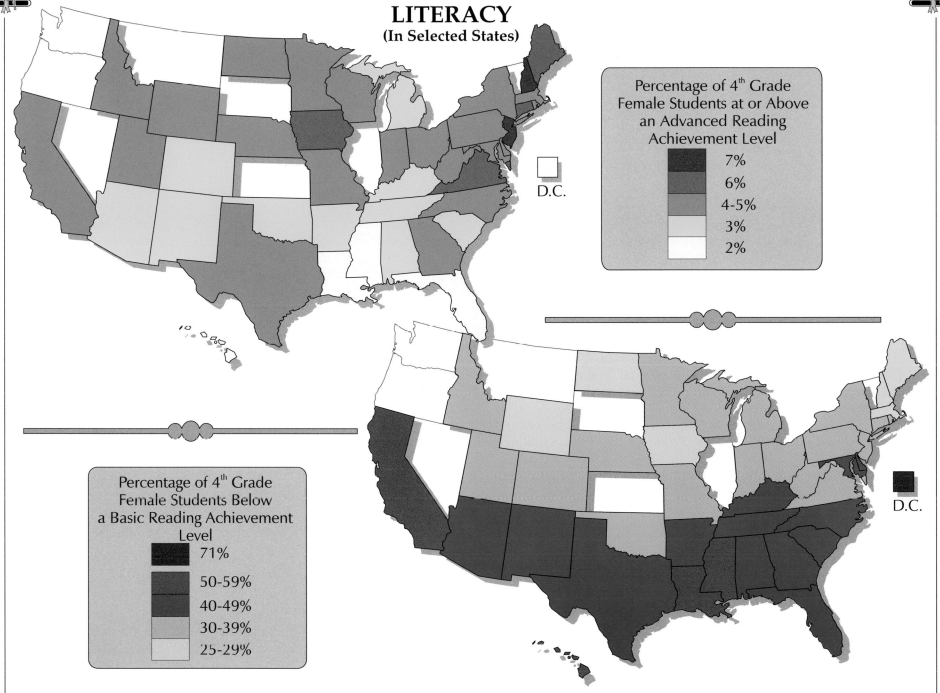

Percentage of 4th Grade Female Students at or Above an Advanced Reading Achievement Level

- 7%
- 6%
- 4-5%
- 3%
- 2%

D.C.

Percentage of 4th Grade Female Students Below a Basic Reading Achievement Level

- 71%
- 50-59%
- 40-49%
- 30-39%
- 25-29%

D.C.

grades, our children are being tremendously short-changed in their education. Reading skills are the most basic building block of learning and without those skills, all others areas of learning suffer.

HIGH SCHOOL

The United States Constitution delegates educational authority to the states and in most states the responsibility for schools rests in the hands of each community's local board of education.

Because of this local autonomy, the percentage of persons graduating from high school is one indicator of a community's attitude toward education. Is there really equal educational opportunity for all? Is education a priority? Do bond issues to support the local schools consistently pass or fail? How do students perform on national achievement tests? The answers to these questions reveal the significance the community places on education.

The first map (High School Graduates) in this section depicts the percentage of women with a high school diploma. The northern states have the highest percentages of women with diplomas and though there are some variations from state to state, this was also the case ten years ago. The southern states show lower percentages of women graduates, just as they did in 1980. Many states have about the same number of graduates as they did a decade ago with declines in the West, southern New England and Texas. Within these regions, seven states (Connecticut, Massachusetts, Texas, Utah, Idaho, Oregon and Washington) exhibited small declines. In four states, Arizona, California,

Nevada and Rhode Island, a decline in the number of female high school graduates of ten or more percentage points was recorded. Only one state, West Virginia, significantly increased the number of female graduates over the past decade. Unfortunately, fewer of our nation's young people are staying in school, a situation that does not bode well for America's future.

On the next map, it is instantly apparent that more males than females receive their high school diplomas. The states with a lesser percentage of women with diplomas than men are shaded pink. Most of the map is shaded pink. Only in South Carolina and the District of Columbia are there more female graduates than male. In five other states, Virginia, North Carolina, Georgia, Florida and Utah, the percentages of male and female graduates are equal. Contrary to what might be expected, all but one of these states where the number of female graduates is greater than or equal to the number of male graduates are located on the Atlantic coast from Delaware south to Florida. With the exception of Delaware and Virginia, these states all have a low percentage of high school graduates for both sexes.

The third map, "Women Minorities—High School Graduates," shows female minority graduates reflect the same proportions as their populations. For example, Native Americans constitute the largest female minority in the Northern High Plains states of Montana, North Dakota, and South Dakota. As would be expected, Native American women make up the largest percentage of women minority high school graduates on these states. The same holds true for African Americans in the Deep South and Hispanics in the West and Southwest.

High school dropout rates are illustrated on the next map on a regional basis for Hispanics, African Ameri-

HIGH SCHOOL GRADUATES

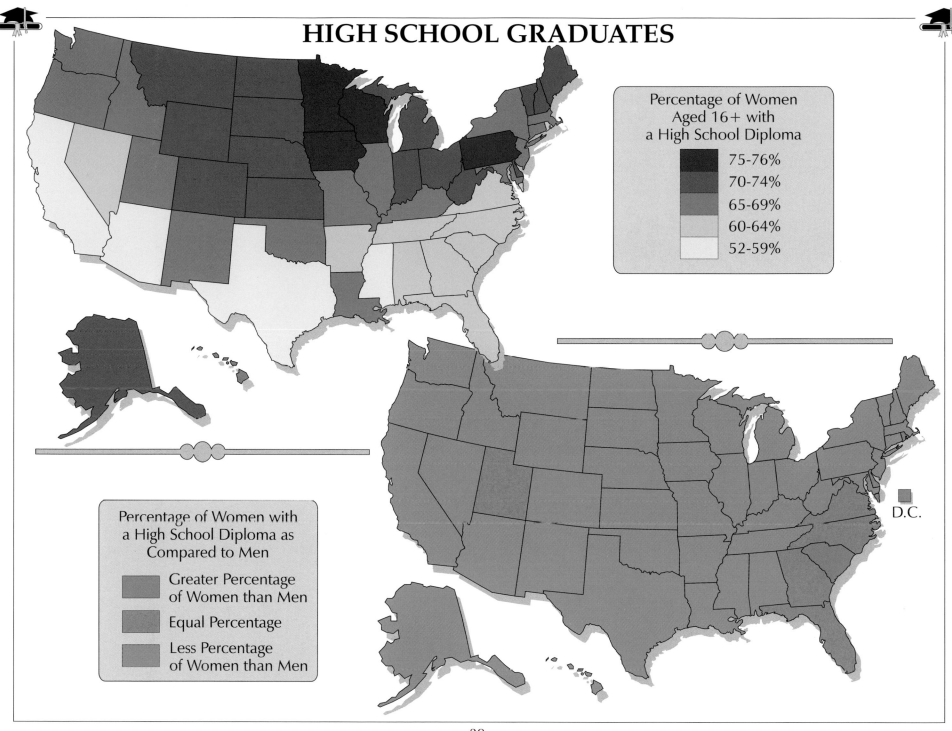

Percentage of Women
Aged 16+ with
a High School Diploma

- 75-76%
- 70-74%
- 65-69%
- 60-64%
- 52-59%

Percentage of Women with
a High School Diploma as
Compared to Men

- Greater Percentage
  of Women than Men
- Equal Percentage
- Less Percentage
  of Women than Men

D.C.

WOMEN MINORITIES
HIGH SCHOOL GRADUATES

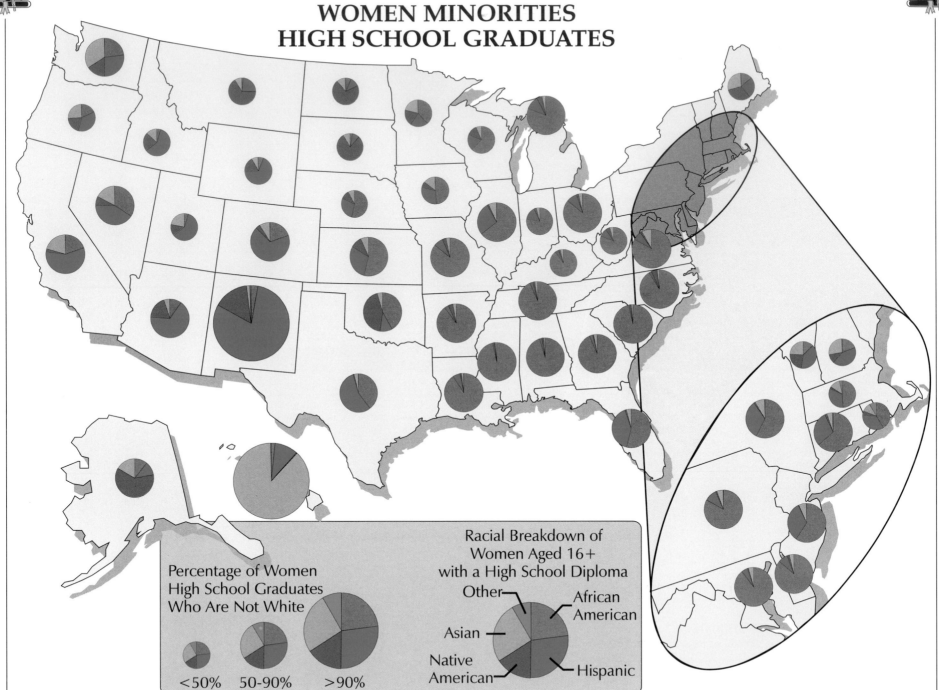

Percentage of Women
High School Graduates
Who Are Not White

<50%   50-90%   >90%

Racial Breakdown of
Women Aged 16+
with a High School Diploma

Other

African
American

Asian

Native
American

Hispanic

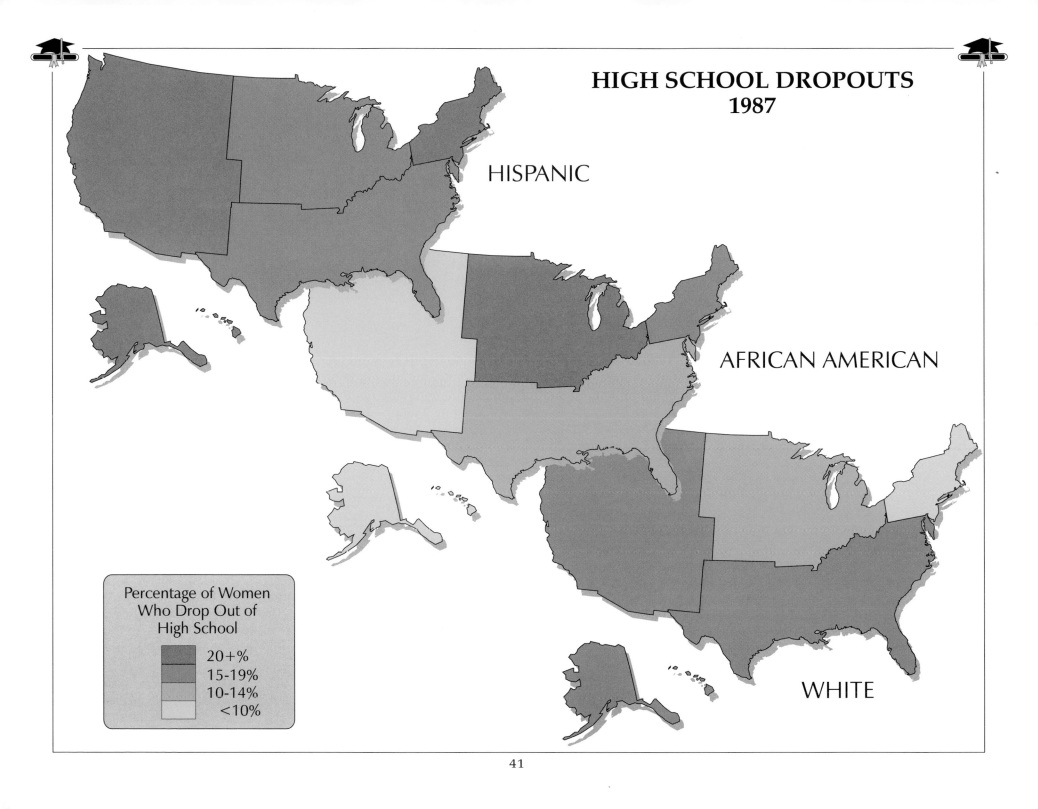

HIGH SCHOOL DROPOUTS
1987

HISPANIC

AFRICAN AMERICAN

WHITE

Percentage of Women
Who Drop Out of
High School

20+%
15-19%
10-14%
<10%

41

cans, and Whites. The data, the most current available at publication, are from 1987. The three maps reveal that Hispanics are at the greatest risk with more than 15% nationwide dropping out of high school. For approximately half of the country, the percentage is greater than 20%. African-American women have the lowest dropout rate in the West. The highest percentage of African-American female dropouts occurs in the Midwest. The South, surprisingly, has the lowest percentage of dropouts. The figures do not improve much for White women. With the exception of the Northeast and New England where the rate is less than 10%, the rest of the United States has a dropout rate of between 10% and 19%. This means that for all three races, one or two out of every ten women drop out of high school.

HIGHER EDUCATION

In 1900 only 500,000 students advanced from elementary school to high school. By 1950, the number had increased to 5,000,000. In the first half of this century, almost three out of every four high school graduates went on to college.[6] Today, unfortunately, the ratio is reversed with only one out of four graduates going on to higher education.

There are two main reasons students do not go on to higher learning. First, many high schools are de-emphasizing a college preparatory curriculum in favor of directing their students toward vocational training. Many students are now able to acquire skills in high school that train them for entry-level employment. Relatively high-paying jobs are also available in industries that require skills acquired in one of these voca-

tional programs. Second, as the price of a college education continues to escalate, many students, without substantial help from family, grants or scholarships, simply cannot afford to attend.

A third, and somewhat more obscure reason may be that there is a generation of students reared in families who did very well for themselves without a college education. They did this by working in what are generally referred to as blue collar jobs in, for example, the automotive, steel and construction industries. These young people see how well their parents have done without higher education and see no reason why the same can't be true for them.

The map, "Enrollment in Colleges and Universities," shows the percentage of college students, by state, who are women. A dramatic change has occurred over the past ten years in the percentage of female college students. In 1980, there were four states, Utah, North Dakota, Iowa and Indiana, where men outnumbered women. By 1990, Utah was the only state where that was the case. From 1980 to 1990 the number of states where more than half of the college students were women increased from 20 to 48.

Even though more women are attending college than ever before, apparently fewer of them want to attend colleges exclusively for women. While some students are willing to go on strike to retain their school's "female only" status, as the students of Mills College in Oakland, California, did in 1990, these institutions generally face reduced enrollment. In the fall of 1991, only ten women's colleges had enrollments of 2,000 or more students. Those institutions remaining are located almost exclusively east of the Mississippi, where, historically, women were obstructed from attending "male only" institutions and had to establish institu-

ENROLLMENT IN
COLLEGES & UNIVERSITIES

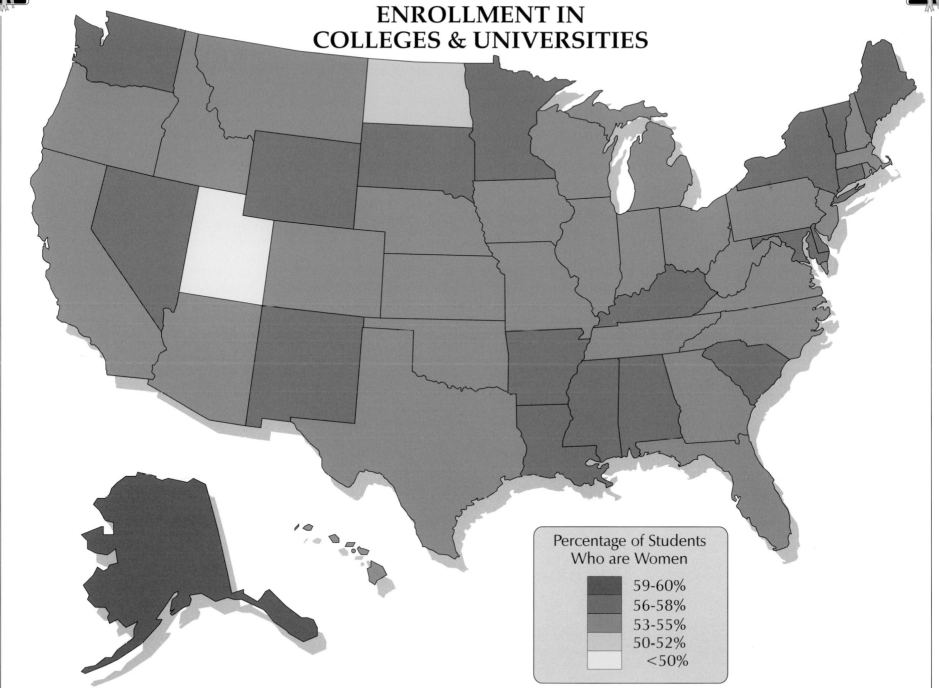

Percentage of Students
Who are Women

59-60%
56-58%
53-55%
50-52%
<50%

tions of their own. Colleges in states west of the Mississippi, with the exception of Missouri, were coeducational from their beginnings, so the need for women's colleges was not so great.

Women's studies programs have been established at many colleges and universities to confirm the importance of women's experiences, values and perspectives, and to foster an understanding of the relationship between women and men in both the academic world and society at large. The map, "Women's Studies Programs—1993," locates the programs in existence in the fall of 1993, when there were 192 colleges or universities offering programs in women's studies. Ten offer master's degrees in women's studies, and two, Clark University in Massachusetts and Cornell University in New York, offer doctorate degrees. Cornell is the only university currently with degree programs at the bachelor, master and doctorate level. Over the past ten years, the number of institutions offering women's studies programs has decreased slightly, probably due to the declining number of women's colleges.

Even though women outnumber men in the classrooms of the nation's colleges and universities, they don't graduate in the same proportions. As is illustrated on the map, "College Graduates," Vermont is the only state where 50% of bachelor's degrees were awarded to women. Of note is North Dakota, which has one of the lowest percentages of female of university students (between 50–52%), but has a comparatively high percentage of women with bachelor's degrees. Another reason the percentages of degreed women compared to degreed men appears to be low in most states is that the overwhelming number of women attending colleges and universities is a relatively recent phenomena. A large proportion of older women

graduated from high school during a time when college attendance was not as acceptable or as available to women as it is now. Possibly, in another decade or two, there will be a smaller gap between the percentage of women attending institutions of higher learning and the percentage of women with degrees.

When comparing the map "Women Minorities with Bachelor's Degrees" to "Women Minorities—High School Graduates," several things become apparent about higher education among the different minorities. For example, let's look at the state of Washington on both maps. On each map there are pie charts representing the number of female minority students. The size of each pie chart represents the percentage of students who are not White. The proportion of each minority is represented by an appropriately sized slice of the pie.

If we examine the high school graduates map for the state of Washington we see that Asian women make up the largest number of high school graduates. The next largest groups are Hispanic, African-American, and finally, Native American women. However, when we examine the map of women minorities with bachelors degrees, the order remains the same, but the proportions drastically change. The same can be said for women minorities with post-graduate degrees. The proportion of Asian women with bachelor's and post-graduate degrees is significantly higher than the proportion of Asian women that are only high school graduates. This indicates that in Washington, at least, a larger percentage of Asian high school graduates go on the obtain degrees than do other minorities. This is a nationwide trend. Asian students consistently perform better academically than students from other cultures. Their culture values higher learning, thus more

WOMEN'S COLLEGES

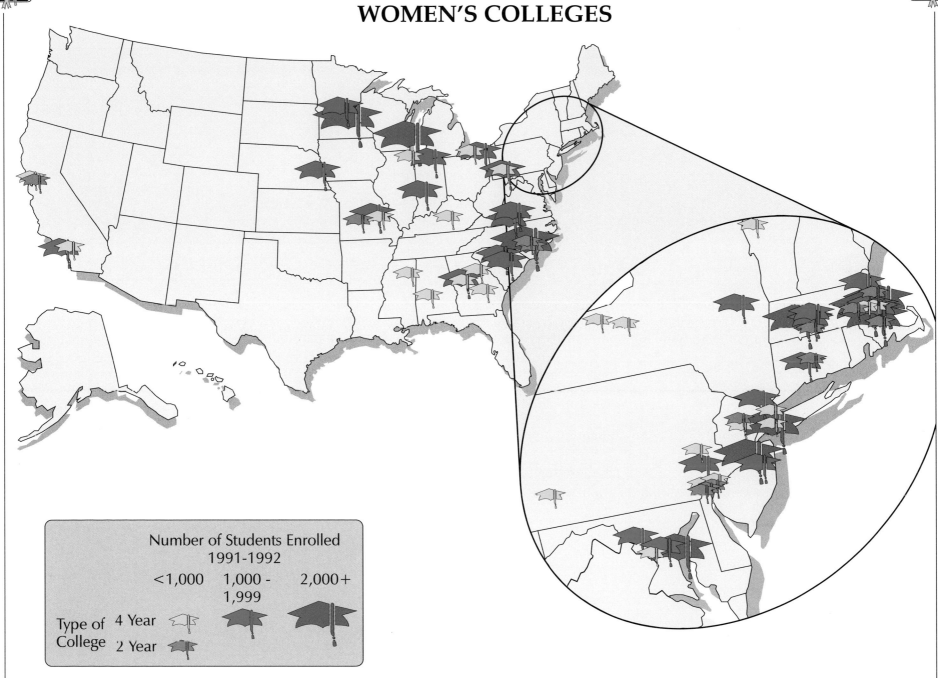

Number of Students Enrolled
1991-1992

<1,000   1,000 -   2,000+
          1,999

Type of   4 Year
College   2 Year

45

WOMEN'S STUDIES PROGRAMS
1993

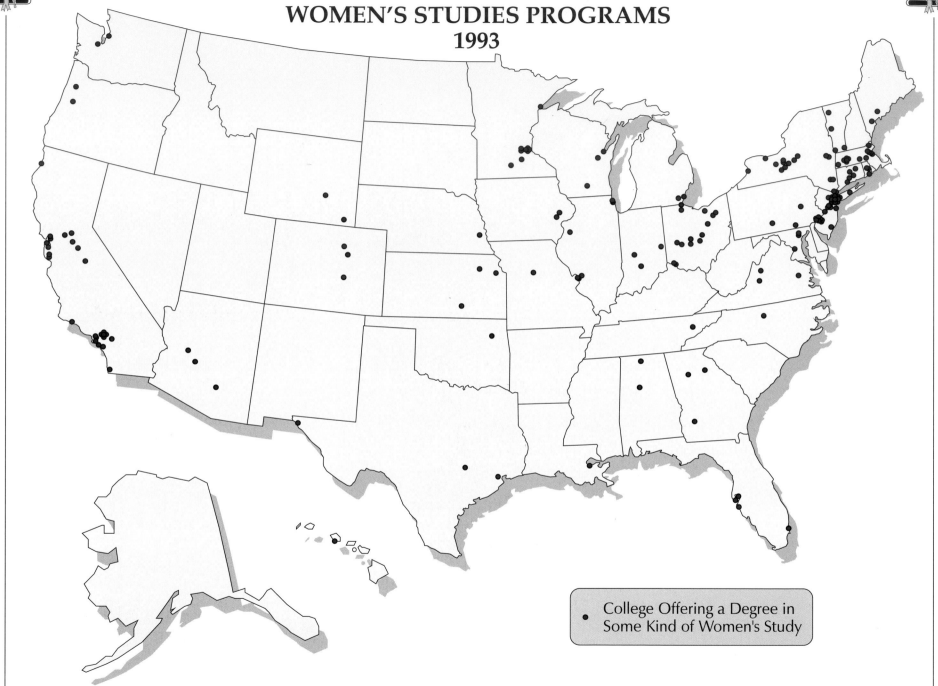

● College Offering a Degree in
Some Kind of Women's Study

COLLEGE GRADUATES

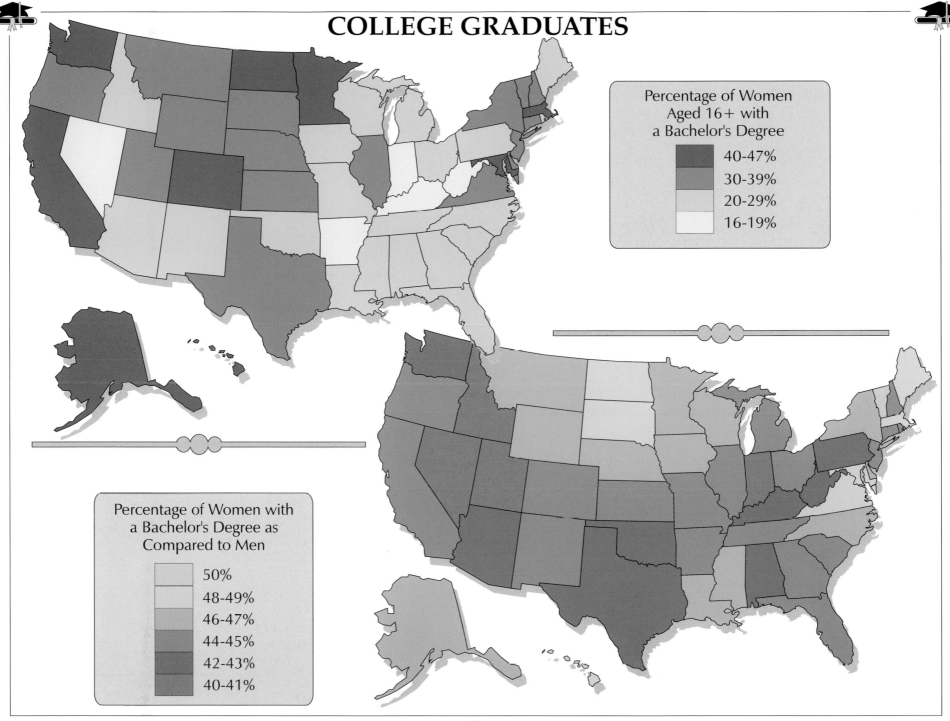

Percentage of Women
Aged 16+ with
a Bachelor's Degree

- 40-47%
- 30-39%
- 20-29%
- 16-19%

Percentage of Women with
a Bachelor's Degree as
Compared to Men

- 50%
- 48-49%
- 46-47%
- 44-45%
- 42-43%
- 40-41%

WOMEN MINORITIES WITH A BACHELOR'S DEGREE

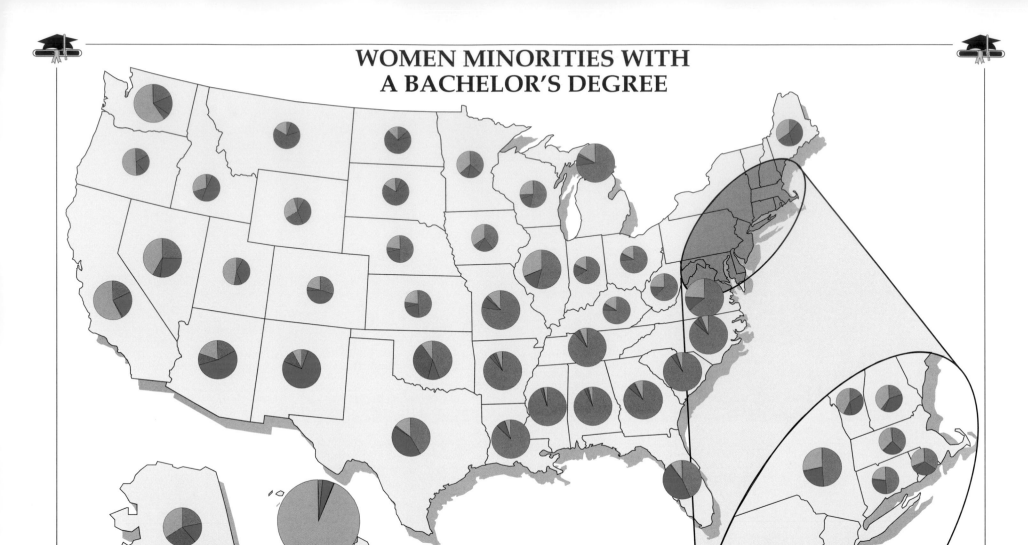

Percentage of Women with a Bachelor's Degree Who Are Not White

<50%   50-90%   >90%

Racial Breakdown of Women Aged 16+ with a Bachelor's Degree

Other

African American

Asian

Native American

Hispanic

is expected of them from their families. Their families also tend to be tightly knit and mutually supportive.

A useful indicator of the depth of women's educational involvement can be found by examining women's attainment of advanced degrees. The maps entitled "Post-Graduate Degrees," illustrate the percentage of women with post-graduate degrees and the percentage of women vs. men with post-graduate degrees. As of 1990, no state had more than 25% of its female population with post-graduate degrees. Not surprisingly, the highest values were found in New York and Connecticut, and also in nearby Maryland, states that also have a large number of institutions offering advanced degree programs. What is surprising is that the states with the highest percentage of women with post-graduate degrees as compared to men were Kentucky at 47%, and Mississippi and West Virginia, both at 45%. These three states ranked among the lowest states as to the percentage of women with a post-graduate degree. The proportion of men with post-graduate degrees in these states is also small. Utah was at the bottom of both categories.

The chart, "Distribution of Degree Specialization of Women and Men," shows in what fields of study both men and women obtained their degrees as of 1990. In two fields of study, Humanities and Education, there was a higher percentage of women earning degrees than men at all three levels. In the case of Education, more than two and a half times as many women as men earned degrees. The obvious question is, if women so overwhelmingly dominate this field of study, why do male teachers earn more and why are men dominating both the instructional and the administrative levels of our nation's schools? While the number of women receiving degrees in fields of physical and social sciences

has increased over the past decade, few women have entered the traditionally male-dominated field of engineering. At the undergraduate level the ratio of men to women studying engineering is 5.3 to one, rising to 5.6 to one at the master's level and to 6.3 to one at the doctoral level.

ROLE MODELS IN THE CLASSROOM

We conclude with several maps examining the role of women as educators. As teaching was one of the first professions open to women, it is not surprising to find that women are well represented as teachers at the elementary and secondary levels. In 1990, more than 75% of our nation's elementary school teachers were women. The maps, "Elementary School Teachers" and "Secondary School Teachers," show the percentage of teachers who are women by state. A strong regional pattern emerges on both maps. The region of the country having the highest percentage of female teachers is virtually the same for both elementary and secondary schools. The most noticeable difference between the two sets of data is the difference in their ranges. Between 75% and 95% of elementary school teachers were women as opposed to 39% and 67% for secondary school. Moving up to the college and university level on the map, "Women Faculty," we see the range is lower still, this time from 19% to 36%. The highest values were still found in the Deep South and Mid-Atlantic regions, just as on the previous two maps. One might believe that these high values were because women are making inroads into the male-dominated

POST-GRADUATE DEGREES

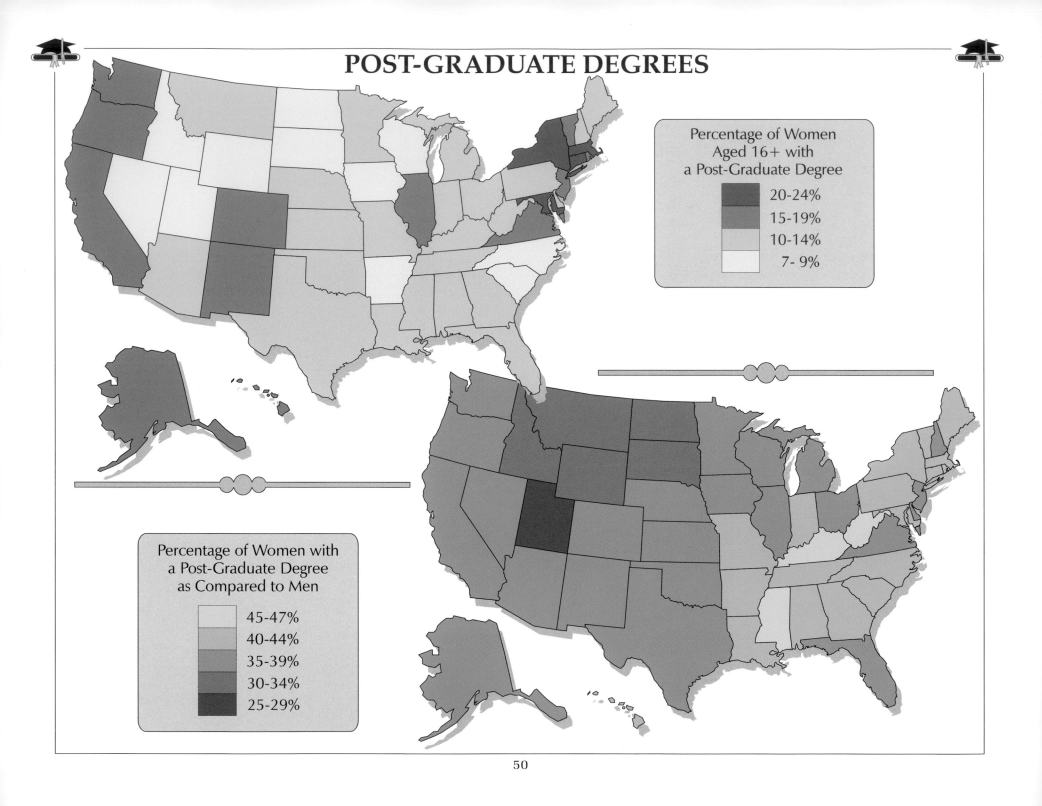

Percentage of Women
Aged 16+ with
a Post-Graduate Degree

- 20-24%
- 15-19%
- 10-14%
- 7- 9%

Percentage of Women with
a Post-Graduate Degree
as Compared to Men

- 45-47%
- 40-44%
- 35-39%
- 30-34%
- 25-29%

WOMEN MINORITIES WITH A POST-GRADUATE DEGREE

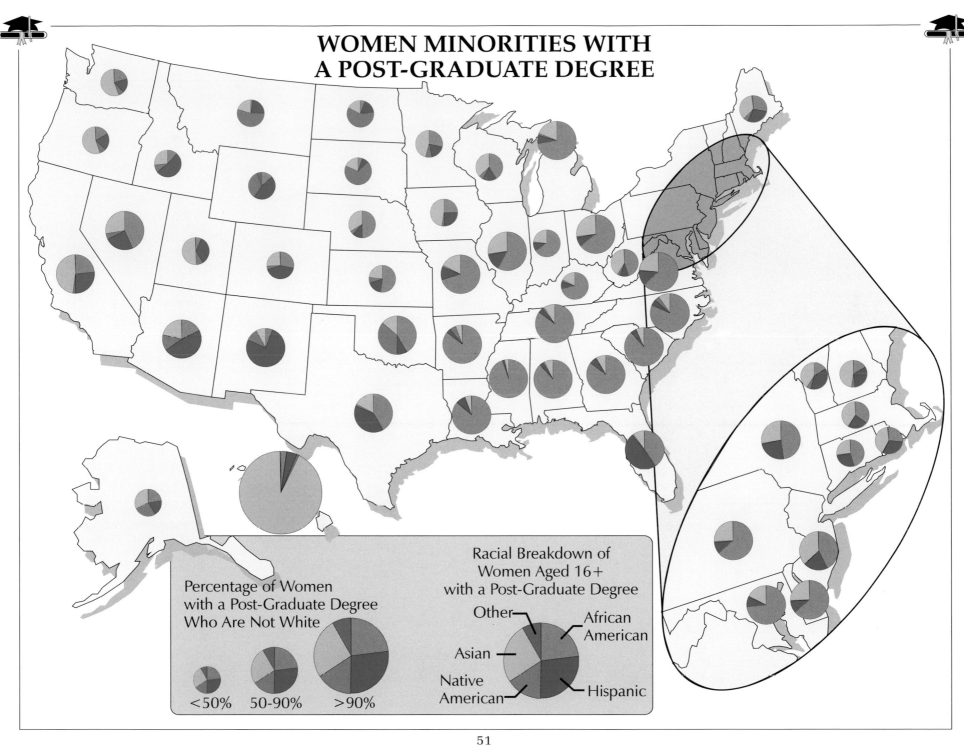

Percentage of Women
with a Post-Graduate Degree
Who Are Not White

<50%   50-90%   >90%

Racial Breakdown of
Women Aged 16+
with a Post-Graduate Degree

Other
African American
Asian
Hispanic
Native American

DISTRIBUTION OF DEGREE SPECIALIZATION
OF WOMEN AND MEN

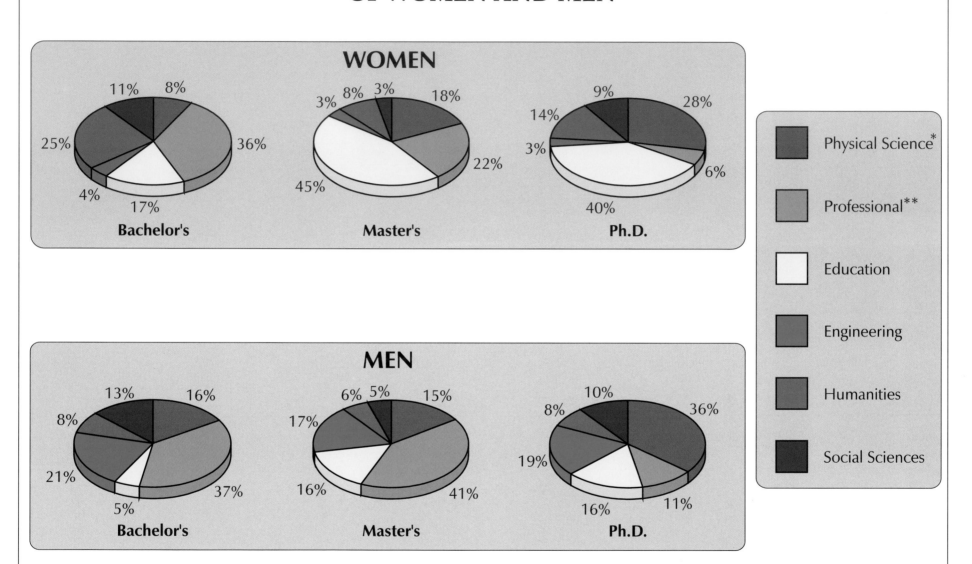

WOMEN

Bachelor's
8%, 36%, 17%, 4%, 25%, 11%

Master's
3%, 8%, 3%, 18%, 22%, 45%

Ph.D.
9%, 28%, 6%, 40%, 3%, 14%

MEN

Bachelor's
13%, 16%, 37%, 5%, 21%, 8%

Master's
6%, 5%, 15%, 41%, 16%, 17%

Ph.D.
10%, 36%, 11%, 16%, 19%, 8%

Legend:
- Physical Science*
- Professional**
- Education
- Engineering
- Humanities
- Social Sciences

* Also includes mathematics & computer science
** Also includes business, theology, speech & hearing sciences

educational hierarchy, but the reason is more likely that salaries in this region are low and don't attract as many men as women. The following map, "Women Minority Faculty in Colleges and Universities," illustrates both the percentage of women faculty who belong to a minority group and also the racial distribution of minority women faculty. The states with the largest percentages of minority faculty were Louisiana at 22% and Maryland (includes the District of Columbia) at 35%. African-American women filled the overwhelming majority of minority-held posts in both states.

During this century and particularly in the past two decades, women have made tremendous strides in their pursuit of education. It can now be said that women have the opportunity to obtain an education on an equal footing with men. As women reach higher levels of learning they become more visible in the work force, participating at levels not dreamed possible when their pursuit for equal educational opportunity began.

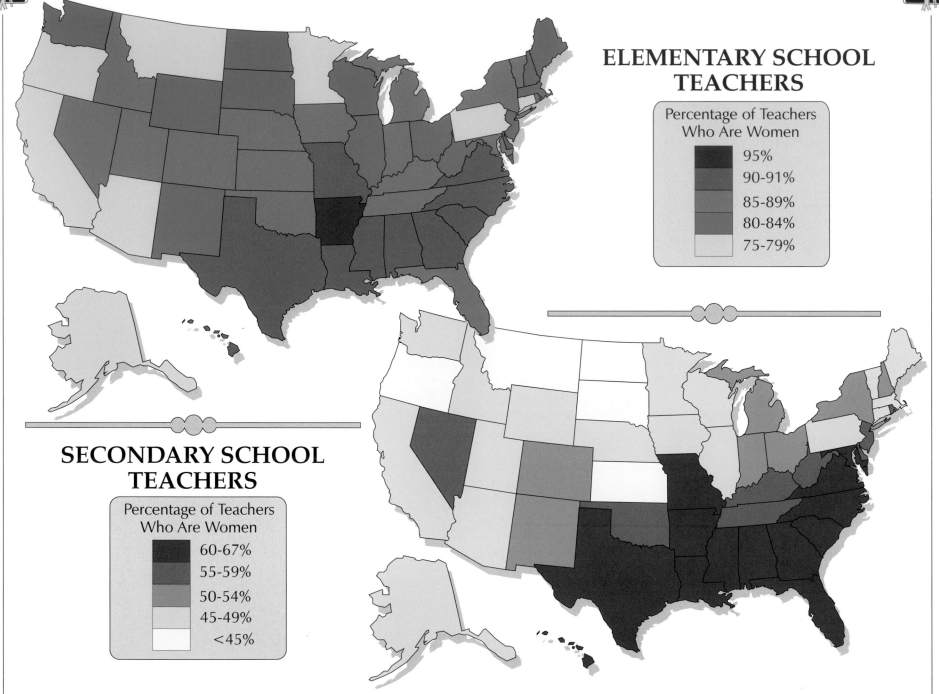

ELEMENTARY SCHOOL
TEACHERS

Percentage of Teachers
Who Are Women

95%
90-91%
85-89%
80-84%
75-79%

SECONDARY SCHOOL
TEACHERS

Percentage of Teachers
Who Are Women

60-67%
55-59%
50-54%
45-49%
<45%

WOMEN FACULTY

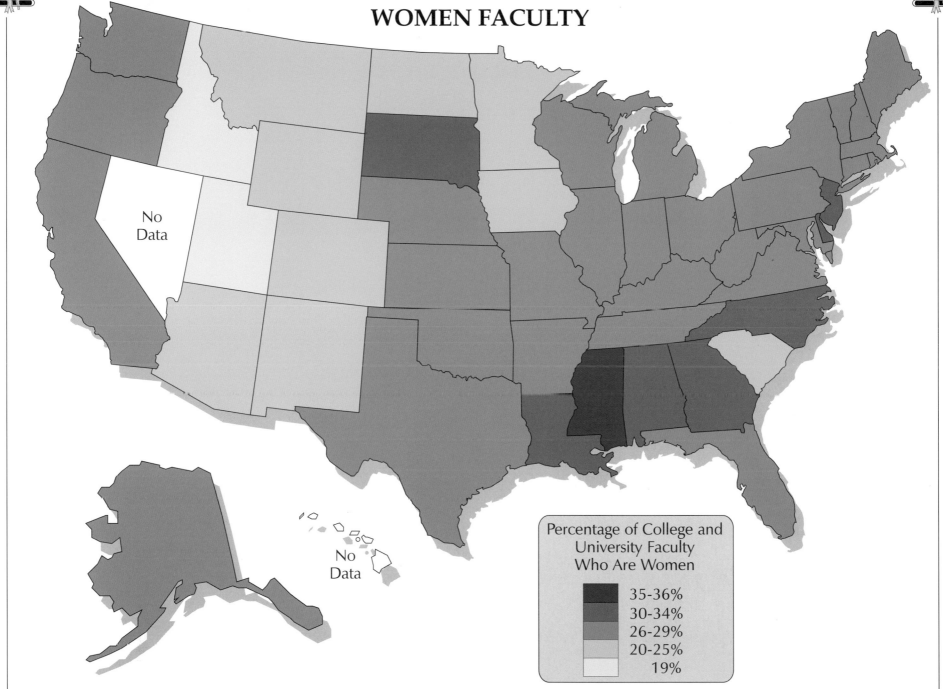

No Data

No Data

Percentage of College and University Faculty Who Are Women

35-36%
30-34%
26-29%
20-25%
19%

WOMEN MINORITY FACULTY
IN COLLEGES AND UNIVERSITIES

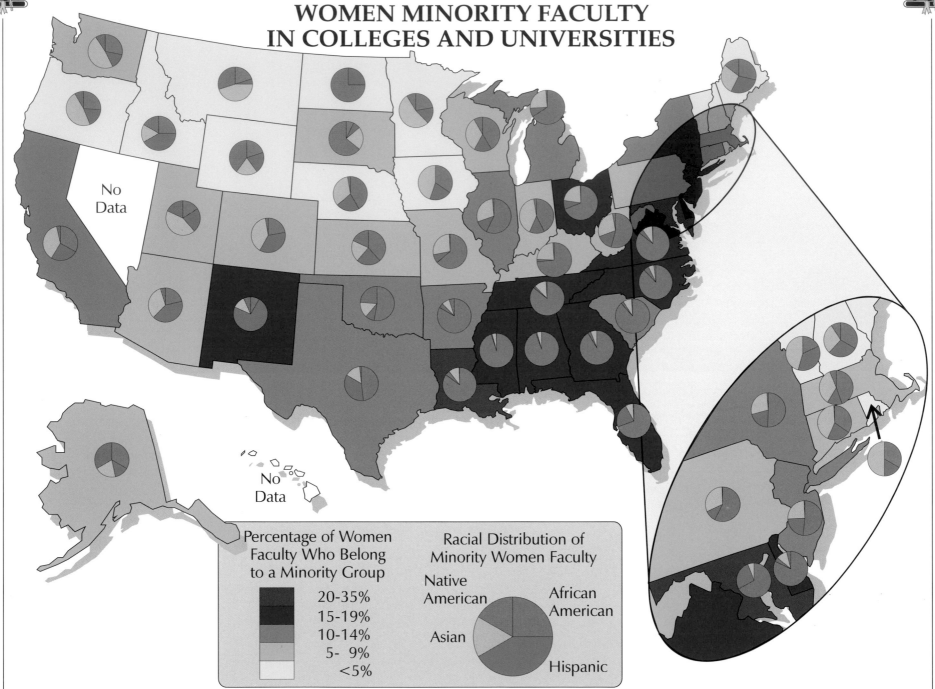

No Data

No Data

Percentage of Women Faculty Who Belong to a Minority Group

20-35%
15-19%
10-14%
5- 9%
<5%

Racial Distribution of Minority Women Faculty

Native American

African American

Asian

Hispanic

EMPLOYMENT

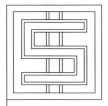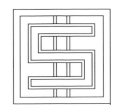

"Women's wages, increasingly, are essential for family survival. At the same time, women have primary responsibility for maintaining their families and households—work outside must be fitted around domestic duties. For many women, this means working a double day."[1]

—Joni Seager and Ann Olson

According to the 1990 Census, 56.8% of all women over the age of 16 were employed. With so many women in the labor force, it is difficult to understand how the stereotypical view that women don't "have to" work, that their incomes aren't needed to support the family, can remain so pervasive. These stereotypes, and others like them, are often the rationale for paying women less, skimping on their educational choices and discriminating against them in the workplace.

The view that a woman's primary role is that of wife and mother is a relatively recent one. In the agrarian society of the pre-industrialized United States, women were seen as valuable contributors to the economic well-being of the family. During much of the 18th century women worked in agriculture, in home-based craft work and in small, family-owned businesses. Every member of the family worked to produce the food, clothing and shelter necessary for survival. All this was done in addition to preparing and preserving food, cleaning, doing laundry, caring for children and often older family members, and other tasks required for the maintenance of the family.

This participation in the economic life of the community and family was largely made possible by the close proximity of home to the workplace, allowing women to supervise children while participating in economic tasks. Mastering these tasks did not require long periods of training, but rather were skills acquired within the family. Much of what the family needed to survive was produced at home or bartered for from other members of the community. Even though women contributed economically to the family, they were not generally considered wage earners.

In Colonial times, one of the few groups of women who were considered wage earners were those working as domestic servants. However, during the post-Revolutionary period from 1780 to 1830, many more women and children entered the work force. Many worked as domestics but a significant number did home work, such as stitching shoes, spinning, weaving cloth and making straw hats.[2] With the arrival of the industrial revolution, these home-based industries were moved to factories and became more specialized and converted to mass production. By 1840 women constituted more than half of those employed in shoe factories, textile mills and millinery shops.[3] Since the workplace and the home were no longer the same, it became difficult, if not impossible, for women to participate in the family's economic activity and to care for children. Women now had to choose between caring for their children and contributing to the economic support of their families.

As the 19th century progressed, the ideology known as the "domestic code" began to take root in our society. Women were to remain home creating a safe haven for husbands and children. Unfortunately, this was not an option for a large number of women. In an era before social security and welfare programs, single women and widows had to provide for themselves and their families. Even in two-parent families, the husband's wages were often so low that women had to work to help in the support of the family. Nevertheless, as the continued development of factories dis-

couraged home production and the increasing flow of immigrants contributed to the labor supply, the "domestic code" took hold and, by 1860, only about 15% of all women were working in the paid labor force. [4]

War is often the instrument of great social change; one change wrought by war is increased employment opportunities for women. As men go off to fight, new job opportunities open up for the women left behind. During the Civil War these jobs tended to be in nursing or clerical work, but with each succeeding war, the jobs filled by women have been increasingly in previously male-dominated fields. At the end of each war, these jobs reverted to men. Even so, each time women gained experience and a new sense of pride knowing they could do the same jobs as men; they gained confidence and greater self-esteem.

In the last few decades of the 19th century, technological advances helped to establish the assembly line factory. Unskilled women, along with immigrants and emancipated slaves, took over jobs previously held by men, primarily because they could be paid lower wages. The work was grueling. The workers put in 10-to-12-hour days, six days a week, in noisy, poorly ventilated and dangerous factories. Labor unions tended to take the view that these jobs belonged to men and that women made their greatest contribution to the family by "attending to the duties of the home."[5] Many states passed protective legislation that dictated what types of jobs women could hold, how many hours they could work, some states even prevented women from working at night. By 1914, protective legislation had been enacted in 27 states.

The late 19th century saw the emergence of the middle class. As family income increased, women were expected to remain in the home, devoting their energies to housekeeping and family. Many women were frustrated by this constricted role. Their devotion to family was unquestionable, but they needed some kind of meaningful work. Yet the stigma accorded employment for women often dissuaded them from seeking paid employment. Instead, many women focused their attentions on a host of social problems—among them abolition of slavery, temperance and women's suffrage. Women often volunteered on an almost full-time basis.

By the mid-20th century, a woman's role in the home had changed. Unlike her 19th century counterpart, she no longer had to produce much of her family's domestic needs, but was now a consumer, purchasing food and clothing for her family. While some women began to find jobs to relieve the boredom or to provide the "extras" their families wanted, more began to seek employment out of economic necessity.

Employment among women has been rising steadily during this century. At the same time we have seen an increase in the average age at which women marry, a decline in family size and a rise in the divorce rate.[6] Employment has empowered women, giving them a greater voice in decisions relating to marriage and family.

Today, more often than not, women work out of economic necessity. Their families depend on them, not just for the "extras," but for necessities. As the cost of living rises at a faster rate than salaries are increased, two or even three salaries may be necessary to support a family. Because of this, women are entering the workplace in increasing numbers. In 1950, about 34% of all women ages 16 to 64 were in the labor force. By 1980, that figure had risen to 52%. In 1990, the number had risen further to 56.8% and this figure may be low, as much of women's work as domestics, child-care providers, and in other home-based industries often goes unreported in labor force statistics. The percentage of women with children under six who are working has risen from 12% in 1950 to almost 60% in 1990 and this number would probably rise significantly if safe, affordable child care were more available.

Despite the influx of women into the labor force, women have tended to work in traditionally female occupations. In 1870 the ten leading occupations for women were domestic servants, agricultural laborers, seamstresses, dressmakers, teachers, cotton mill operators, laundresses, woolen mill operators, farmers and nurses. By the 1920s there was an increase in "white collar" jobs as women became telephone operators, clerks, bookkeepers and typists. Nursing, library work and social work were also seen as good fields for women, complementing their roles as wives and mothers.[7] Currently, the majority of women are employed in 20 of the 420 occupations listed by the Bureau of Labor Statistics. Five of the top ten women's occupations are clerical and sales jobs characterized by low wages and little opportunity for advancement.[8]

The increase in women-owned businesses since 1977 has been dramatic. Between 1977 and 1987 the percentage of all businesses owned by women rose from 7% to 30%. Much of the increase is attributable to the large number of women who have begun home-based businesses. Women who run such businesses can more easily meet family responsibilities than if they worked outside the home.

In 1989, women earned 67 cents for every dollar earned by men. By 1993 women were earning 70.6 cents for every dollar a man made.[9] While this is an improvement, a huge discrepancy still exists between the wages earned by women and men. Why? First, women as a group are less unionized than men because many of the jobs women perform are difficult to unionize. Second, many women's employment history is more intermittent as they leave the work force periodically to bear and raise children. Even while on the job, a working mother's obligations to home and family usually come first. She finds it more difficult to work overtime or travel.[10]

The result is that it takes women longer to gain the experience necessary to qualify for higher paying jobs. Finally, women tend to work more frequently than men in part-time, lower paying jobs, in order to meet family obligations. The down side of part-time work, however, is that it restricts women's future job choices and offers few, if any, benefits. More than 70% of part-time workers in the United States are female.[11]

Women continue to account for a disproportionately large percentage of those living in poverty. Ten percent of all families in this country have incomes below the poverty line. Although only 16% of these families are headed by women, they account for more than 48% of all poor families.[12] This trend—termed the "feminization of poverty"—has several causes. The disparities in pay and employment previously discussed put women at a financial disadvantage. Women are more likely to be employed at low-paying jobs with few benefits or pension plans.

Also, much of government policy is structured with the stay-at-home wife and mother as the norm. The lack of child-care facilities and public policy in support of families leave women with fewer options in the work force than their male counterparts.[13] The recent passage of the Family Leave Act might have been a step in the right direction, but the failure to add guaranteed pay during leave and the exclusion of firms with fewer than 50 employees from its provisions have considerably limited its benefits to the majority of women.

About 35% of women live below the poverty line. Those most likely to be in this situation are women with children but no husband present, accounting for almost half of all families in poverty. The increasing number of single, teen-aged women having babies and the high number of divorced women with children means that more women than ever before are responsible for the sole support of their families. Young teen-aged mothers usually don't have the training or education necessary to get a good job. Divorced women who have been full-time homemakers are at a distinct disadvantage when trying to enter the job market, perhaps for the first time. Even those who have been employed during the marriage find that their salaries don't cover all their expenses. Child support payments should help the financial status of these families, but often those entitled to child support do not receive it, although some states are passing laws requiring employers to deduct child support payments from father's wages. In addition, the lack of affordable child care means that many mothers are forced to rely on public assistance for their income.

Another group, those women over the age of 65, commonly live in poverty. According to the 1990 Census, 14.7% of all women in the United States were over the age of 65. Of the 12.8% of all persons over 65 living in poverty, the overwhelming majority, 73.2%, were women.[14] This is because the two primary sources of income for retired persons, pension plans and social security, are designed more with men in mind than with women. Half of the women now working do not have a pension plan and 80% of retired women are not eligible for pension benefits.[15] Because women frequently work part-time or leave the work force periodically to meet family obligations, they are often ineligible for pension plans and cannot always rely on the transfer of their husbands' pension plans should the husband die. Although social security benefits can be paid with as few as 10 years of employment, many women, because of breaks in employment to care for children, will fall short of the 35 years of paid full-time work necessary to qualify for full social security benefits upon their retirement. Thus, social security benefits, calculated against tenure in the work force and average earnings, are lower for women than men. Since women's salaries are lower, their benefits are usually inadequate to support themselves. On the average, retired women receive only 76 cents for every dollar received by retired male workers from social security.[16]

The recognition that sex-based discrimination has contributed to women's lower earning rate has resulted in legislation prohibiting sex discrimination in both employment and pay. The 1963 Equal Pay Act was the first federal law to prohibit discrimination in pay on the basis of sex. Then, in 1964, Title VII of the Civil Rights Act prohibited discrimination in employment on the basis of race, creed, national origin or sex. This act gave women the vehicle they needed in the struggle to eliminate the use of protective legislation to discriminate against women.

WORKING WOMEN

We begin this section with four maps and one chart illustrating women's participation in the labor force. The Census Bureau has defined the labor force as all persons 16 years and over who were either at work or actively looking for work. Members of the armed forces are included, but students, housewives, househusbands and retired workers are not. The graph, "Labor Force Through Time," charts out what percentage of the labor force was comprised of men and women from 1890 until 1988. In 1890 women made up only 17% of the labor force. Their share didn't substantially increase until after 1920 when the percentage of employed women rose steadily. This was the trend until 1980 when there was a small decline, probably because of an economy in recession.

The map, "Women in the Labor Force," displays the percentage of the total labor force that was female in each state in 1990. There is only a 6% difference between the lowest (West Virginia) and the highest values (Colorado, Maryland and the District of Columbia) with most of the higher values located along the eastern seaboard and in the Midwest. In certain states there seems to be a correlation between the percentage of women in the labor force and the number of women vs. men in the state. For example, California and Nevada have a relatively low percentage (44%) of women in the labor force and are two of only four states where men outnumber women in the population. The same is true in Idaho, Utah and Wyoming. In the eastern United States, however, no such correlation appears. States having higher percentages of women in the labor force tend to have higher percentages of women with high school diplomas. Oklahoma, Louisiana, Alabama and West Virginia, while having low percentages of women in the work force, have some of the highest populations of women as compared to men. A stronger correlation exists between the number of women in the labor force and the percentage of women with high school diplomas. Perhaps the most dramatic change in these figures over the past

LABOR FORCE THROUGH TIME

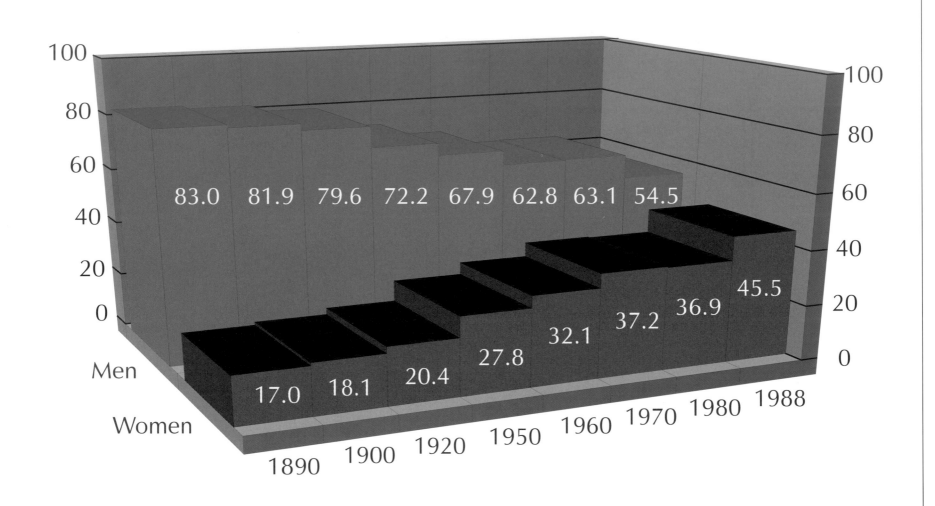

62

WOMEN IN THE LABOR FORCE

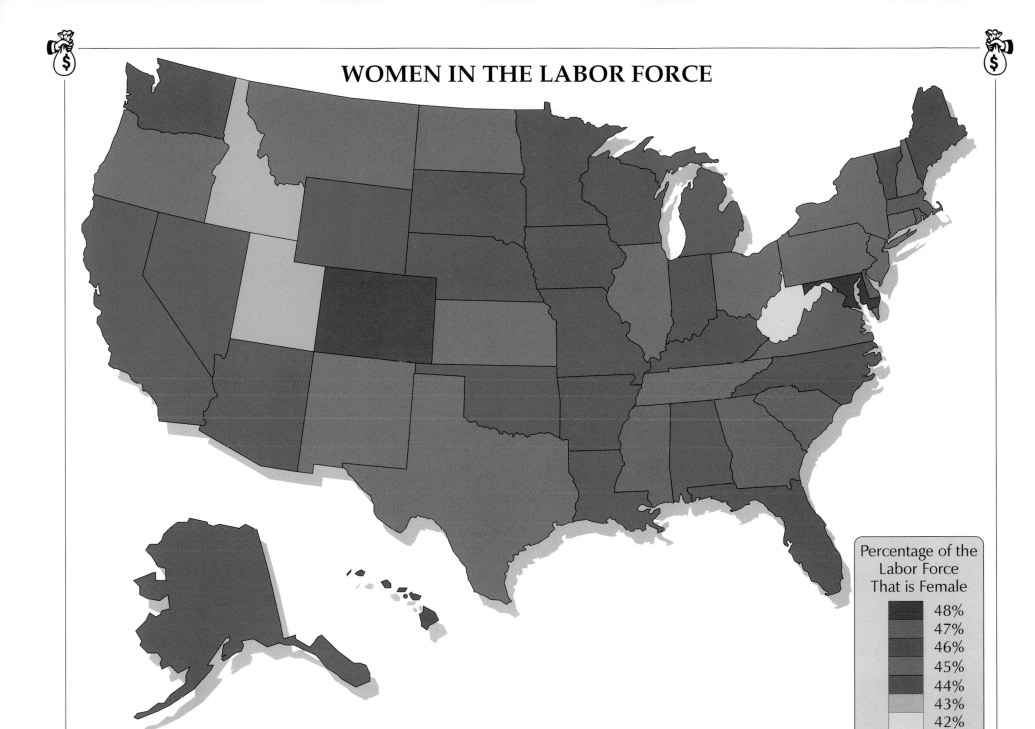

Percentage of the
Labor Force
That is Female

48%
47%
46%
45%
44%
43%
42%

WORKING WOMEN

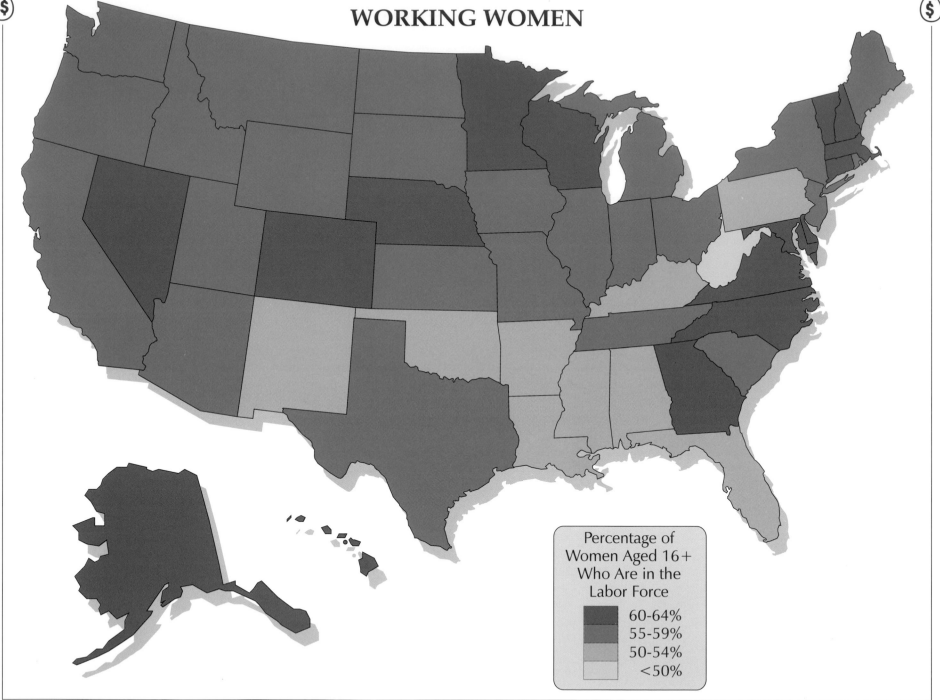

Percentage of
Women Aged 16+
Who Are in the
Labor Force

60-64%
55-59%
50-54%
<50%

WOMEN IN THE LABOR FORCE
IN MAJOR CITIES

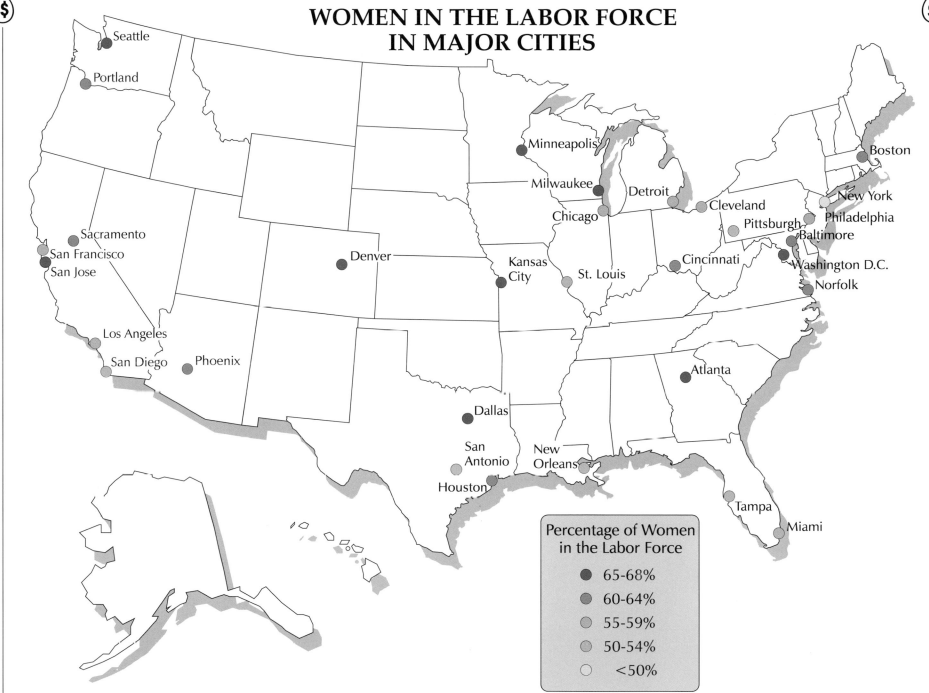

Seattle
Portland
Minneapolis
Milwaukee
Detroit
Cleveland
Boston
New York
Chicago
Pittsburgh
Philadelphia
Baltimore
Sacramento
San Francisco
San Jose
Denver
Kansas City
St. Louis
Cincinnati
Washington D.C.
Norfolk
Los Angeles
San Diego
Phoenix
Atlanta
Dallas
San Antonio
New Orleans
Houston
Tampa
Miami

Percentage of Women in the Labor Force

- 65-68%
- 60-64%
- 55-59%
- 50-54%
- <50%

ten years is in the range of data. In 1980 the range of percentages of women in the labor force went from 37% to 45%. In 1990 the values ranged from 42% to 48%, with an increase in virtually every state.

The next map in this section, "Working Women," shows the percentage of women age 16+ who are in the labor force. In 49 of the 50 states, the exception being West Virginia, more than half of the female population aged 16 and older were in the work force; in 1980, 18 states had less than half of this age group of women in the labor force.

Major cities with high percentages of women in the labor force are almost invariably located in states with a high percentage of working women. On the map, "Women in the Labor Force in Major Cities," the percentages of women in the labor force in 31 major cities across the country are identified. Cities with high values are located in states with corresponding high values, however the opposite is not always true. Certain cities, for example New York City (the only major city with less than 50% of women over 16 in the labor force) is located in New York State, which has a relatively high percentage of women in the labor force. Also, San Diego and San Antonio, both with low percentages of women in the labor force, are located in California and Texas, states with high values. However, the percentage of women in the labor force in major cities is almost always higher than the percentage for the states in which they are located.

UNEMPLOYMENT

From 1950 to the present, women's unemployment rates have exceeded men's. The map, "Unemployment in Major Cities," breaks down unemployment rates for women in major cities by race, showing the percentages of women in the labor force who are unemployed for White, African-American and Hispanic women. Since women make up the majority of the "discouraged" workers (those who are no longer looking for employment and remain uncounted in unemployment statistics), the percentage of women who are unemployed is probably higher than shown. The lowest unemployment rates are for White women, ranging from 2% to 7%. In only one major city that we examined, San Antonio, Texas, was the unemployment rate for White women higher than 7%.

Although a number of cities did not have unemployment data for African-American and Hispanic women, enough cities are represented to show a trend. The unemployment rates for Hispanic and African-American women were higher than for White women in every major city examined. African-American women have the worst rates, higher than both White and Hispanic women. In only three cities, the District of Columbia, Philadelphia and New York were the unemployment rates for African-American women in the 2–7% range.

PART-TIME WORK

Two maps, entitled "Full-Time vs. Part-Time Employment," show us the breakdown for full-time vs. part-time employment for both women and men. In the nation as a whole, between 19% and 35% of women who are employed work part-time. The rate for men working part-time falls between 6% and 13%. Nationwide, women are almost three times as likely as men to

WHITE WOMEN

UNEMPLOYMENT
IN MAJOR CITIES

AFRICAN-AMERICAN WOMEN

HISPANIC WOMEN

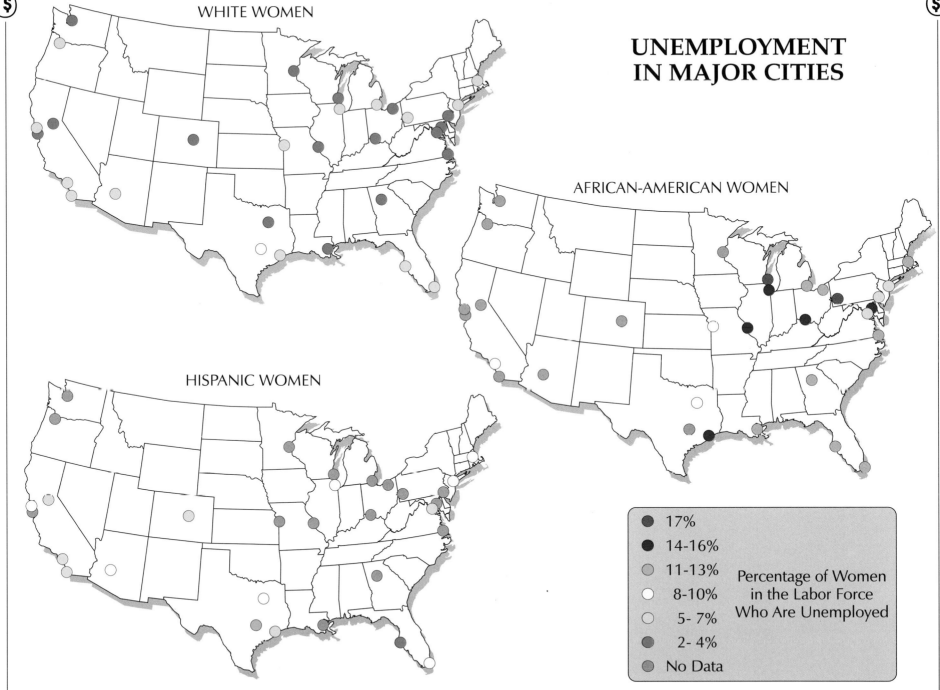

- ● 17%
- ● 14-16%
- ● 11-13%
- ○ 8-10%
- ○ 5- 7%
- ● 2- 4%
- ● No Data

Percentage of Women
in the Labor Force
Who Are Unemployed

67

FULL-TIME VS. PART-TIME EMPLOYMENT

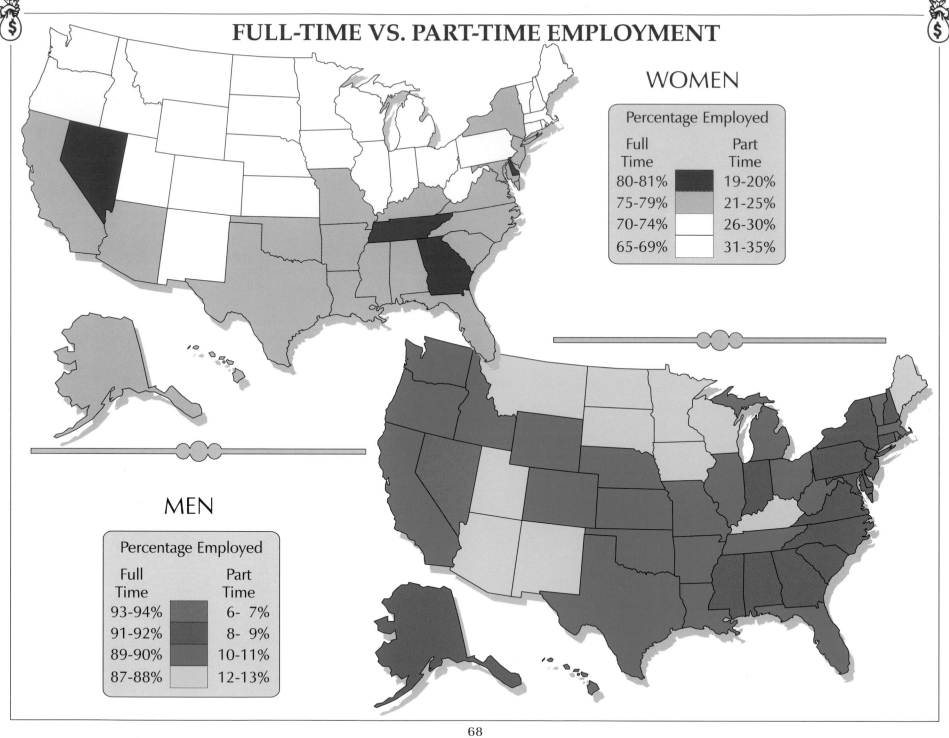

WOMEN

Percentage Employed

Full Time		Part Time
80-81%		19-20%
75-79%		21-25%
70-74%		26-30%
65-69%		31-35%

MEN

Percentage Employed

Full Time		Part Time
93-94%		6- 7%
91-92%		8- 9%
89-90%		10-11%
87-88%		12-13%

be working in part-time positions. Women in the northern half of the country are more likely to be part-time employees than women in the southern half. We believe this is attributable to the tendency for salaries to be lower in the South, thus requiring women to work full time to meet their economic needs.

Part-time work, for both sexes, can be a double-edged sword. But for women, the long-term disadvantages can outweigh the short-term advantages. Women often work part-time to enable them to be more available for their families. However, part-time employees are usually ineligible for most of the benefits that come with full-time employment. Lack of an employer-sponsored insurance plan, paid sick and vacation days and the like are a problem, but the lack of pension contributions often has the most devastating effect on women in the long term. Upon retirement, women who have spent their lives in the part-time labor force generally don't have much in savings, don't qualify for full social security benefits and don't have an income from a private pension. Often their golden years are especially lean ones.

MOTHERS ON THE JOB

In the 35 years between 1955 and 1990, the percentage of employed mothers with preschool-aged children increased threefold. The increase for mothers with children under age 18 was slightly less. The graph, "Working Mothers Through Time," depicts the percentages of employed mothers increasing from 1965 through 1975 at twice the rate of the decade before. From 1975 to 1985 there were 15% more mothers working than in the previous ten years. A steady in-

crease in employment rates for mothers means that more mothers than ever are employed for a variety of reasons. As women become more educated, they are less content to "stay at home with the kids." Also, in a society with rapidly changing technology, women frequently remain in the work force after having children because they fear the loss of job skills if they remain off the job for an extended time. But the overwhelming reason mothers are in the work force is that the financial well-being of their families depends on their employment.

Examining the map "Employed Mothers," we see that the states with the highest percentages of working mothers are in the Northern High Plains and the Midwest. Generally, the states having among the lowest median incomes for men and women have the highest percentages of working mothers. This is certainly true for the four states, Nebraska, North Dakota, South Dakota and Iowa, where between 65% and 68% of mothers are employed. Median annual incomes for men in that region range from $21,000 to $25,000 and for women from $14,000 to $16,000. These are among the nation's lowest incomes and thus two or even three incomes are needed to support a family.

States having a low percentage of employed mothers fall into two categories, those with high unemployment rates and low median incomes and those with relatively low unemployment rates and higher median incomes. The high unemployment rates in the first category mean that women (and men) have difficulty finding jobs, particularly at pay levels that would enable them to pay for child care. The second category's low unemployment and higher median incomes mean that mothers in these states often have husbands who can earn enough to support the family and enable them

WORKING MOTHERS THROUGH TIME

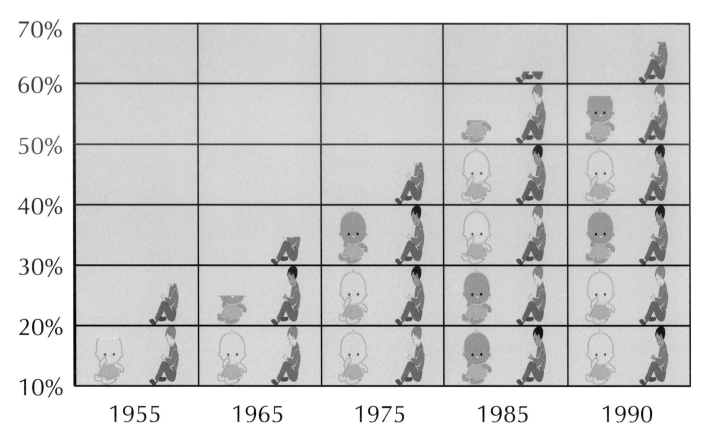

Percentage of Mothers Who Are Working

With Children < 6

With Children < 18

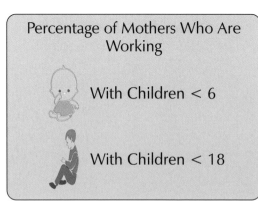

70

EMPLOYED MOTHERS

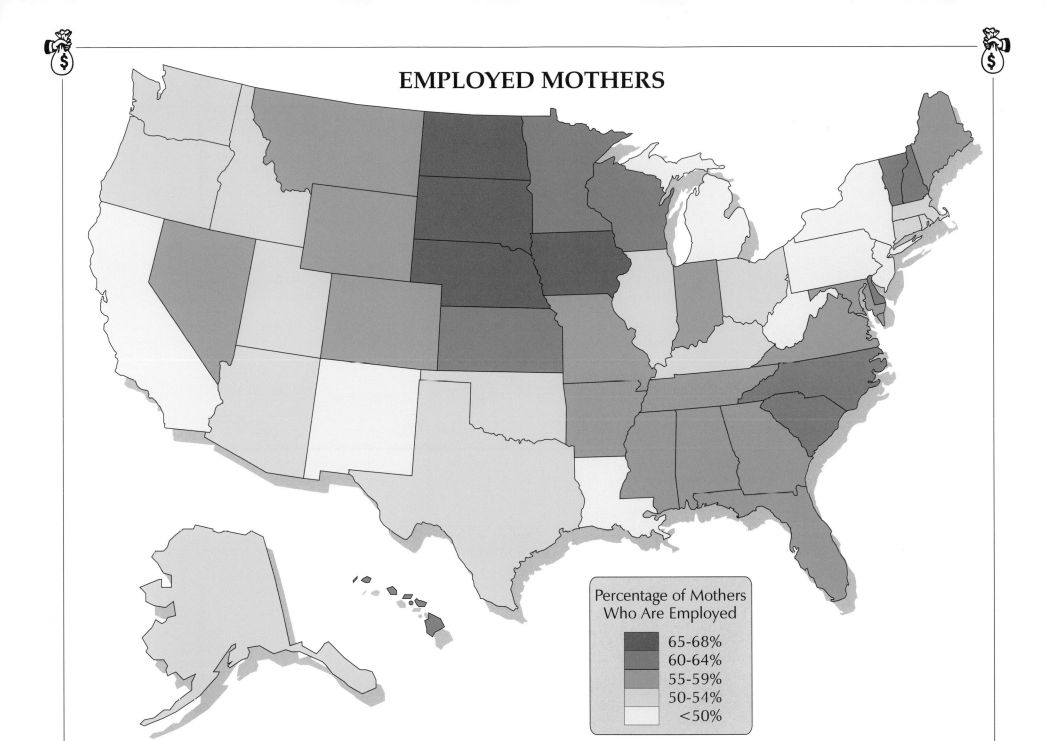

Percentage of Mothers
Who Are Employed

65-68%
60-64%
55-59%
50-54%
<50%

TWO-INCOME FAMILIES

Percentage of Families with Two Incomes

- 50-55%
- 45-49%
- 40-44%
- 37-39%

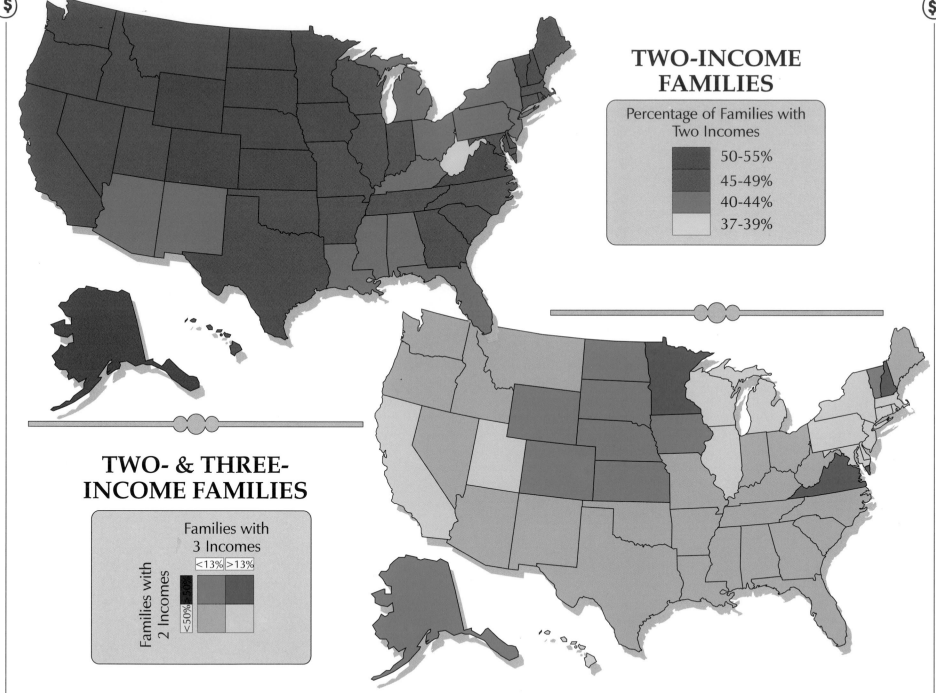

TWO- & THREE-INCOME FAMILIES

Families with 3 Incomes

	<13%	>13%
Families with 2 Incomes >50%		
<50%		

MEDIAN INCOME

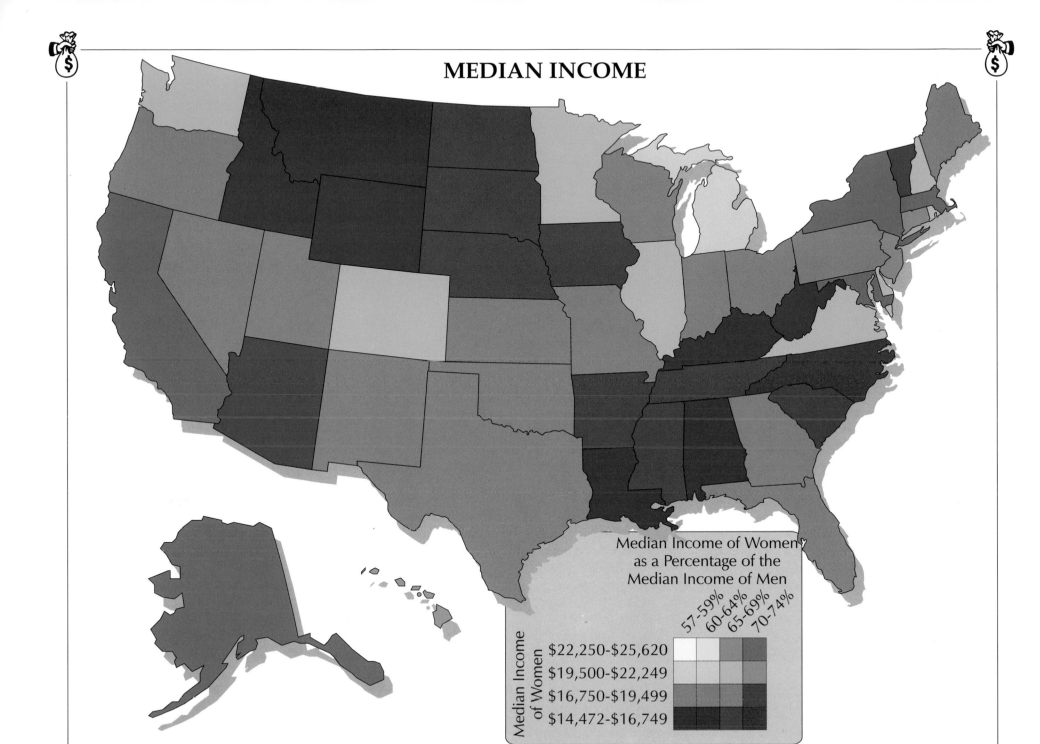

Median Income of Women as a Percentage of the Median Income of Men

	57-59%	60-64%	65-69%	70-74%
$22,250-$25,620				
$19,500-$22,249				
$16,750-$19,499				
$14,472-$16,749				

Median Income of Women

to remain at home with their children. Another consideration is the availability of day care for young children. All but one of the states with fewer than 50% of mothers working also have the lowest number of day-care facilities per 1,000 children under age five. Employment for mothers is frequently not a question of the availability of jobs, but of the availability of affordable, quality day care.

Many of the states with high percentages of working mothers also have high percentages of families earning two and three incomes, as illustrated on the maps, "Two-Income Families" and "Two- & Three-Income Families." Again, states with the higher percentages of two- and three-income families tend to be areas with lower median incomes or states with high median incomes but very high costs of living, as in Alaska.

The map, "Median Income," depicts the median income of women by state. Median income is a reflection of a region's cost of living, thus examining median income of women alone is not a good indicator of how women are valued in the work force. A better indicator of women's value in the work force is how women's income compares to that of men. In some states, such as Vermont and Arizona, where median income is low, women earn 70% or more of what men earn. There is, however, a correlation between high median income and high median income compared to that of men. Eight of the ten states where women earn 70% or more of what men earn are also states with the highest male and female median incomes. It is unfortunate that differences in median incomes between the sexes is an issue at all. Although the gap between incomes is narrowing, the inequalities still exist.

Elaborating further on the subject of earnings for men and women we can examine the graph "Median Earn-

ings Through Time, Women vs. Men." From 1960 until 1980, women's median income as a percentage of men's remained steady at about 60%, although the median incomes for both steadily rose. After 1980, incomes increased more rapidly and the percentage of women's income as compared to men's increased to 68%. Even though women's income as compared to men's is increasing, a very real gap—almost $9,000—exists between the median income of women and that of men.

Women in Poverty

To aid in our discussion of women in poverty is an illustration presenting three graphs. The first ("Poverty Levels") is a graph depicting the poverty level as established by the Social Security Administration (SSA) for a family of four. The concept of a "poverty line" was created in 1963 by employees at the SSA.

Using 1955 data that the average American family spent approximately one-third of its income on food, the SSA took a low-cost food budget prepared by the United States Department of Agriculture, multiplied it by three and thus created the "poverty line." This formula has become the basis for benefits for the decades that followed. This method ignores the fact that the food budget used for calculation is considered to be nutritionally inadequate for the long term.[17] The official poverty line for a family of four rose from an annual income of $3,000 in 1964 to $12,675 in 1989, an increase of 426%. If the rise in median income can be used as an indicator of increasing costs of living, then compare the 426% increase in the poverty line to a

MEDIAN EARNINGS THROUGH TIME
WOMEN VS. MEN

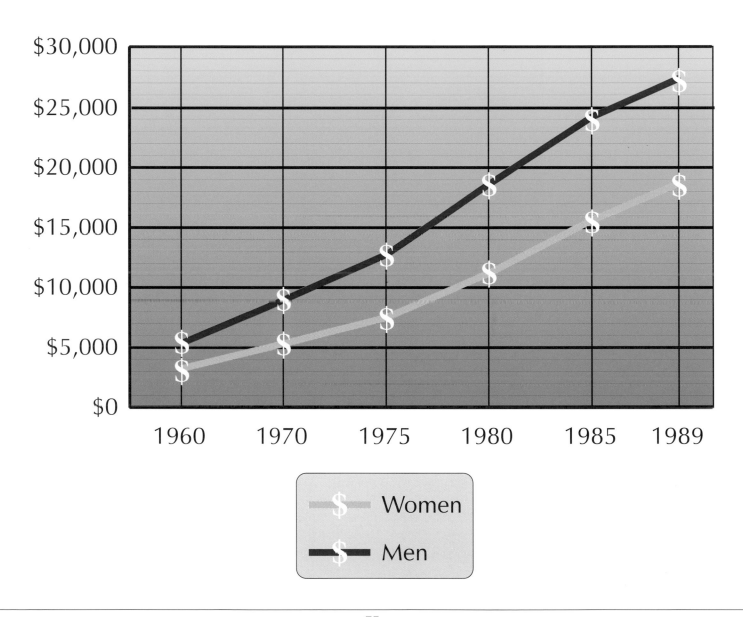

	Women	Men

POVERTY LEVEL
(FAMILY OF 4)

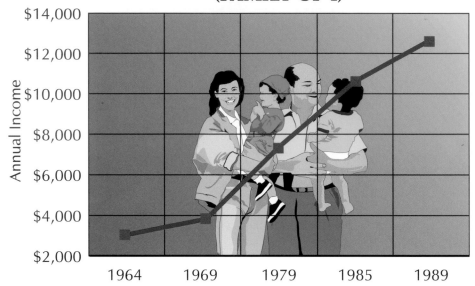

Annual Income

$14,000
$12,000
$10,000
$8,000
$6,000
$4,000
$2,000

1964   1969   1979   1985   1989

CONSUMER PRICE INDEX

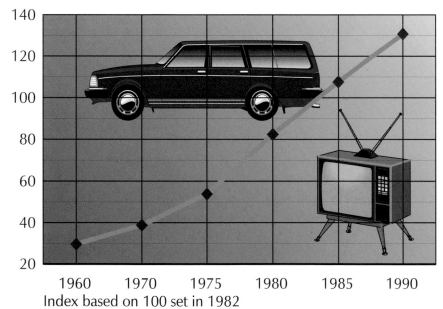

140
120
100
80
60
40
20

1960   1970   1975   1980   1985   1990

Index based on 100 set in 1982

MINIMUM WAGE

$4.00
$3.00
$2.00
$1.00
$0.00

1950 1955 1960 1965 1970 1975 1980 1985 1990

470% increase in women's median income and a 528% in men's median income over the same time frame (see "Median Earnings Through Time—Women vs. Men"). Clearly the poverty line has not increased at a rate that can even approach meeting a family's needs. To put it in more practical terms, the 1989 poverty line allows $2.89 per person per day for food, an amount that is inadequate to feed anyone, especially a growing child.

The next graph ("Consumer Price Index") illustrates the rise in the consumer price index over the past 30 years. The consumer price index is a measure of living costs based on changes in retail prices. The goods and services in a typical "market basket" are periodically priced and their prices are combined in proportion to the relative importance of the goods. This set of prices is compared with the prices collected in the base year, 1982, to determine the percentage increase or decrease. The consumer price index has been rising at a faster rate than the poverty level in the last few decades, making it more and more difficult to exist at poverty-level incomes.

The minimum wage (see chart, "Minimum Wage") in 1994 is $3.80 an hour. In 1965, when the minimum wage was $1.25 per hour, a person working forty hours per week for 50 weeks of the year earned, before taxes, $2,500 per year. This amount was $500 below the poverty level (83% of poverty level) and inadequate to support a family. By 1989, minimum wage had risen to $3.80 per hour so that an annual income for a person earning minimum wage would be $7,600 or $5,075 less than the poverty level, 60% percent of what the federal government says a family of four should be able to subsist on. Clearly, the failure of the minimum wage to increase at a rate at least equal to increases in the poverty

level has meant that those people forced to work at jobs earning minimum wage are unable to earn enough to provide for a small family.

The next two maps examine various aspects of women in poverty. The first map, "Women in Poverty," displays the percentage of female-headed households with no husband present living below the poverty level. Not surprisingly, states with a high percentage of women below the poverty line also have low median incomes for women. Unemployment rates are frequently higher than in states with lower poverty rates. Conversely, states with low poverty rates tend to have lower unemployment rates. One notable exception is Alaska, with a low poverty rate but high employment rate. Alaska is one of only four states where men outnumber women and is known for its rugged climate, not a place most women would chose to raise their families alone.

In 30 states the majority of female-headed households living in poverty are White as illustrated on the map "Racial Distribution of Women in Poverty." African Americans are the next largest racial group represented with African-American women making up the largest percentage of the poor in the Deep South and Mid-Atlantic regions. As Hispanic people can be of any race, Hispanics were not included in the data. Asian women, even when they make up a large percentage of the minority population, have very low percentages of female-headed families living in poverty.

In 1991, an average couple with both partners on social security would receive $1,022 a month. That means a yearly income of only $12,264, an amount below the poverty line. Although some of these people also receive additional income from private pension plans, the unsettling fact is that 12.8% of the elderly

WOMEN IN POVERTY

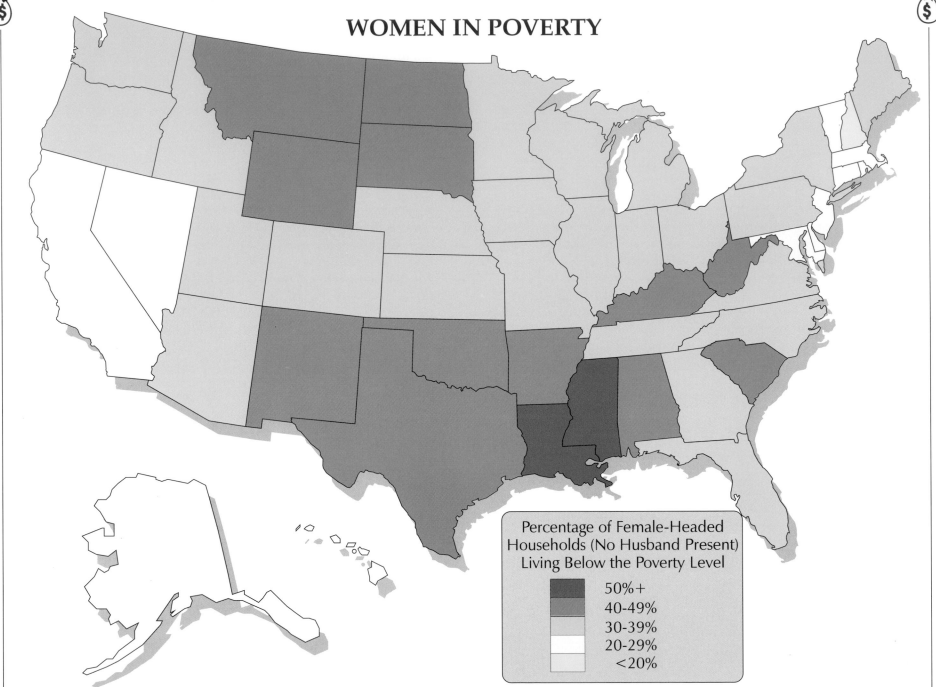

Percentage of Female-Headed
Households (No Husband Present)
Living Below the Poverty Level

50%+
40-49%
30-39%
20-29%
<20%

RACIAL DISTRIBUTION OF
WOMEN IN POVERTY

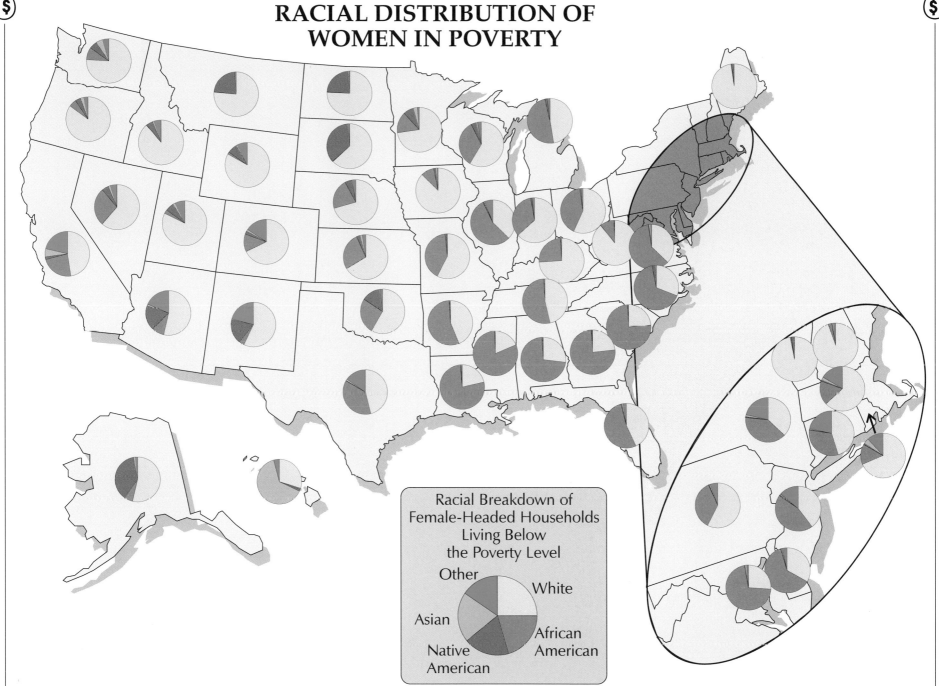

Racial Breakdown of
Female-Headed Households
Living Below
the Poverty Level

Other

White

Asian

Native
American

African
American

WOMEN ON SOCIAL SECURITY

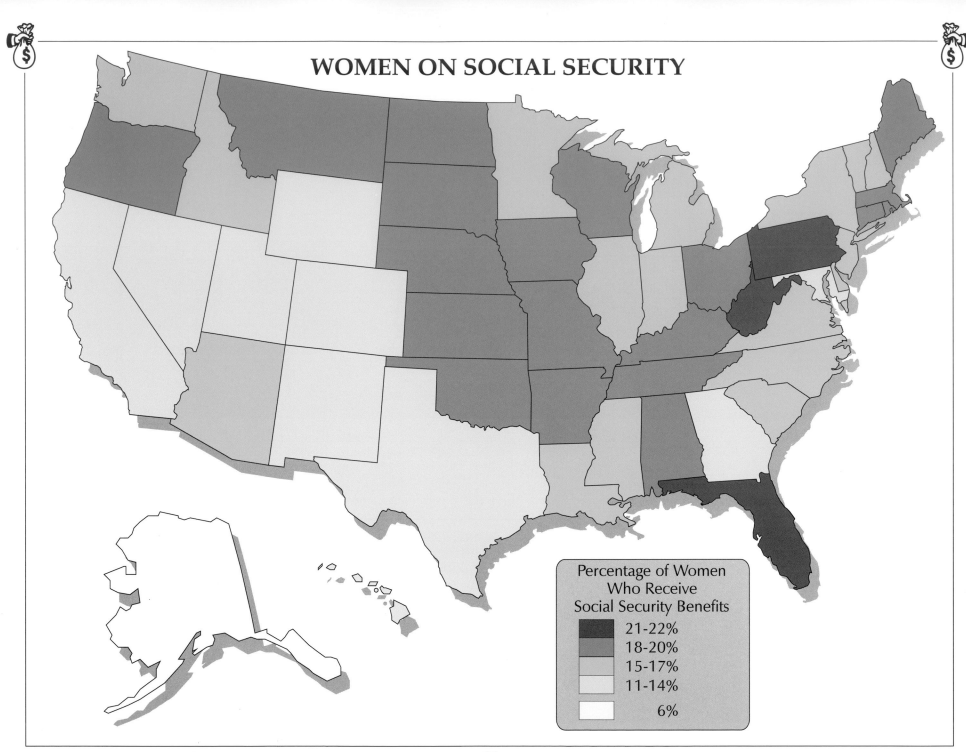

Percentage of Women
Who Receive
Social Security Benefits

21-22%

18-20%

15-17%

11-14%

6%

live in poverty and almost three-quarters of them are women. The map, "Women on Social Security," shows the percentage of women in each state receiving social security. As expected, states having the highest percentages of women receiving social security benefits are states with a large percentage of their female population over age 65. For example, between 21% and 22% of women in Florida, Pennsylvania and West Virginia receive social security benefits. Women over 65 make up 22%, 18% and 17%, respectively, of the female population of these states, well above the national average of 15%. There is a direct relationship between the size of the elderly population and the number of people receiving social security benefits. With this knowledge, predicting the future draw on the social security system—by examining the sizes of younger populations, their death rates and their income statistics—is easy.

CHILD CARE

Ruth Sidel, in her book, *Women and Children Last*, says, "There is little doubt that the absence of a high-quality, coherent, comprehensive day-care policy is a key factor in the perpetuation of poverty among women and children. Without access to affordable day care, women with young children are frequently unable to enter the labor force."[18] The map entitled "Child Day Care" shows the number of child day care establishments in each state per 1,000 children under the age of five (preschool age). In 1990, 58.2% of women with preschool aged children were in the work force. Since many of the states with high percentages

of employed mothers are woefully short on day care establishments, the majority of these mothers must entrust their children to friends, relatives or home day care.

WOMEN IN BUSINESS

In the past, discrimination against women in the work force has been evident in unequal pay structures, unfair hiring practices and diminished opportunities for advancement. As recently as 1992, discrimination on the basis of sex was prohibited in all but nine states, Wyoming, Arkansas, Georgia, Virginia, Texas, Louisiana, Mississippi, Alabama and North Carolina. The first four states on the list do, however, have laws requiring equal pay in minimum wage jobs. Protective legislation, a remnant from an earlier time, still exists in various forms in five states, as illustrated on the map, "Selected State Laws Affecting Women In Private Industry, 1992." Fortunately, the majority of the states have laws requiring equal pay and prohibiting sexual discrimination.

Although women compose almost half of the work force, they hold only 3% of top management positions among Fortune 500 corporations. In fact, the number of women in top executive positions at America's 1,000 largest corporations has increased by only 4.5% in more than a decade.[19] The following map, "Women in Management," shows both the percentage of managers who are women in each state and the percentage of women who are managers. Only seven states and the District of Columbia have management forces that are more than 30% women. Why, if women are almost

CHILD DAY CARE
1987

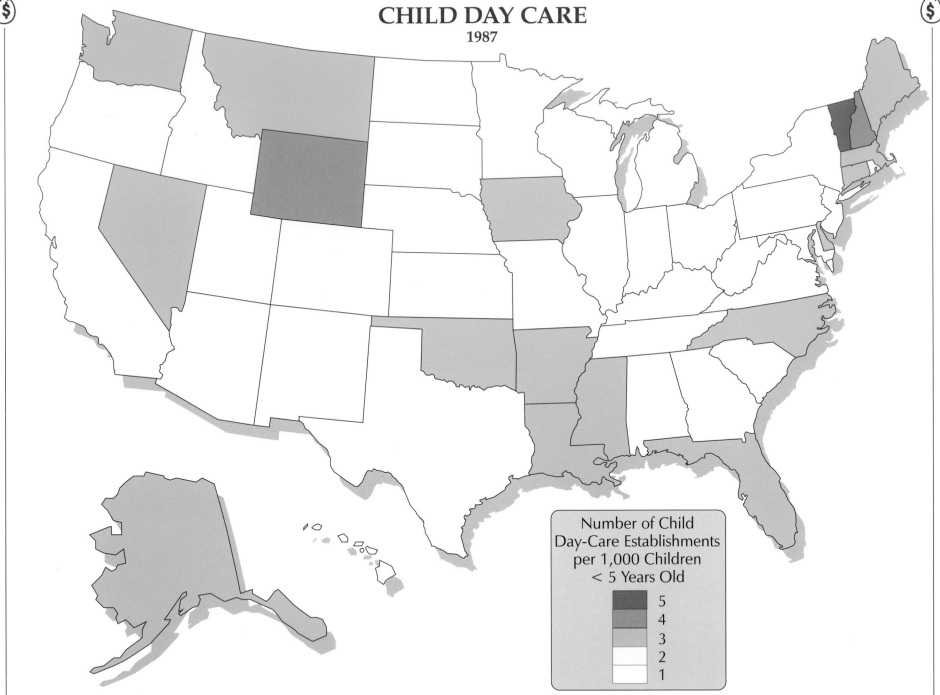

Number of Child
Day-Care Establishments
per 1,000 Children
< 5 Years Old

5
4
3
2
1

SELECTED STATE LAWS AFFECTING WOMEN
IN PRIVATE INDUSTRY, 1992

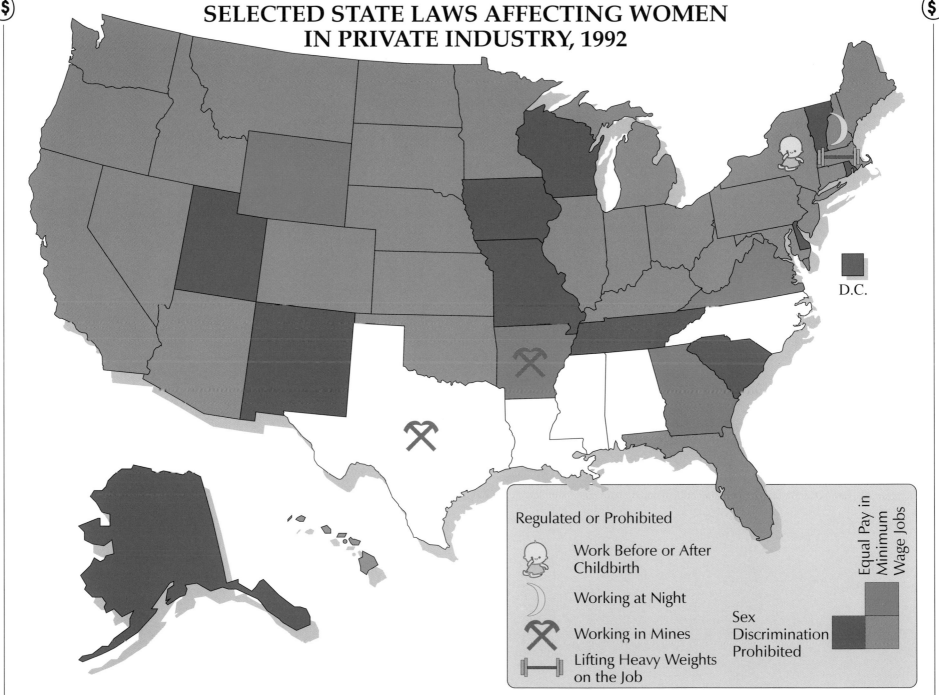

D.C.

Regulated or Prohibited

Work Before or After Childbirth

Working at Night

Working in Mines

Lifting Heavy Weights on the Job

Equal Pay in Minimum Wage Jobs

Sex Discrimination Prohibited

half of the labor force, do they hold only an average of 26% of the management positions? Why are only an average of about 6.3% of women in the work force in management positions? If only 6.3% of the female work force fills 26% of management positions, that speaks well of women's management skills. A recent study found that female managers tend to share power and information, trying to enhance their employees' sense of self-worth, while male managers use their positions of power to reward or punish employees based on bottom-line performance.[20] Women tend to get stuck or hit the "glass ceiling" at lower management levels than men. This is partly because corporations often don't pursue qualified women for top-level jobs and partly because women, because they have often taken time off for family obligations, aren't always seen as having the accumulated experience to handle top-management positions. This is an area of great potential growth for women in the future.

The number of women-owned businesses in the United States increased from 2,613,000 in 1982 to 4,115,000 in 1987. Businesses owned by women made up 30% of the total number of firms in the United States and accounted for 14% of total sales and receipts.[21] While California had the largest number of women-owned businesses, it did not rank high when considering the number of women entrepreneurs per 1,000 women in the population. The map, "Women-Owned Businesses," depicts the number of businesses owned by women per 1,000 women age 14+. The state with the highest rate of women-owned businesses was Alaska (75 per 1,000 women), closely followed by Colorado (68) and Wyoming (64). The state with the lowest rate of women-owned businesses was Mississippi where only 28 per 1,000 women were in business for themselves. More women were in business for themselves in the north central part of the United States than in the West and the South. The Deep South had a particularly low rate of women-owned businesses. Average gross sales and receipts are also displayed on the map with businesses in New Jersey and New York showing the highest average sales.

The last map in the section, "Volunteer Work," examines the percentage of women who do volunteer work. Before it was acceptable for women to be in the paid work force, they were a formidable presence in a variety of volunteer causes, often doing work that would challenge any of the nation's top male managers. Contrary to what one might expect, a trend toward greater volunteerism is evident in states with high percentages of women in the work force. States with low percentages of women in the work force, most notably in the Deep South, also have low percentages of women who do volunteer work.

WOMEN IN MANAGEMENT

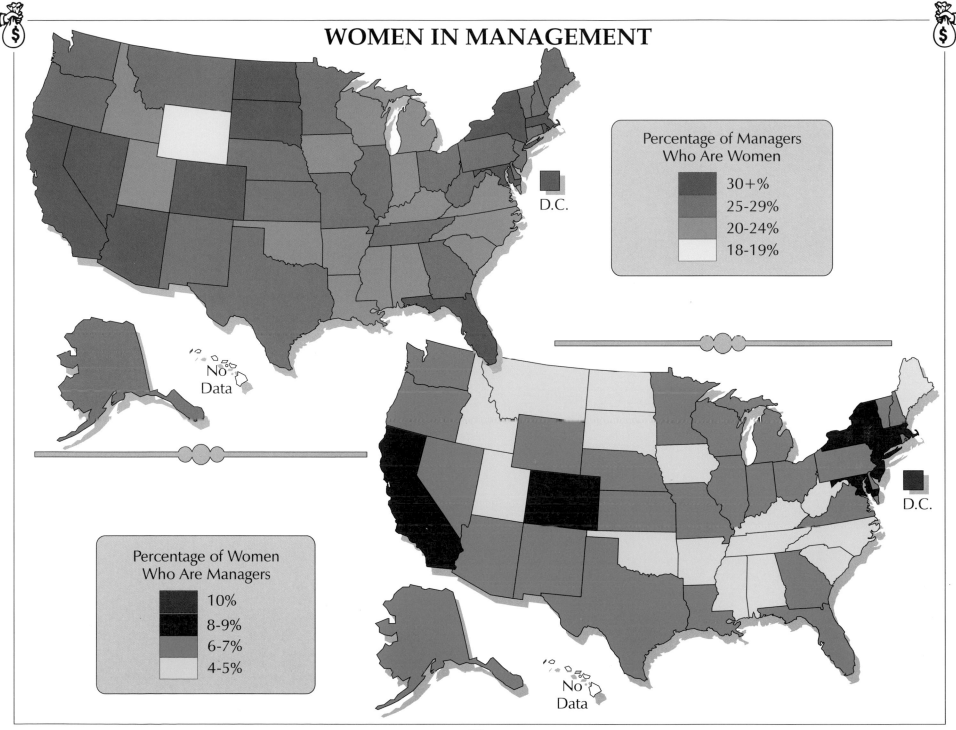

Percentage of Managers
Who Are Women

- 30+%
- 25-29%
- 20-24%
- 18-19%

D.C.

No
Data

Percentage of Women
Who Are Managers

- 10%
- 8-9%
- 6-7%
- 4-5%

D.C.

No
Data

WOMEN-OWNED BUSINESSES
1987

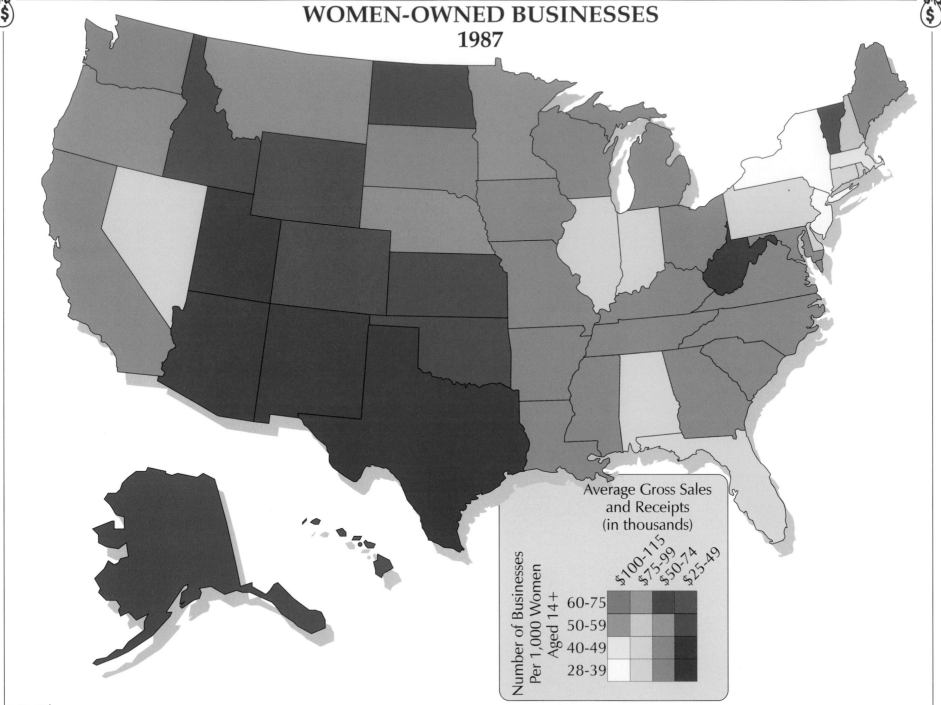

Average Gross Sales
and Receipts
(in thousands)

$100-115 $75-99 $50-74 $25-49

Number of Businesses
Per 1,000 Women
Aged 14+

60-75

50-59

40-49

28-39

VOLUNTEER WORK

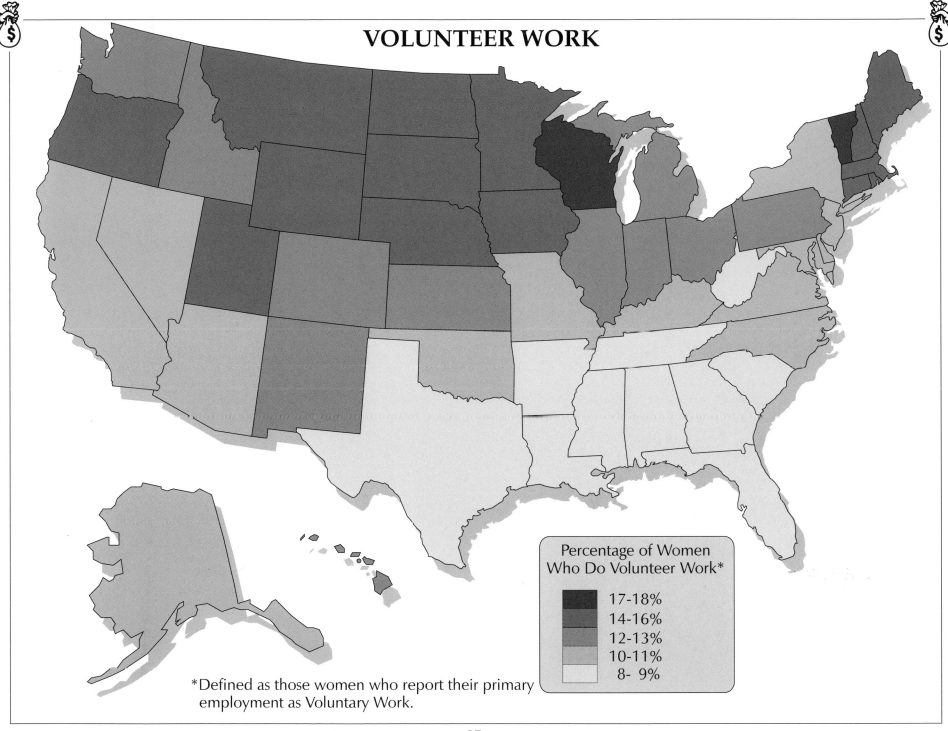

Percentage of Women
Who Do Volunteer Work*

- 17-18%
- 14-16%
- 12-13%
- 10-11%
- 8- 9%

*Defined as those women who report their primary
employment as Voluntary Work.

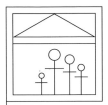
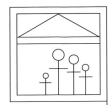

FAMILY

"Most other countries of the developed world do much more to help families than we do and they have better statistics on divorce, infant mortality, and adolescent problems. I think there's a connection. Politicians have viewed family issues as worth mentioning in speeches but not worth addressing in policy."[1]

—Pat Schroeder

Will Rogers once said, "Family is where you go at night and they have to let you in." But today the definition is not so simple. Among individuals and politicians, real disagreements arise about what the family is and what government's role in aiding it should be. Do we subscribe to the "Ozzie and Harriet" version with a Dad bringing home the paycheck and Mom staying home to care for house and children? The truth is almost no one's family is or ever was like that. Real life is more complex. Families are changing and must struggle to find a way of life that works for them; each one is unique. Women's roles in the family are changing as well, and the struggle to break free of old, out-dated, stereotypical ideas of women's "place" continues.

Women's every step forward—the right to vote, the right to equal pay, the right to decide for themselves about reproductive issues—has been greeted with forecasts of the end of the American family. Such doomsaying has proved wrong. Over the last 300 years the American family has weathered change by changing itself.[2] A woman's traditional role as wife, mother and homemaker is different than it was even 20 years ago. Women increasingly must work outside the home, not just for their own personal gratification, but in most cases to either help support or totally support their families. Thus, the family, and women's roles in it, must constantly be redefined.

At the heart of this redefinition process is the issue of child care. If women are to be able to have the opportunity to work outside the home, then they can no longer be solely responsible for the care of children in the family. Acceptable alternative child care must be available. With no national child care policy, child care remains the most difficult aspect of maintaining a working family. A hodgepodge of solutions ranging from home care and day-care centers to friends and relatives is all that most families have to rely upon. Parents constantly worry if their children are being well cared for and if the delicate balance of their lives will collapse if their child or child care provider becomes ill. Cost of day care is almost as large an issue as availability, and cost is often so high as to prohibit women from entering the work force. The availability of affordable day care is the single largest roadblock for many women attempting to enter the work force.

State and federal funding has been made available to support some child-care facilities, most noticeably for low-income women so they can return to work. Unfortunately, such programs were massively cut back during the Reagan administration and demand outstrips the number of available spaces. Why has this situation been allowed to grow worse year after year? According to Congresswoman Pat Schroeder, it is because society cannot decide how to treat the working woman. It has considered child care a "women's" issue rather than a family issue.[3]

Societal changes have resulted in changes in household structure. The Census Bureau divides households into two types, family and non-family. A family household is made up of two or more persons living together who are related by birth, marriage or adoption. Examples include a married couple with or without children, a single mother with children or an adult living with a elderly parent. The number of family households has declined from 80% of all households in 1970, to 73% in 1980, to 70% in 1990. The number of married-couple households as a percentage of all households has also declined steadily from 69% in 1970, to 60% in 1980, to 56% in 1990.[4]

Although the percentage of married-couple households has declined, the percentage of female-headed family households with no husband present has remained stable. Female-headed family households with no husband present accounted for 16.5% of all family households in 1990 with no change since 1980. This group is the majority of female-headed families; 74% of female-headed family households have no husband present, down from 82% in 1980. Fifty-seven percent of female-headed households had children under the age of 18, about the same percentage as in 1980.

The changing needs of society are redefining the family. Fewer families are composed of the traditional two parents with children. For an increasing number of people, a household shared with non-family members fulfills many of the functions of a family, specifically, those of companionship and shared economic responsibility. A non-family household consists of a person living alone or with unrelated roommates. Non-family households were about 20% of all households in 1970, rose to 27% in 1980, and by 1990 an estimated 30% of households were of this type. About 82% of these non-family households consisted of a person living alone; 59% of those living alone were women. Women over age 65 make up almost one-third of those living alone.

The past few decades have seen a change in the composition of households in the United States. The increasing number of divorced and never married single mothers has resulted in more women assuming the position of household head. Both the 1980 and 1990 censuses gave married couples the choice of assigning "head of household" status to either partner, thus an increasing number of female household heads are married and living with their spouses. The proportion of women heading their own households has increased between 1980 and 1990 from 25% to 32%. Women headed about 22% of family households in 1990, reflecting a 5% rise since 1980. More than half (56%) of non-family households were headed by women, showing little change from a decade earlier.

Many factors contribute to the changes in household structure. Women on the average are marrying later or not at all. One of the results of later marriage is that more women are living on their own or with roommates. In addition, half of all marriages end in divorce, resulting in a greater number of female-headed households.

The high rate of births to teen-age mothers has added to the growing number of female-headed families. In 1988, about 96 of every 1,000 women between the ages of 15 and 19 gave birth. The birthrate, after a 30-year decline from 2.41 in 1950 to 1.57 in 1981, began to increase in the late 1980s and by 1992 had reached 2.1. The onset of this "baby boomlet" can be attributed partly to the large number of "baby boomers" who postponed motherhood until their 30s or 40s and partly to the increase in the birth rate among teenagers. Cutbacks in family planning programs during the Reagan and Bush administrations reduced spending for family planning efforts by almost two-thirds and re-

stricted access to abortions, contributing to a high teenage birth rate.[5]

Further contributing to the rise in female-headed households are the growing numbers of elderly women living alone. As women continue to outlive men and the average age of the population rises, the proportion of this group compared to the general population will continue to increase.

WOMEN ON THEIR OWN

The first map in this section, "Women Living Alone," shows the percentage of women who are living alone. The percentages vary from a low of 6% in Mississippi to a high of 13% in West Virginia. Nationwide, a little more than 10% of all women live alone. With a few exceptions, states having high percentages of women living alone have a high proportion of women over age 65. For example, 12% of women in Pennsylvania live alone. Women over age 65 account for 18% of the total female population of the state and more than a third of this age group (37%) live alone. In every state, between 30% and 42% of women over age 65 live alone.

The next illustration ("Single Women"; "Married Women") has two maps using 1990 data, one showing the percentage of single women over age 15 and the other showing the percentage of married women over age 15. The percentages of single women varied from a low of 17% in Oklahoma to a high of 30% in Massachusetts. In 11 states, California, Connecticut, Delaware, Hawaii, Illinois, Maryland, Massachusetts, Michigan, New Jersey, New York and Rhode Island, at least one in four women over age 15 were single. The six states

WOMEN LIVING ALONE

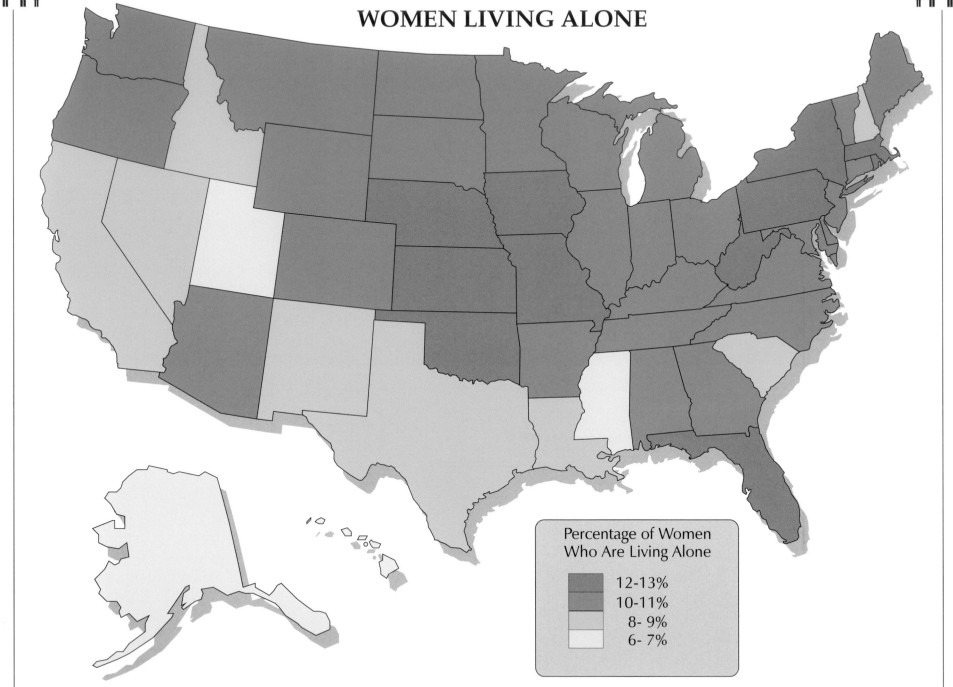

Percentage of Women
Who Are Living Alone

12-13%
10-11%
8- 9%
6- 7%

SINGLE WOMEN

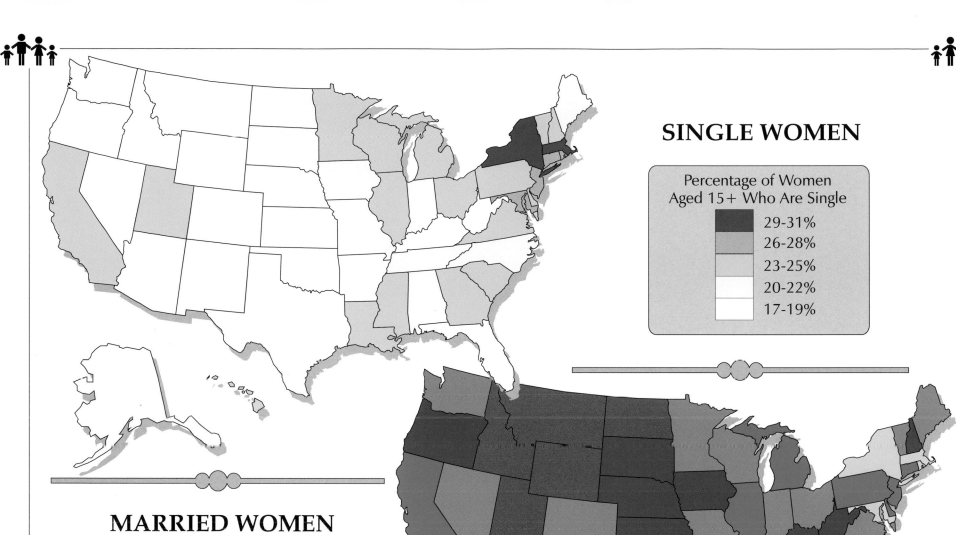

Percentage of Women
Aged 15+ Who Are Single

- 29-31%
- 26-28%
- 23-25%
- 20-22%
- 17-19%

MARRIED WOMEN

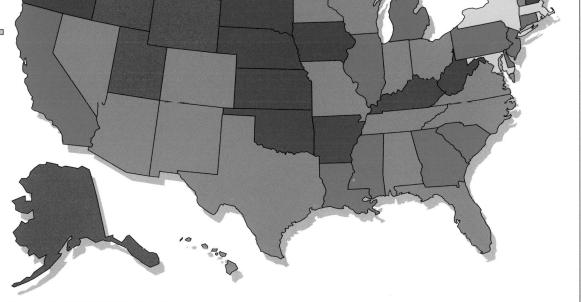

Percentage of Women
Aged 15+ Who Are Married

- 59-61%
- 56-58%
- 53-55%
- 50-52%
- 47-49%

SINGLE WOMEN VS. SINGLE MEN

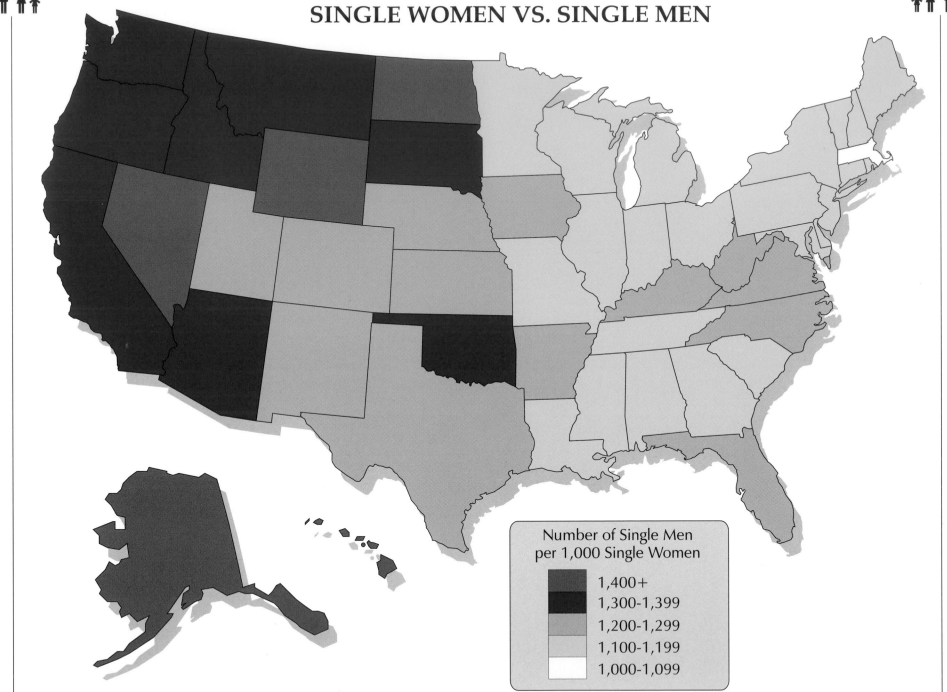

Number of Single Men
per 1,000 Single Women

- 1,400+
- 1,300-1,399
- 1,200-1,299
- 1,100-1,199
- 1,000-1,099

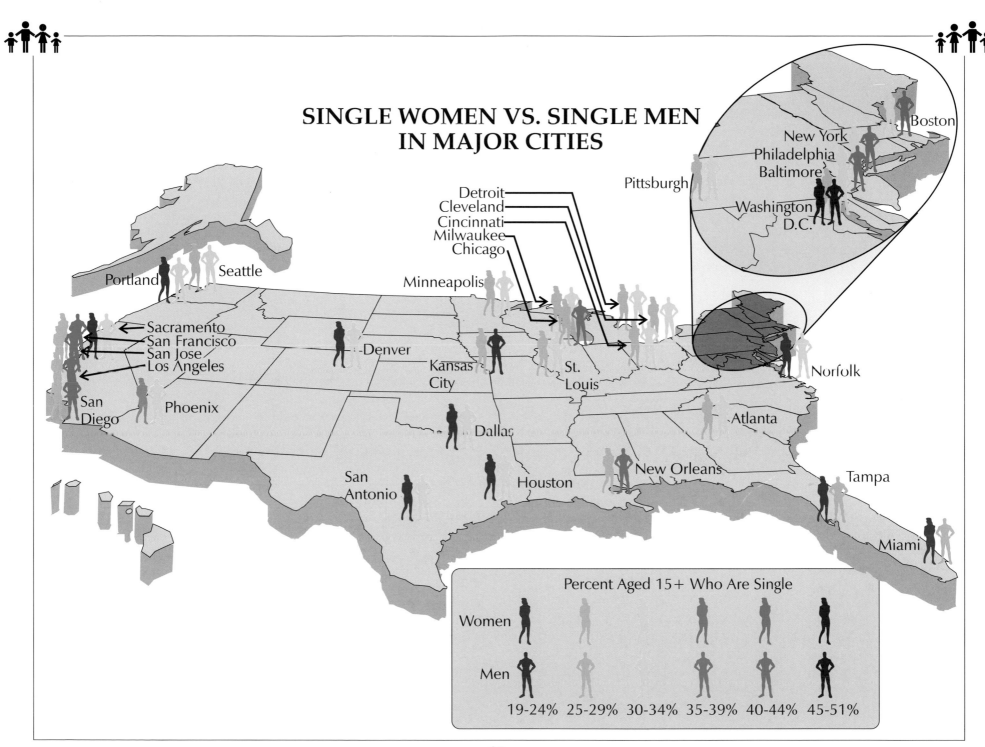

SINGLE WOMEN VS. SINGLE MEN IN MAJOR CITIES

Detroit
Cleveland
Cincinnati
Milwaukee
Chicago

Pittsburgh

Boston
New York
Philadelphia
Baltimore
Washington D.C.

Seattle
Portland

Minneapolis

Sacramento
San Francisco
San Jose
Los Angeles

Denver

Kansas City

St. Louis

Norfolk

San Diego

Phoenix

Dallas

Atlanta

San Antonio

Houston

New Orleans

Tampa

Miami

Percent Aged 15+ Who Are Single

Women					
Men					
19-24%	25-29%	30-34%	35-39%	40-44%	45-51%

95

having the highest values are located in the Northeast and are near large urban areas. Urban areas generally offer a wider selection of career and educational choices for women.

The percentages of women aged 15+ who are married range from a low of 47% in New York to a high of 61% in Idaho and Wyoming. As expected, states having higher percentages of single women have lower percentages of married women. In only four states, Maryland, Massachusetts, New York and Rhode Island, were fewer than half of the women in this age group married.

The "Single Women vs. Single Men" map compares the number of single men per 1,000 single women in the age group 15 years and older. The states having the highest proportions of single men to single women are North Dakota, Wyoming, Nevada, Alaska, and Hawaii. The data show a strong east–west division. States with more equal numbers of single men and single women are located in the east, while in the west, the proportion of single men to single women is much greater. In states where a large percentage of the female population was single, the ratio of single men to single women tended to be low. For example, Massachusetts had the highest percentage of single women in the country with 30% of women over age 15 being single; it also had the lowest ratio of single men to single women. Important to remember is that single people tend to be younger than the average adult population, and it is in these younger groups that men are most likely to outnumber women.

Single people interested in living in areas where there are large concentrations of other singles should consider living in urban areas, which generally have more singles. On the map, "Single Women Vs. Single Men in Major Cities," the percentages of women (and men) over the age of 15 who are single are displayed for selected urban areas. The District of Columbia had the highest percentages of single people of both sexes. In every major city single men outnumbered single women. Cities having the highest percentages of singles were concentrated in the Northeast and in California. Even though, in all cities examined, the percentages of single men were higher than the percentages of single women, it is still possible for single women to outnumber single men. Even though 51% of the men over age 15 in the District of Columbia were single (compared to 45% of women), the city has more single women than single men.

LEGAL ISSUES

During the past 30 years we have seen a change in society's attitude toward couples who decide to cohabitate without marrying. As society grows more tolerant of this arrangement, the number of men and women living together has increased. Common-law marriages are quite common in other cultures where formal marriage demands costly ceremony or economic exchange. This method of contracting a marriage was particularly useful on the frontier when civil or religious officials were not always available.

The map, "Common-Law Marriage and Cohabitation," indicates those states recognizing common-law marriage and those states in which cohabitation is illegal. Twelve states and the District of Columbia recognize the legal rights of a couple agreeing to live as husband and wife by making it legal to enter into a common-law marriage. Some other states disagree with this philosophy and not only do not recognize the legality of common-law marriage, but have statutes making cohabitation illegal. Paradoxically, Idaho recognizes common-law marriages, but makes cohabitation illegal.

The companion map, "Sexual Intercourse," gives the legal age of consent for women to have sexual intercourse. In two states, Mississippi and North Carolina, women can legally consent to have intercourse at the age of 12, while in seven states the age is 18. Laws in 21 states say that the age of consent is 16 and one state, Connecticut, has no law setting the age.

WEDDED BLISS

In all states, women over the age of 18 are free to marry without parental consent. Although the median age at first marriage has risen in the past 40 years, a significant number of women marry as teenagers. The "Teenage Marriage and Age of Consent" map illustrates both the minimum age of consent for women to marry (with parental permission) and the percentage of women aged 15 to 17 who are married. Sixteen is the minimum age favored by most states for marriage with parental permission. If court permission is obtained, it is often possible to marry at a younger age than specified on the map.

Nationwide the percentage of women aged 15 to 17 who are married is relatively low, ranging from 1% to 4%. These marriages, however, are often under greater pressure than marriages involving older couples. Women who marry young are often unable to complete their education and compete in the job market. Teenagers who marry often do so as the result of pregnancy and are under the added stress of becoming parents before they have grown up themselves. The "Teenage Marriage and Age of Consent" map does not always show a correlation between the number of teenage marriages and the age of consent. Only four states in the south (Georgia, Alabama, Mississippi and Texas) have a low age of consent coupled with a high percentage of teenage marriages.

Observing the changes in the ratios of marriages to divorces throughout the century is an indication of society's growing acceptance of divorce. The rise of the divorce rate throughout our recent history is not so much an indication of more unhappy marriages than at the turn of the century, but that women and men are less likely to stay in a marriage that is unsatisfying. Some have suggested that the rise in divorce rates is directly related to the women's movement and there is some truth in that belief. As women have gained more rights in society, they have become more empowered in their domestic situations. Changes in divorce laws, the so-called "no fault" divorce, have also been responsible for an increase in the rate of divorces. These laws, however, have tended to benefit men and impoverish women. Sociologist Lenore Weitzman found some disturbing results of the liberalization of divorce laws. She found that the "no-fault" divorce laws have largely eliminated alimony and forced the sale of the family home, typically causing a 73% drop in the standard of living of women and their children after a divorce while the former husband's standard of living increases 42%.[6] So the high rate of divorce can be attributed not only to women who have become empowered to leave bad marriages, but also to men who are no

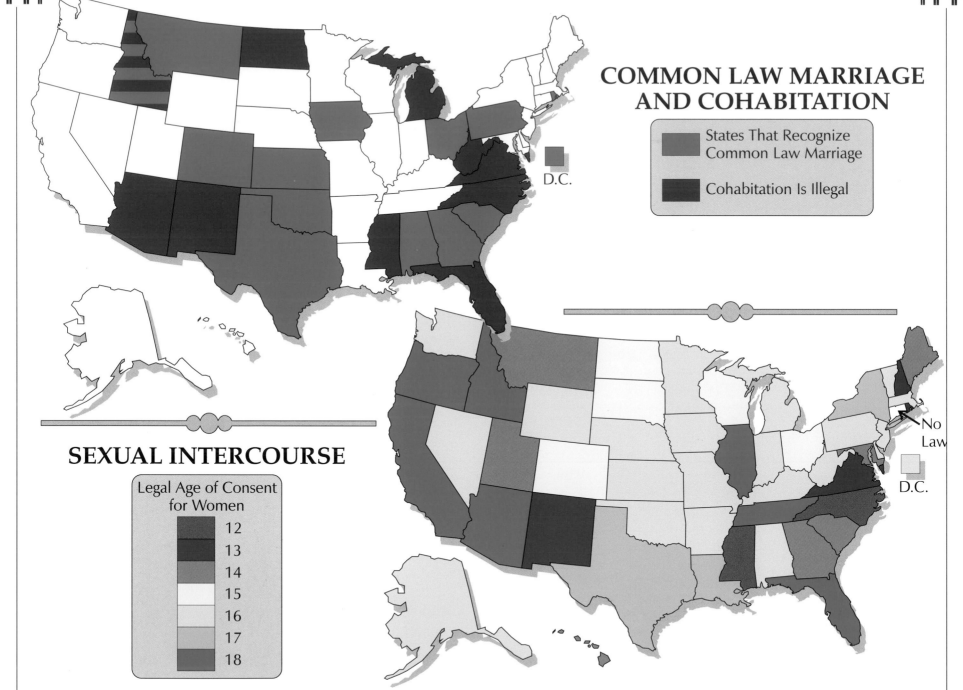

COMMON LAW MARRIAGE AND COHABITATION

- States That Recognize Common Law Marriage
- Cohabitation Is Illegal

D.C.

SEXUAL INTERCOURSE

Legal Age of Consent for Women

- 12
- 13
- 14
- 15
- 16
- 17
- 18

No Law

D.C.

longer held as responsible for the support of their families. The chart, "Marriage/Divorce Rates," compares the marriage and divorce rates at seven different intervals throughout the twentieth century. The marriage and divorce rates are expressed as the number of marriages or divorces in a given year per 1,000 persons. The marriage rate is generally related to the median age at first marriage. The marriage rate rose from 9.3 to 11.1 between 1900 and 1950 as the median age at first marriage decreased for women from 21.9 to 20.3 years and for men from 25.9 to 22.8 years. A rise in the median age for first marriage between 1970 and 1990 was accompanied by a decline in the marriage rate from 10.6 per thousand to 9.4.

There has been a steady increase in the rate of divorce since 1900 from 0.7 divorces per thousand to 4.7 in 1990. Between 1900, when one in 13 marriages ended in divorce, and 1950, the divorce rate tripled. It doubled from one in four in 1950 to one in two in 1980 and has remained fairly steady since that time.

As would be expected, the distribution of married women is related to that of single women. Areas such as the Northeast having a high percentage of single women have a relatively low number of marriages per 1,000 people, as indicated on the map, "Marriages." The astronomically high rate of 105 marriages per 1,000 people in Nevada, well-known for its numerous Las Vegas wedding chapels, is due to the lenient marriage laws that permit couples to marry with no waiting period. Marriage rates in the other 49 states range from a low of 7.2 in Pennsylvania and West Virginia to a high of 16 in South Carolina.

Divorce rates, as indicated on the map, "Divorces," go from a low of 3 per 1,000 marriages in Massachusetts to a high of 11 in Nevada. The Northeast, Midwest and Northern Plains States have a lower incidence of divorce than other areas of the country. Louisiana also ranks very low. While Nevada's liberal divorce laws explain its high rate, a number of factors are responsible for the low rates in other states. Religious beliefs are a major influence in an area's divorce rate, as evidenced by the low rate of predominantly Catholic Louisiana and the Lutheran influence in the northern Midwest. In addition, states having a low marriage rate tended to have among the lowest divorce rates.

To facilitate the comparison of marriage and divorce rates, we have used a two-variable choropleth map entitled "Marriage vs. Divorce" to combine the information. Each state's marriage and divorce rates are classified as being either above or below the national averages of 9.4 and 4.7, respectively. This allows us to classify the states into four categories: those with both marriage and divorce rates higher than average; those with both rates lower than average; states with high marriage rates but low divorce rates, and states with low rates of marriage and high rates of divorce. Twenty states, clustered in the Deep South, the Southwest and the West, fell into the first category with marriage and divorce rates both above the national average.

The second category, with both rates below the national average, had 14 states. With the exception of California, all were located in southern New England, the Northeast and around the Midwest. Four states, Maine, Maryland, Virginia and South Dakota, with high marriage rates and low divorce rates, made up the third category. North Carolina, West Virginia, Mississippi, Kansas, New Mexico, Montana and Oregon were the seven states with low marriage rates but high divorce rates in category four. One state, New Hampshire,

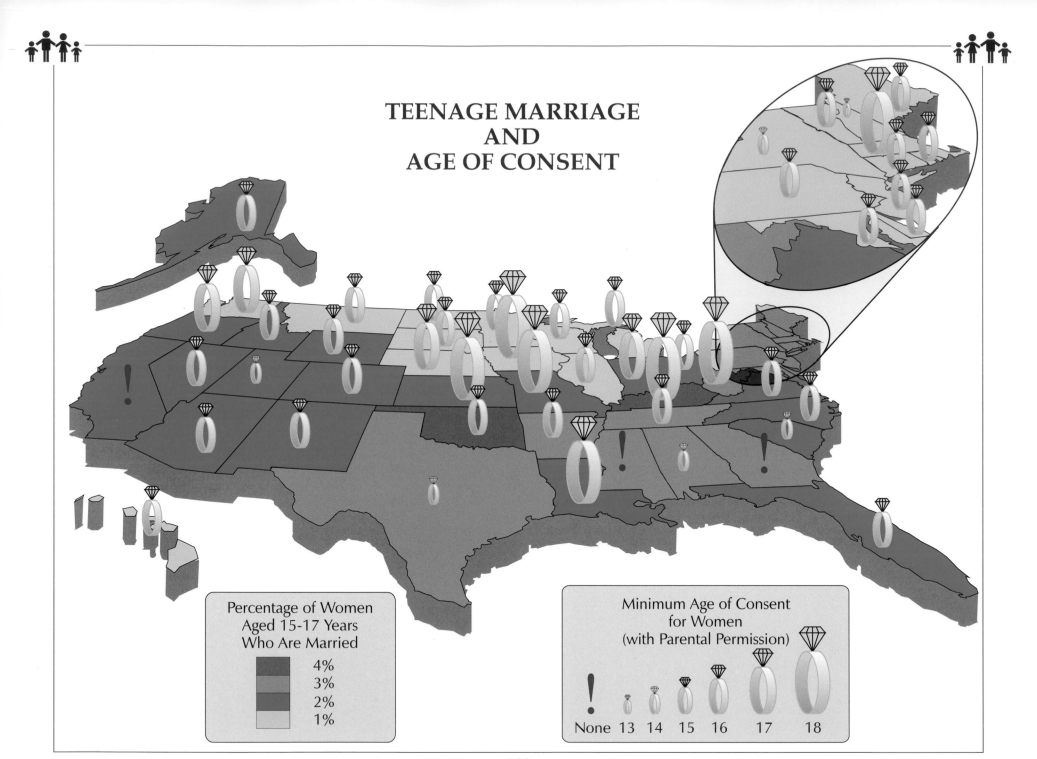

TEENAGE MARRIAGE
AND
AGE OF CONSENT

Percentage of Women
Aged 15-17 Years
Who Are Married

4%
3%
2%
1%

Minimum Age of Consent
for Women
(with Parental Permission)

None 13 14 15 16 17 18

MARRIAGE / DIVORCE RATES

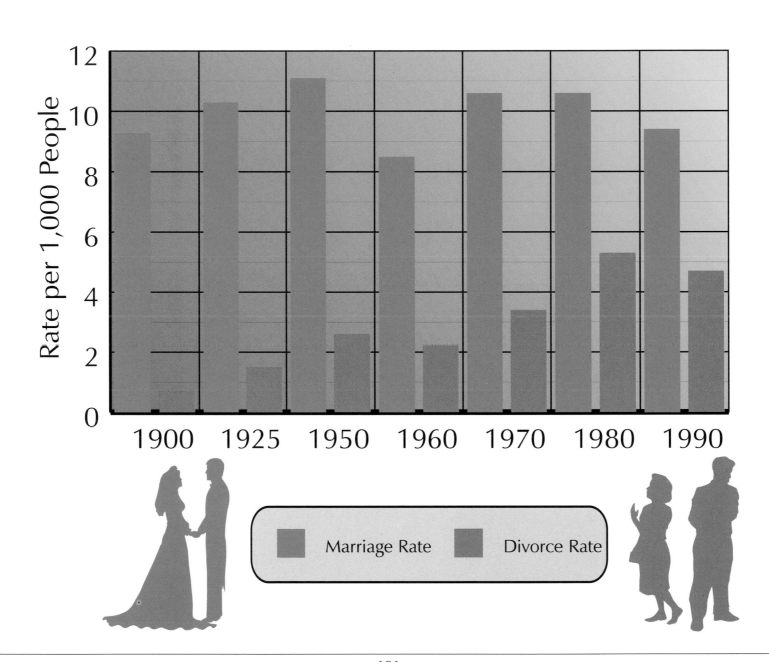

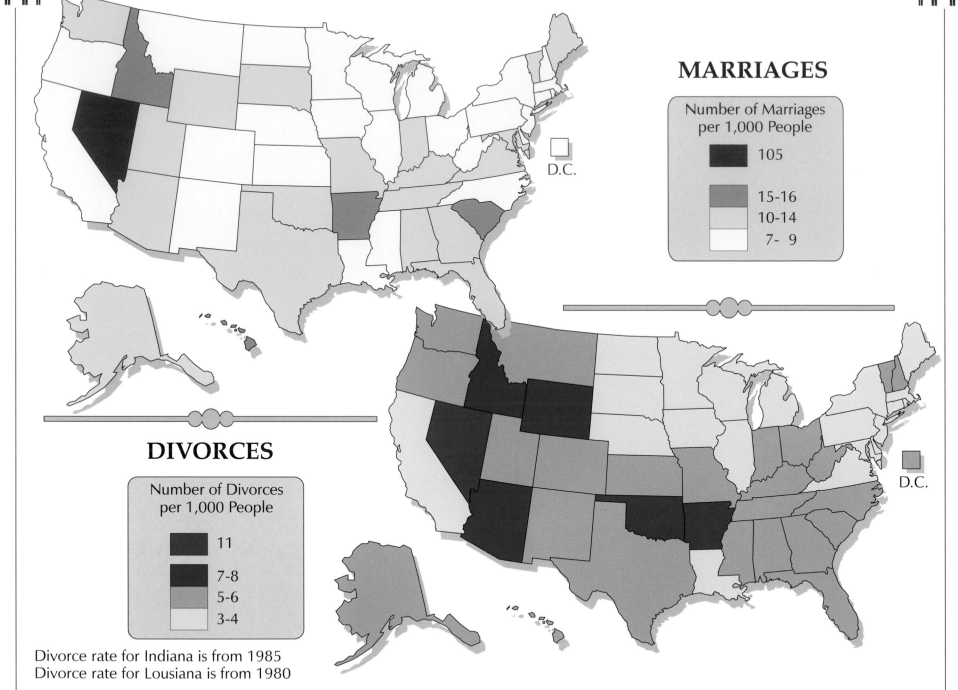

MARRIAGES

Number of Marriages
per 1,000 People

■	105
▨	15-16
▨	10-14
□	7- 9

D.C.

DIVORCES

Number of Divorces
per 1,000 People

■	11
■	7-8
▨	5-6
□	3-4

D.C.

Divorce rate for Indiana is from 1985
Divorce rate for Lousiana is from 1980

MARRIAGE VS. DIVORCE

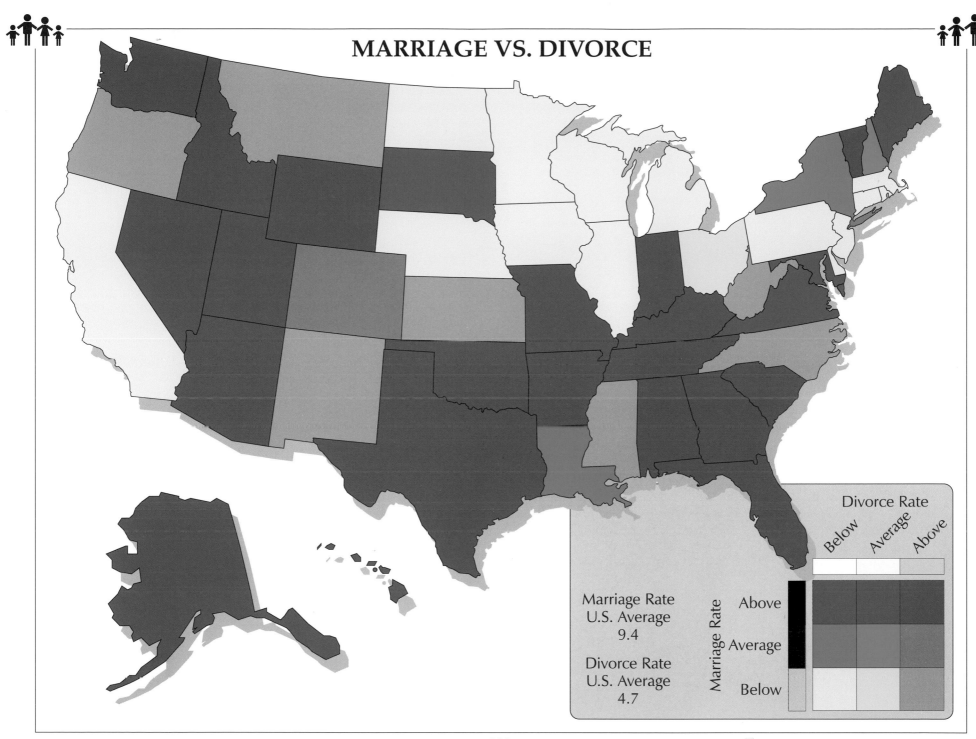

Divorce Rate

Below   Average   Above

Marriage Rate
U.S. Average
9.4

Divorce Rate
U.S. Average
4.7

Marriage Rate

Above

Average

Below

had rates of marriage and divorce equal to the national average. As one would expect, states with the highest percentages of single women (for example, Massachusetts, Connecticut, Rhode Island, New Jersey, Maryland and New York) were among those states with low or average rates of divorce.

IT'S OVER

The first map of this section, "Divorced Women," shows the percentage of women age 15 and over who were currently divorced in 1990. Women who had been divorced but had remarried were counted as married women. States with the highest proportions of divorced women were located in the western half of the United States. Nevada, where 15% of women age 15+ were divorced, had the highest percentage of divorced women. By contrast, North Dakota, South Dakota, New Jersey and Pennsylvania had the lowest percentages of divorced women, varying from 6% to 7%. Throughout the country, states with similar percentages of divorced women appear in clusters, suggesting that there are regional influences on the divorce rate.

The percentages of separated women age 15 and over are much lower than the percentages of divorced women. Since a trial separation is often the first step toward divorce, most of the women in this group will eventually join the ranks of divorced women. The data for the map, "Separated Women," fall in concentric semi-circles going outward and centered around North Dakota. The innermost states had values around 1% increasing to values around 4% in the coastal areas.

Many states, especially those concentrated in the Atlantic coastal region, with low divorce rates had relatively high percentages of separated women. This suggests that even if divorce is not an option for religious or other reasons, a woman may choose not to live with a spouse.

Continuing the discussion on divorce, a map entitled "Average Duration of Marriage Before Divorce" is included. On this map, selected states for which data were available are shaded according to the average length of marriages before divorce. The values extended from a low of seven years to a high of eleven. It is not surprising that states with low values, around seven or eight years, on this map all had higher-than-average divorce rates. The opposite is also true. With the exception of South Carolina and New Hampshire, all the states where the average divorced couple had been married ten or more years before divorce, had either average or lower-than-average divorce rates.

ALONE AGAIN

What happens after a divorce? As mentioned earlier, women and children generally lose the most economically when a family breaks up. The next three maps will attempt to show how a woman and her children are affected. The first map of the section, "Divorces With Children," illustrates what percentage of divorces involved children for the selected states for which data were available. Sadly, in the overwhelming majority of states, more than half of the divorces involved children. With children involved, divorce becomes a

DIVORCED WOMEN

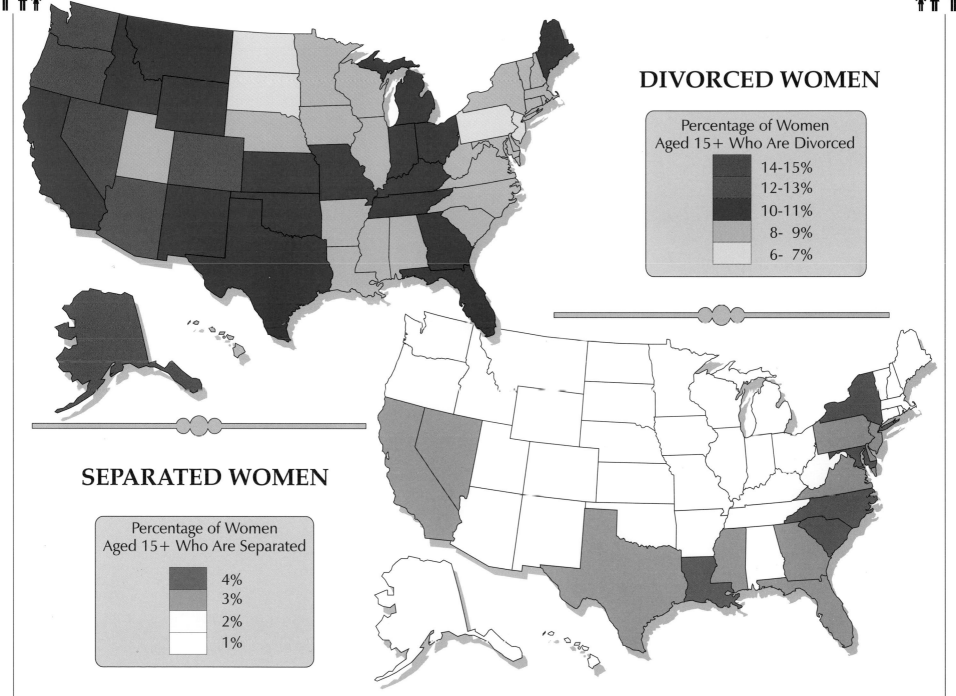

Percentage of Women
Aged 15+ Who Are Divorced

- 14-15%
- 12-13%
- 10-11%
- 8- 9%
- 6- 7%

SEPARATED WOMEN

Percentage of Women
Aged 15+ Who Are Separated

- 4%
- 3%
- 2%
- 1%

AVERAGE DURATION OF MARRIAGE BEFORE DIVORCE
(In Selected States)

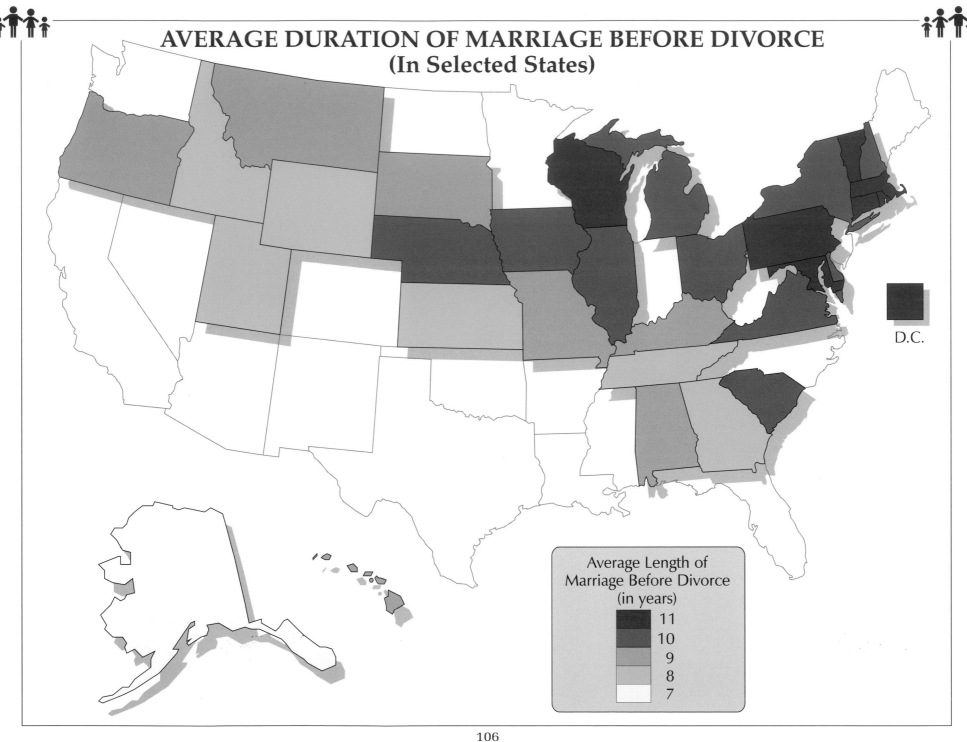

D.C.

Average Length of
Marriage Before Divorce
(in years)

11
10
9
8
7

much more complex affair, necessitating the resolution of custody and child support issues as well as spousal support and property distribution.

The following maps, "Laws Regulating Child Support and Custody," show which states have laws regulating child support and custody issues in four areas: states that allow the garnisheeing of wages for child support; states with statutory custody guidelines; states that consider the child's wishes for custody; and states with joint custody laws. As of 1990, all but two states, Mississippi and New Jersey, had laws allowing a parents wages to be garnisheed for payment of child support. Thirty states had statutory guidelines to be used by court officials in establishing matters of custody. Thirty-nine states had laws requiring the courts to consider a child's wish as to which parent has custody and 37 states had laws that allowed for joint custody.

No-fault divorce laws have meant that fewer and fewer woman receive spousal support after a divorce. At first glance this may seem to be a fair and equitable arrangement. After all, the women's movement has been working toward more independence for women. However, women who have either remained out of the work force or have limited their careers in order to devote themselves to their families, are rarely able to earn enough to even approach the economic level they had while married. All too frequently, these women wind up in poverty. The illustration, "Spousal Support," has four maps addressing state laws for separate issues considered before determining spousal support.

The first map shows which states are community property states (meaning that the property of the marriage is divided 50–50, barring the existence of a premarital agreement) and which states provide for equitable distribution of property. The majority of

states are of the latter type, allowing the courts much greater latitude in distributing property. Mississippi has no laws regarding property distribution.

A second map shows which states have laws allowing spousal support to be denied on the basis of marital misconduct and which states do not consider marital fault. Twelve states have statutes allowing for the modification or ending of spousal support if the party receiving support cohabitates with a member of the opposite sex. The final map in this illustration indicates which states allow contribution to a spouse's professional degree to be considered before determining property and spousal support awards.

Between 10% and 15% of all women age 15 and over are widowed. The map, "Widows," displays the percentage of women aged 15+ who are widowed in each state. Widows accounted for between 10% and 15% of all women in 46 states, up from 42 states in 1980. Widows were a smaller proportion of the population in the western states. Obviously, states with a higher proportion of widows tended to have populations of older women in proportions higher than states having a lower percentage of widows. Alaska had the lowest proportion of widows, representing only 5% of the female population age 15 and over. West Virginia ranked highest at 15%.

Women live longer than men. This means that women are the predominant residents in nursing homes. The percentages for all 50 states are presented on the map, "Women in Nursing Homes." Nationwide between 3% and 10% of all women aged 65 and over are living in nursing homes. Hawaii has the smallest percentage of women in nursing homes, only 3%, due in part to the disproportionately large Asian population with strong traditions of families caring for their

DIVORCES WITH CHILDREN
(In Selected States)

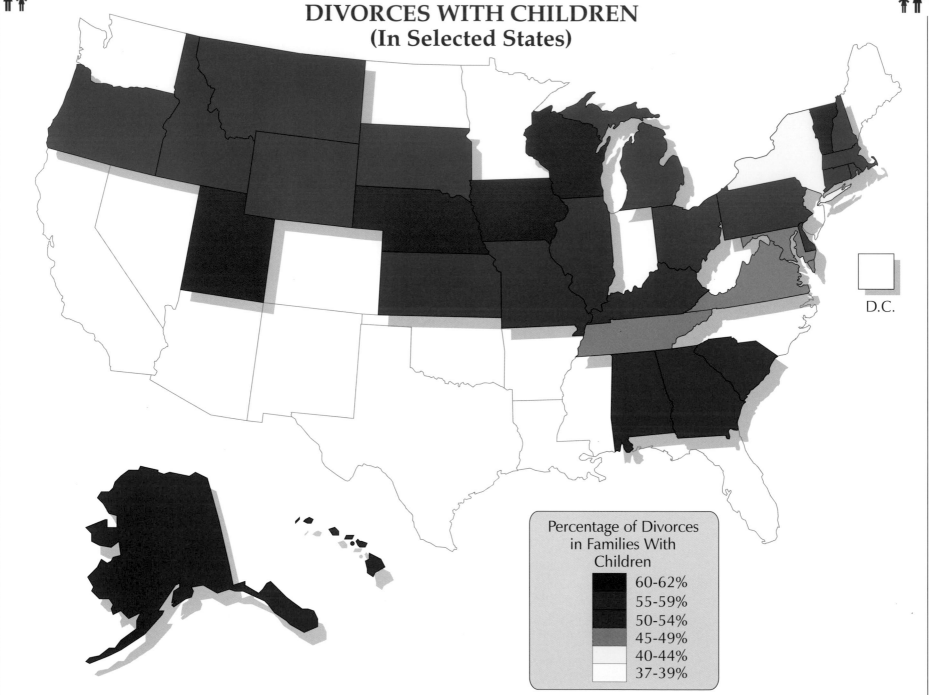

D.C.

Percentage of Divorces
in Families With
Children

60-62%
55-59%
50-54%
45-49%
40-44%
37-39%

LAWS REGULATING CHILD SUPPORT AND CUSTODY

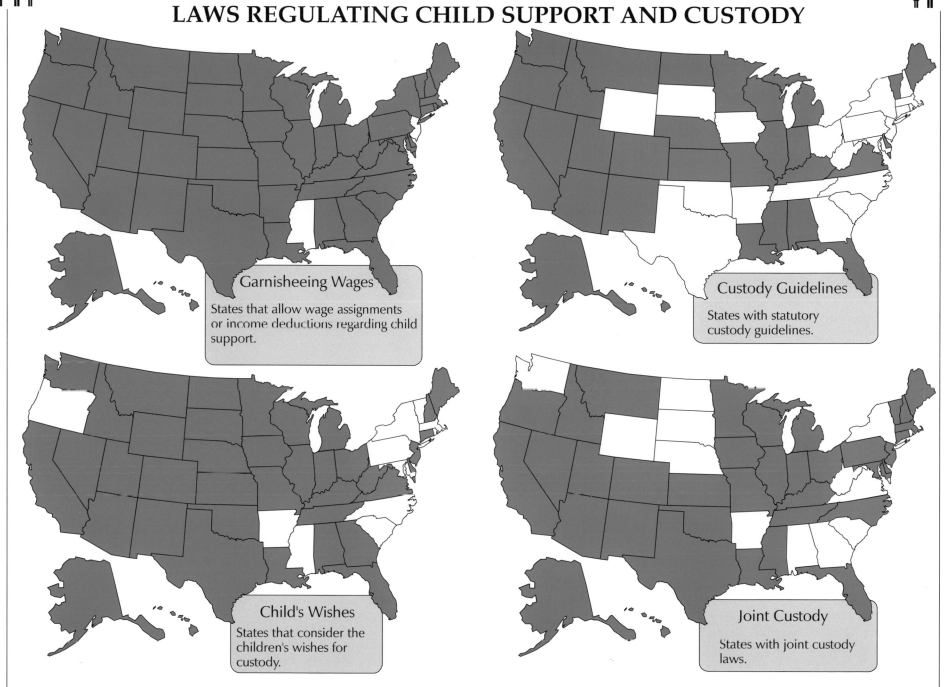

Garnisheeing Wages

States that allow wage assignments or income deductions regarding child support.

Custody Guidelines

States with statutory custody guidelines.

Child's Wishes

States that consider the children's wishes for custody.

Joint Custody

States with joint custody laws.

SPOUSAL SUPPORT

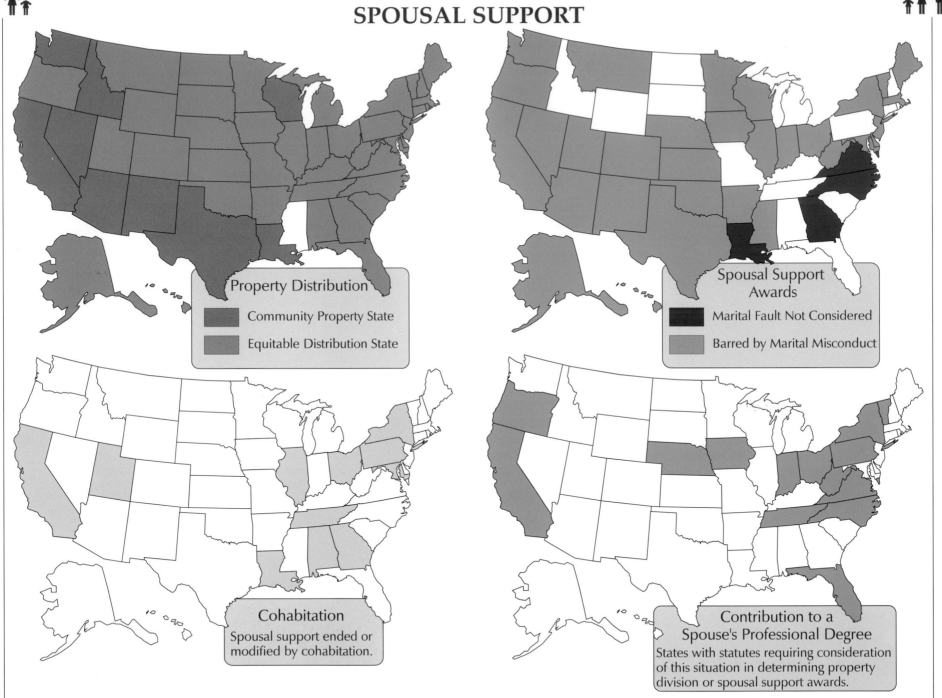

Property Distribution

- Community Property State
- Equitable Distribution State

Spousal Support Awards

- Marital Fault Not Considered
- Barred by Marital Misconduct

Cohabitation
Spousal support ended or modified by cohabitation.

Contribution to a Spouse's Professional Degree
States with statutes requiring consideration of this situation in determining property division or spousal support awards.

WIDOWS

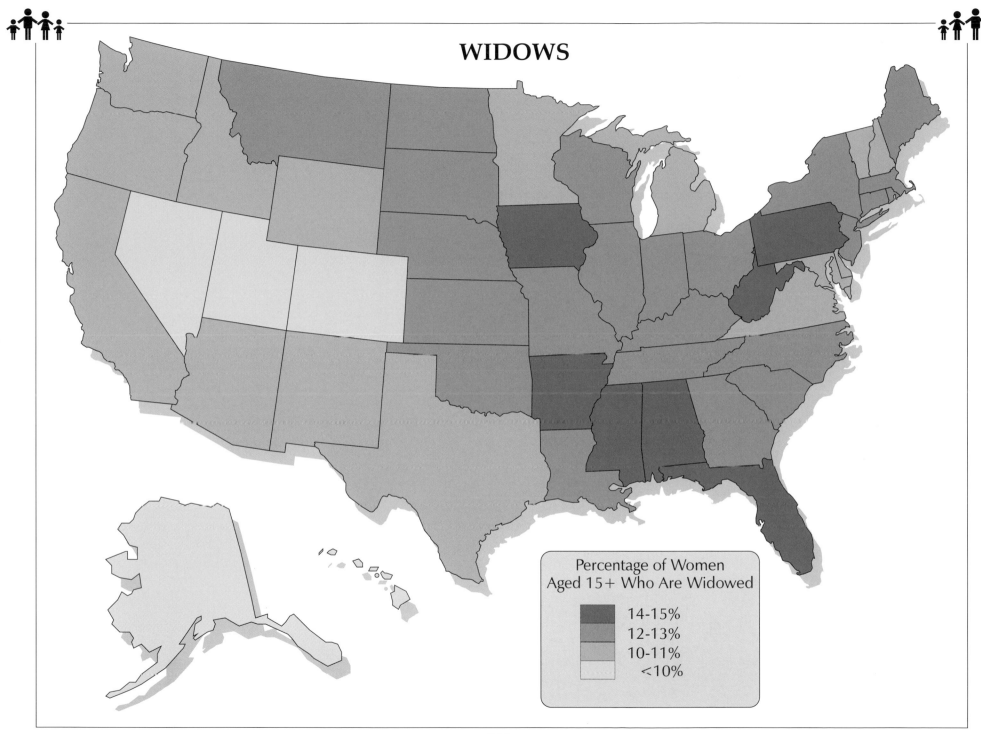

Percentage of Women
Aged 15+ Who Are Widowed

- 14-15%
- 12-13%
- 10-11%
- <10%

WOMEN IN NURSING HOMES

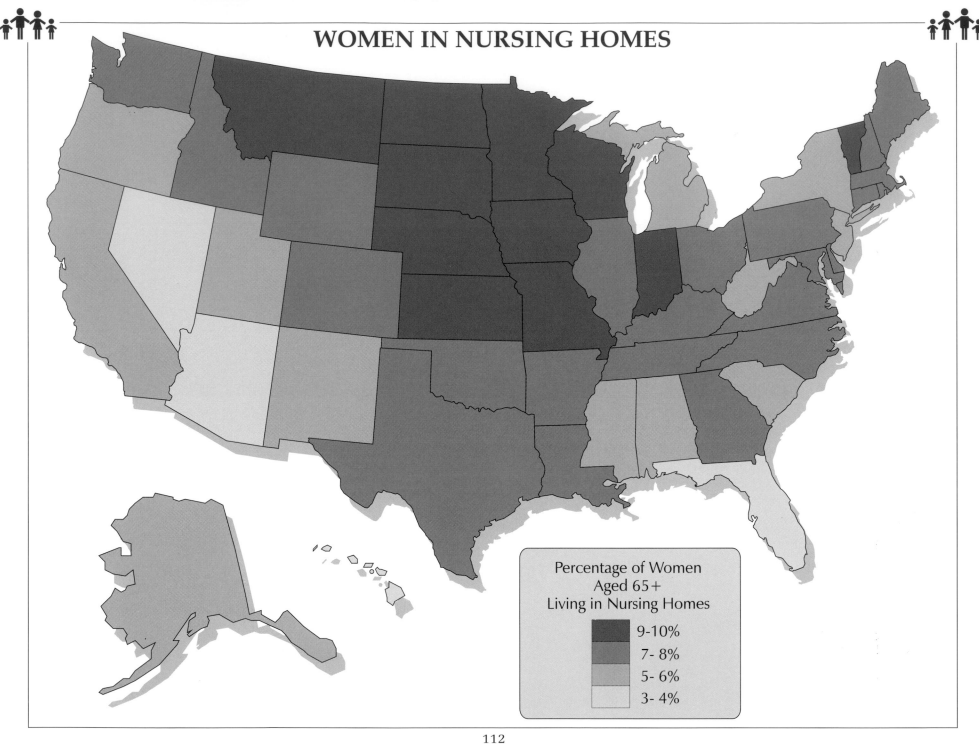

Percentage of Women
Aged 65+
Living in Nursing Homes

9-10%

7- 8%

5- 6%

3- 4%

elders. The highest values are in Vermont and in states located in the Midwest and Northern High Plains. A contributing factor to these high values could be the greater-than-average percentage of women over the age of 65 residing in these states. Availability of quality care facilities could also be a contributing factor.

AND BABY MAKES...

The fertility ratio is a measure of the number of children under age 5 per 1,000 women of childbearing age (considered to be ages 15 through 44). The distribution of the fertility ratio for each state is shown on the map, "Fertility Ratio." The low values in the Northeast coincide with a low percentage of women who were married in this region. In most cases, states having high fertility ratios, such as South Dakota, Idaho, Utah and New Mexico, had female populations with a greater-than-average proportion of married women. The reverse, however, was not always true. Some states, such as Mississippi and California, had relatively high fertility rates and only half of the women over age 15 were married. In this case we can look ahead to the map "Births to Unmarried Women" and observe that these states have a high rate of births to unmarried women. Closely related to the fertility ratio is the birth rate (see "Birth Rate" map).

The United States' birth rate is now on the rise after a long period of decline. The birth rate had climbed to 2.1 by 1992, the highest in the industrialized world, from its low of 1.8 in the 1980s. Alaska had a high birth rate, partly because is was the only state where more than half of the female population was of child-bearing age. Utah's rate can be largely attributed to religious beliefs, which encourage large families, of its largely Mormon population. The other four states with high values were California, Arizona, New Mexico and Texas, all bordering Mexico and all with relatively high rates of births to unmarried mothers along with a large population of Catholic Hispanics with cultural and religious encouragement of large families.

Increasingly, financially secure older women are choosing to have children even though they may be unmarried. This group, however, contributes very little to the birthrate for unmarried women. Teenagers make up a disproportionately large number of never married mothers. The rate of pregnancies among teenagers has soared, especially among the poor and less educated. In three out of four unplanned pregnancies involving teenagers, no form of contraception was used. In fact, the United States has the highest adolescent pregnancy, abortion and birth rates among developed countries.[7] The map, "Births to Unmarried Women," tracks the birth rate for unmarried African-American women, unmarried White women and then combines the rates for unmarried women of all races. Nationwide, between 10% and 40% of all births were to unmarried women and the east tended to have higher rates than the west. Predictably, Utah and Idaho, states with large Mormon populations, had the lowest rates of births to unwed mothers—accounting for 12% and 14%, respectively, of all births. Mississippi had the highest rate with 38%. When you examine the rates for African-American women, the rates increase dramatically. For instance, in Mississippi more than half (665 out of every 1,000 births) of all African-American births were to unmarried women. Five states had rates even higher than that, with the highest being a rate of 765 (more

FERTILITY RATIO

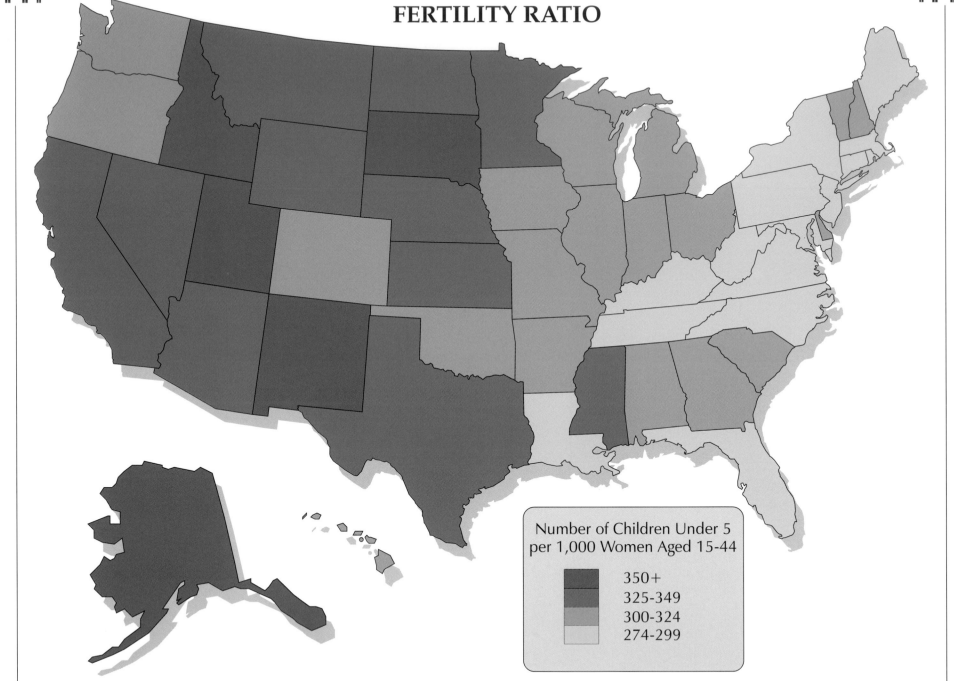

Number of Children Under 5
per 1,000 Women Aged 15-44

350+
325-349
300-324
274-299

BIRTH RATE

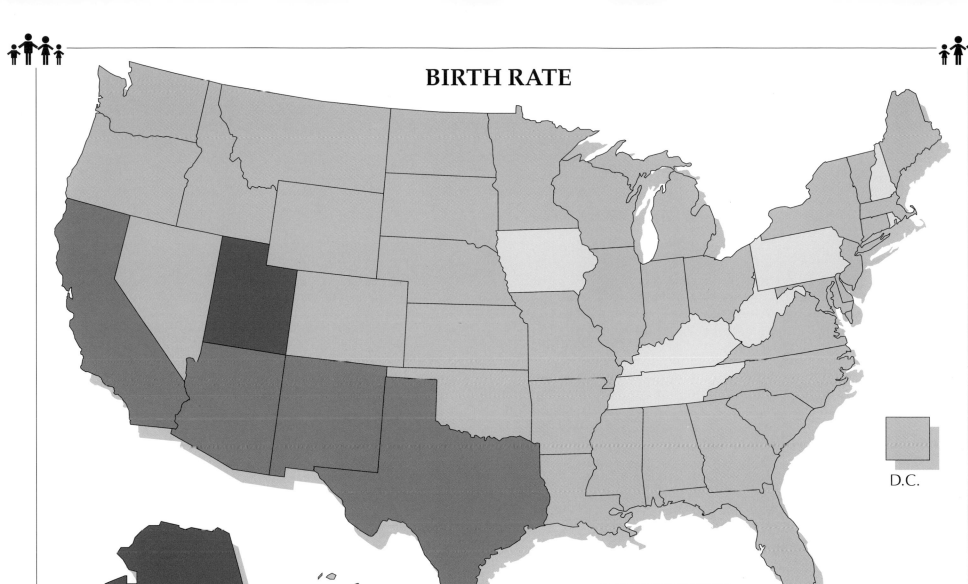

D.C.

Number of Births
per 1,000 People

■	21
■	18-20
■	15-17
☐	12-14

than three-quarters of all African-American births) in Wisconsin.[8] Many of the states with high rates have relatively large numbers of rural women living in poverty as in the Deep South or major cities with a large number of urban poor as seen in New York and Ohio. Clearly, these states need to make information about and availability of birth control a greater priority.

The focus of the following maps of "Teenage Pregnancy/Birth/Abortion Rates" is the rate of pregnancy, birth and abortion for women age 15 to 19. The pregnancy rate will, of course, be the highest rate as pregnancies can end by birth, miscarriage (less than 2% in this age group), or abortion. The United States as a whole had 111 pregnancies per 1,000 women aged 15 to 19 in 1988. This means than 11% of the nation's teenaged women became pregnant that year. California had the highest teen pregnancy rate at 154 while North Dakota, at 57, had the lowest.

Birth rates for teenagers, as well as pregnancy rates, are higher in the southern half of the United States. Birth rates varied from lows of 31 per 1,000 in North Dakota and Minnesota to a high of 73 per 1,000 in Mississippi. As one would expect, there appears to be a direct relationship to birth rates and abortion rates. For example, in Mississippi, 69% of pregnancies in this age group resulted in birth and 15% ended in abortion. By contrast, in Massachusetts, only 33% of pregnancies resulted in birth while 55% ended in abortion, a percentage considered to be lower than the actual rate because a parental involvement law was in effect and minors may have obtained abortions in other states. This is also the case in seven other states. Abortion rates are higher in the Northeast, where large urban areas have less restricted access to abortion than in rural areas. Rates were also high in California and

Nevada. The sum of births and abortions usually equals only about 86% of the pregnancy rate. Pregnancy rates in the data are rounded to the nearest ten. Miscarriage rates and other inaccuracies in data collection contribute to the failure of the rates to add up to 100%.

Related to maps portraying unwed mothers and teenage pregnancy rates is the map "Maternity Homes for Unwed Mothers" on which the number of women aged 15 to 44 living in homes for unwed mothers is represented. The various shades of yellow and green represent the number of residents per 100,000 women. These women constitute a very small percentage of the population of unwed mothers and an even smaller percentage of the population of women of childbearing age. Alaska has the greatest proportion of unwed mothers living in maternity homes, at 20 per 100,000 women. Arizona has the lowest with fewer than one woman per 100,000. Perhaps more unmarried, pregnant women would choose to live in one of these homes if more homes were available. However, the stigma attached to a pregnant, but unmarried, woman is a thing of the past; women who were once compelled to disappear during their pregnancies can now continue their normal lives. Also, many of the women who might choose to go to such a home cannot afford to do so.

At the other end of the spectrum we have a map entitled, "Births to Older Mothers." Here we show the number of live births for women over 40 per 10,000 births. The numbers are relatively low, starting with a low of three per 10,000 (0.03%) in Virginia to the maximum of 992 per 10,000 (9.9%) in Alaska. While still a small percentage of total births, births to women in this age group have increased in recent years. Baby

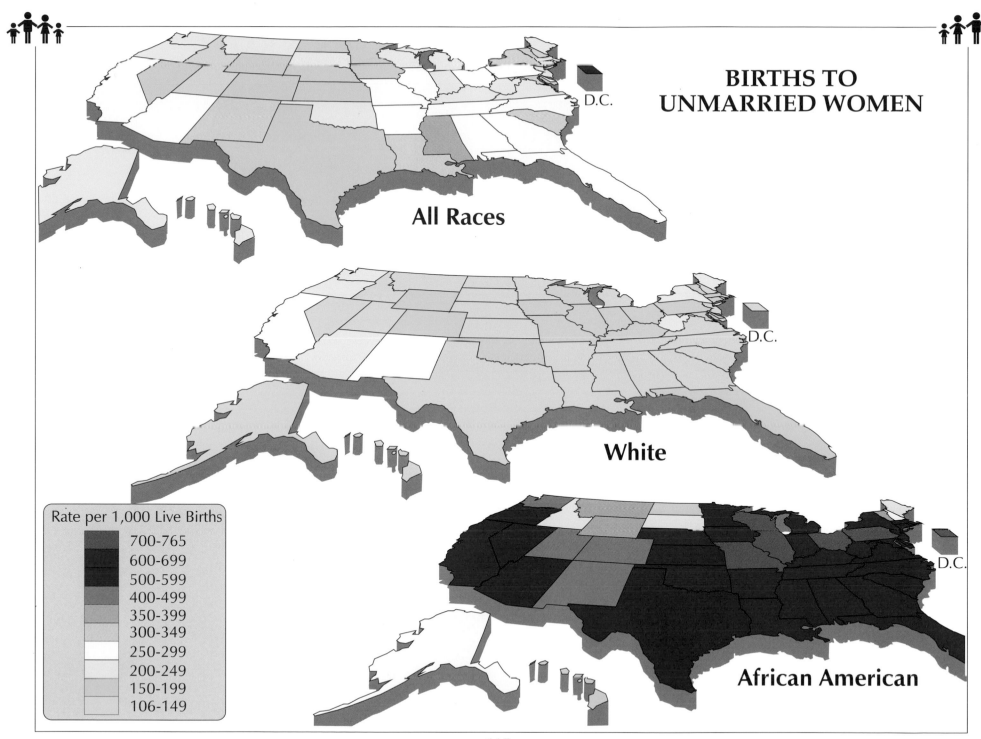

BIRTHS TO UNMARRIED WOMEN

All Races

White

African American

Rate per 1,000 Live Births

700-765
600-699
500-599
400-499
350-399
300-349
250-299
200-249
150-199
106-149

TEENAGE PREGNANCY / BIRTH / ABORTION RATES
1988

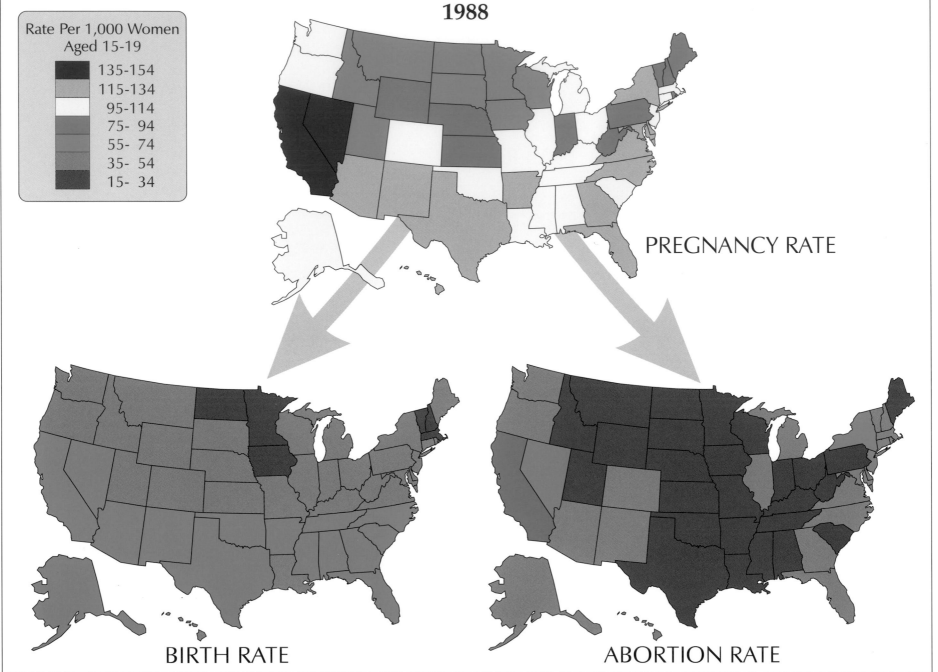

Rate Per 1,000 Women
Aged 15-19

135-154
115-134
95-114
75- 94
55- 74
35- 54
15- 34

PREGNANCY RATE

BIRTH RATE

ABORTION RATE

118

MATERNITY HOMES FOR UNWED MOTHERS

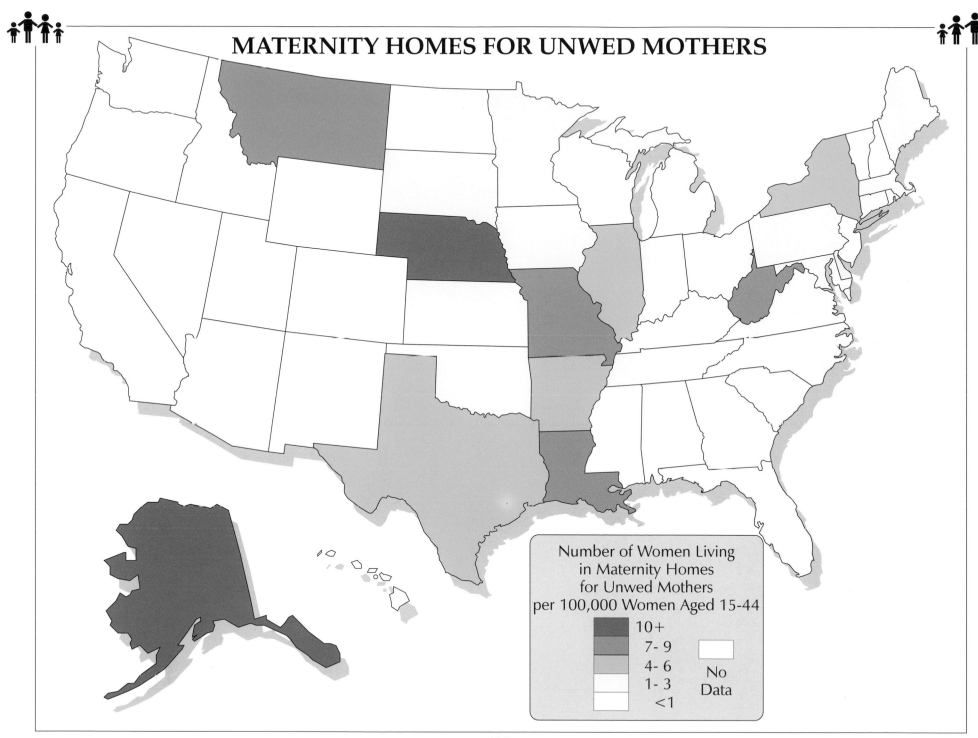

Number of Women Living
in Maternity Homes
for Unwed Mothers
per 100,000 Women Aged 15-44

- 10+
- 7- 9
- 4- 6
- 1- 3
- <1
- No Data

BIRTHS TO OLDER MOTHERS
1988

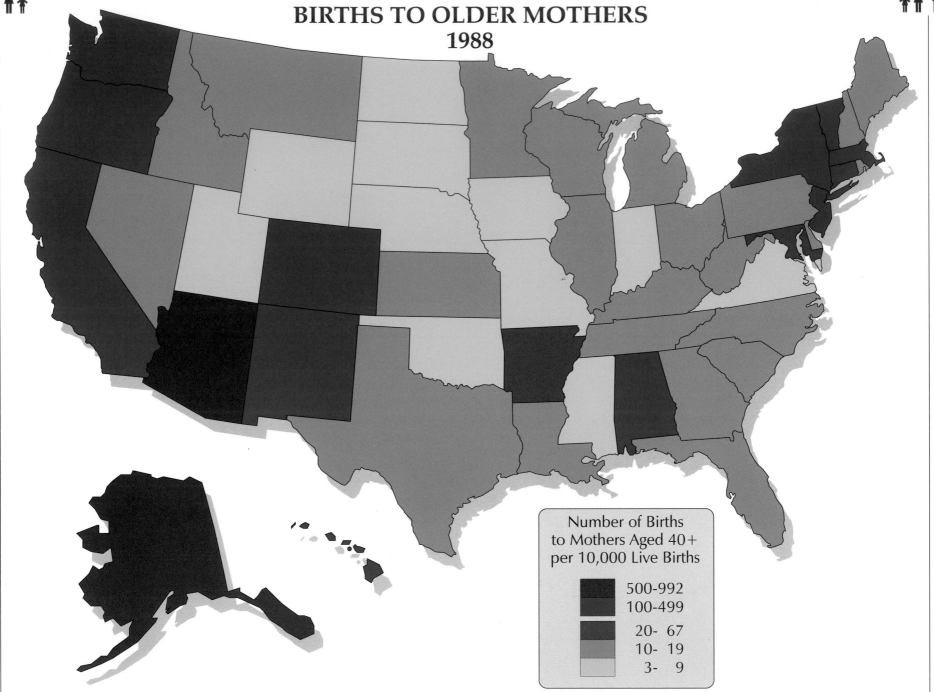

Number of Births
to Mothers Aged 40+
per 10,000 Live Births

500-992
100-499
20- 67
10- 19
3- 9

boomers who postponed parenthood while building careers in the 1970s and 1980s have begun to have children. The highest rates for women in this age group appear in the Northeast and the West, generally in states with large urban populations. Alaska, without a large urban population, has a birthrate in this age group that is nearly twice as high as Arizona, the state with the second highest rate. Eleven states had rates between three and nine per 10,000 live births.

FAMILY ARRANGEMENTS

As mentioned earlier, the American family is being re-defined. Half of the nation's families do not fit the stereotype of the "typical" family, a married couple with children. Many alternative households are being formed, tailored to the needs of the people involved. Some alternative household types include divorced women (and men) with or without children, never-married women with children and women or men who live alone or with unrelated roommates. The next four illustrations in this section will focus on some of these household arrangements.

Married-couple households represented only 56% of all households in 1990, a 4% drop from 1980.[9] Married-couple households and married couple families with a female head of household are represented on the maps entitled "Married-Couple Families." In only four states, Idaho, Utah, Wyoming and New Hampshire, did more than 60% of the families fit into the married-couple household category. Barely 50% of all households in New York did. A north–south strip running through

the middle of the country, including a section in the mid-south, shows where this "traditional" type of family is more common. Men were still overwhelmingly the heads of such households, but a growing number of women, from 3% to 11%, were assuming this role. Women as the household head in married-couple households were more common in the Northeast and less common through the nation's midsection.

Households headed by women are the focus of the next set of maps. The first, "Female-Headed House-holds," uses shaded states to indicate female-headed households as a percentage of all households. The proportion of family (two or more related persons) and non-family (one or more unrelated persons) households that make up these female-headed households in each state is represented by a pie chart. The family household component is shaded green and the non-family household component is blue. Female-headed households represent between 25% and 39% of all households. The specifics of this map are best explained by using an example. In New York State, 38% of all households are headed by women. Of that number, about half are family households and half are non-family households. High percentages of female-headed households are found in the Northeast and Deep South with lower values throughout the nation's midsection and the West. In fact, in most states east of the Mississippi River more than 30% of all families are headed by women. States having high proportions of married-couple families tended to have low proportions of female-headed families. The pie charts indicate that in the West, Midwest and Northeast women were slightly more likely to head non-family households, while in the South they were more likely to head family households.

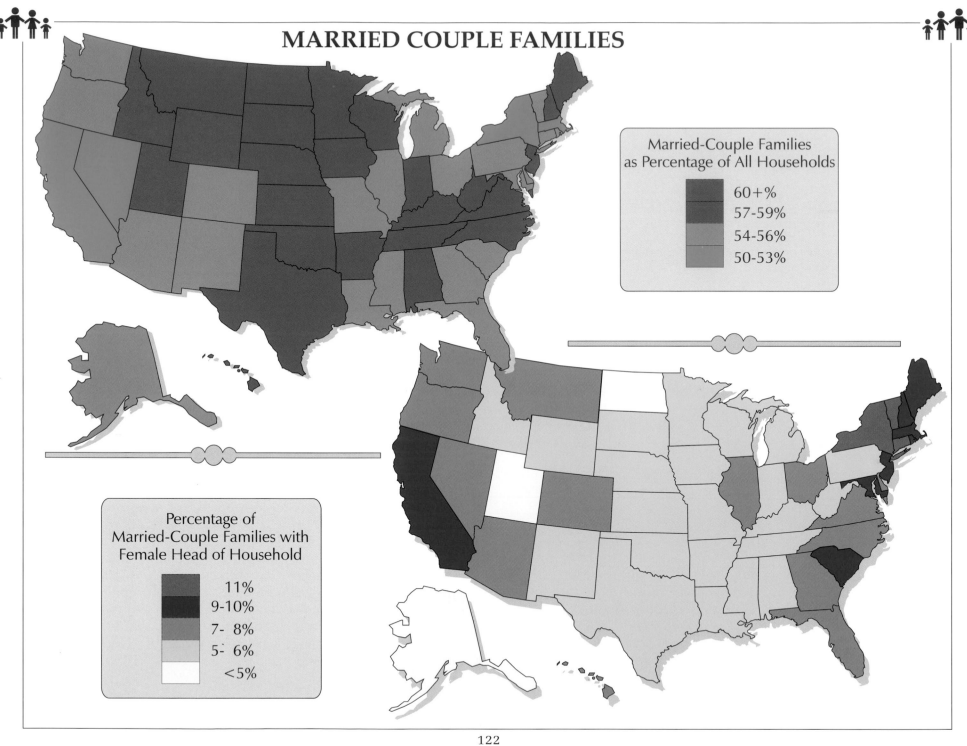

Married-Couple Families
as Percentage of All Households

- 60+%
- 57-59%
- 54-56%
- 50-53%

Percentage of
Married-Couple Families with
Female Head of Household

- 11%
- 9-10%
- 7- 8%
- 5- 6%
- <5%

FEMALE-HEADED HOUSEHOLDS

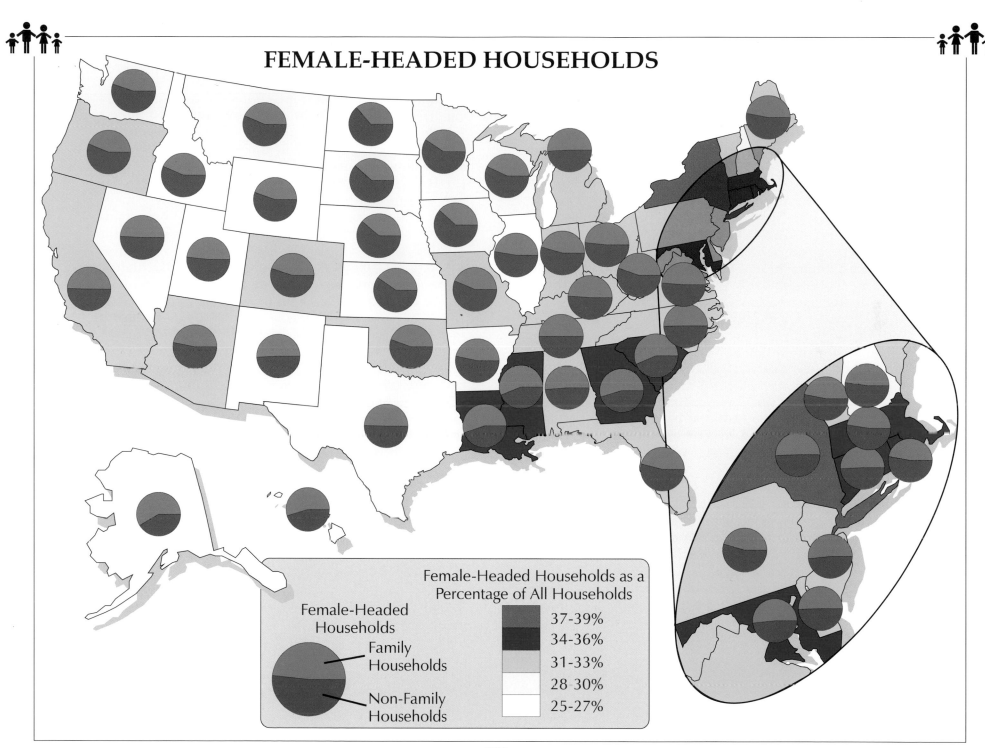

Female-Headed Households as a Percentage of All Households

Female-Headed Households

Family Households

Non-Family Households

- 37-39%
- 34-36%
- 31-33%
- 28-30%
- 25-27%

"Female-Headed Family Households (No Husband Present)" is the subject of the next map. States are colored in various shades of blue to indicate the percentage of all families that are headed by women with no husband present. In 1990 this group represented almost 17% of all family households. Nationwide, almost three-quarters of the families headed by women were of this type. In more than half of the states, more than 10% of all families were headed by women with no husband present. The Deep South, Maryland, New York and Michigan had the highest percentages in the nation, while six states in and around the Northern High Plains had the lowest values.

Children in female-headed households are the subject of the next two maps. On "Children in Female-Headed Households (No Father Present)," the upper map shows the percentage of female-headed households (no husband present) with children and the lower map shows the percentage of children who live with their mother (no husband present). Nationwide, 67% of these female-headed households had children. In Wyoming, 77% of women with no husband present had children living with them, the highest percentage in the nation. The lowest value, 56%, is found in New Jersey. In Mississippi, almost one in every four children lived in this type of household. By contrast, in Idaho and Utah only one in ten children had a family of this type. The map showing the percentage of children living with their mothers closely resembles the previous map of female-headed family households. Notice that in western states where female householders without husbands were more likely to have chil-

dren, those children represented a proportionally smaller number of all children than in the east, where female householders were less likely to have children.

Finally, we look at homeless women. The 1990 census attempted to make the first national count of people living on the street and in shelters. Though the very nature of this task assured inaccuracies in the count, it was, nonetheless, the first attempt ever made at enumerating the homeless. The first map shows the number of visibly homeless women living on the street as a rate per 100,000 women. New York ranks highest in number of homeless women on the streets with 29 out of every 100,000 (0.03%) living outside. Three states, Minnesota, Nebraska and Arkansas had rates that were less than one per 100,000. The map illustrating the number of women living in shelters reveals that, again, New York has the highest percentage in the category. The rate for women in shelters in New York was 132 per 100,000 women. The state with the lowest rate was Arkansas, with only 12 out every 100,000 women living in a homeless shelter.

The majority of homeless people congregate in large cities. The final map in this chapter, "The Homeless in Major Cities," uses pie charts to represent the proportions of women, men, families and unaccompanied youths that make up the homeless population. The proportion of the charts represented by families is frightening. Men, in all cases, are more greatly represented in homeless ranks than are women. San Francisco, with 25%, has the largest percentage of women in the homeless population; Kansas City, at 4%, the smallest.

FEMALE-HEADED FAMILY HOUSEHOLDS
(NO HUSBAND PRESENT)

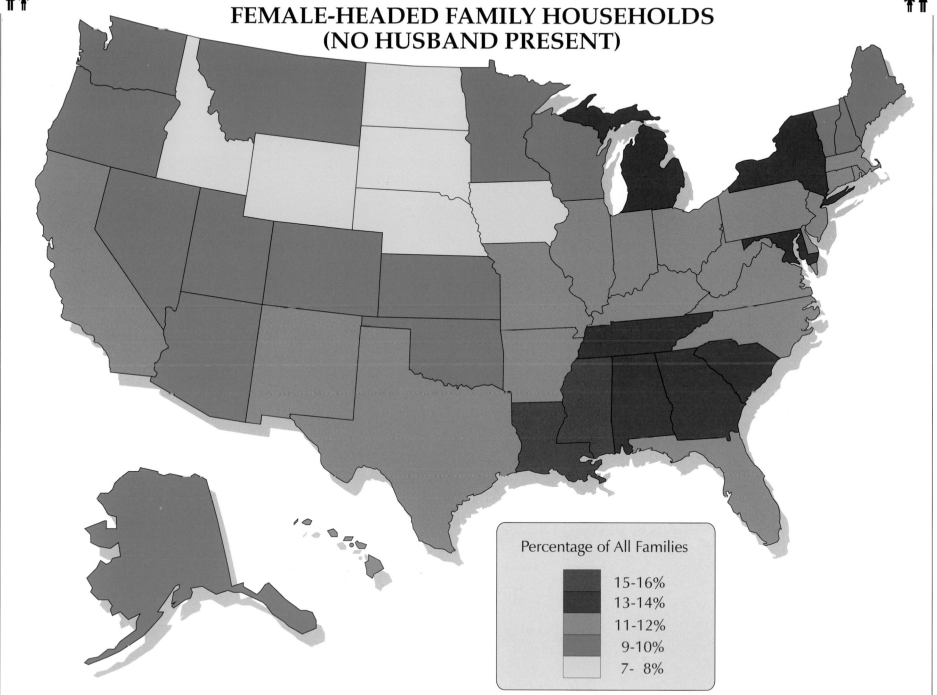

Percentage of All Families

15-16%
13-14%
11-12%
9-10%
7- 8%

CHILDREN IN FEMALE HEADED HOUSEHOLDS
(NO FATHER PRESENT)

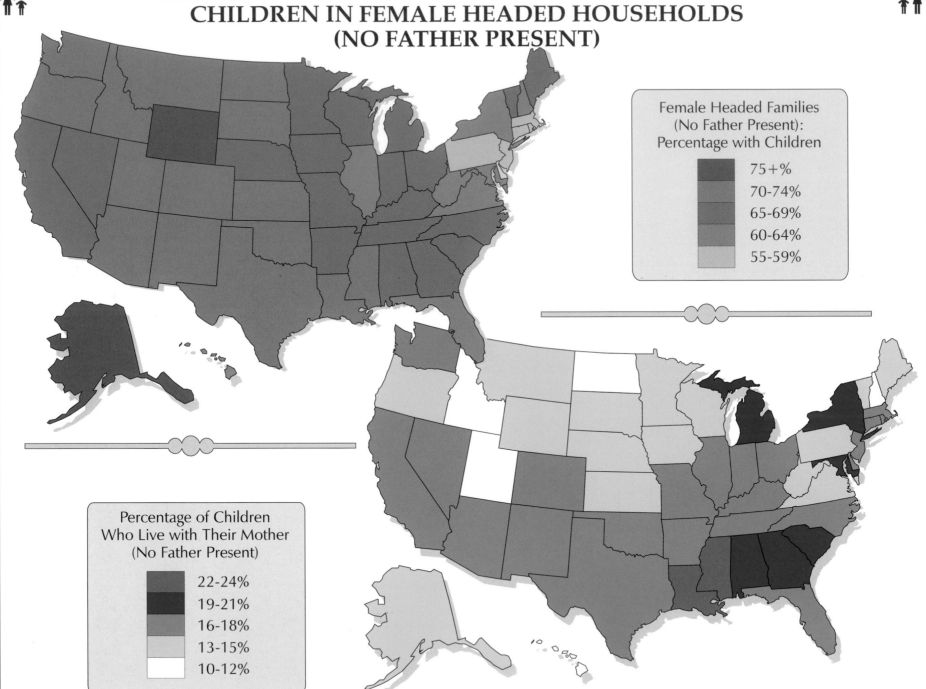

Female Headed Families
(No Father Present):
Percentage with Children

75+%
70-74%
65-69%
60-64%
55-59%

Percentage of Children
Who Live with Their Mother
(No Father Present)

22-24%
19-21%
16-18%
13-15%
10-12%

HOMELESS WOMEN

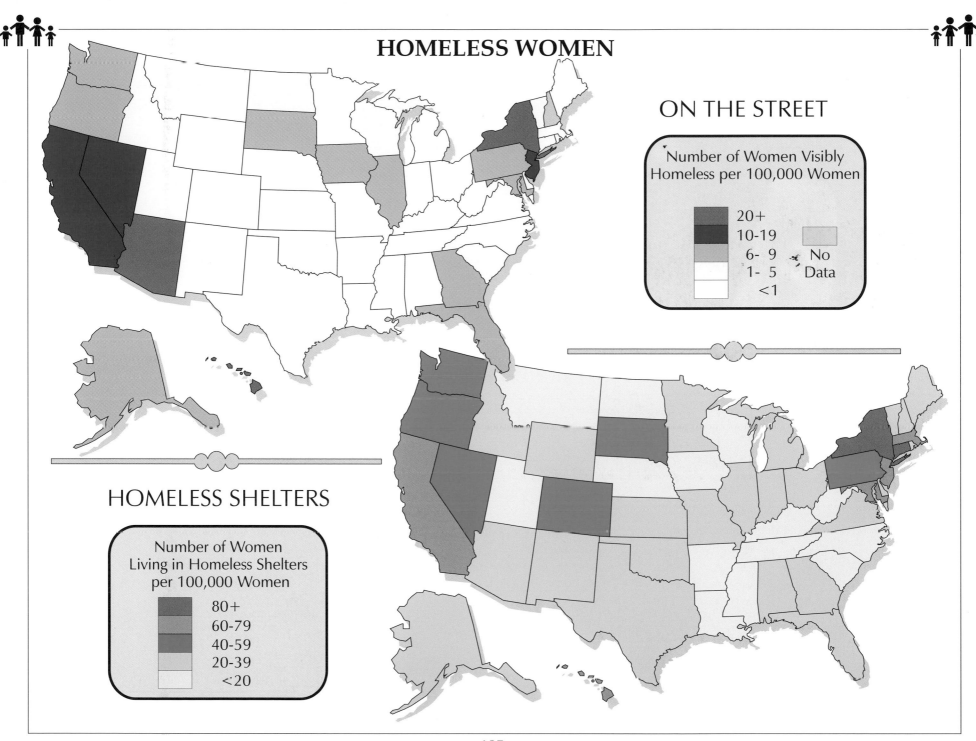

ON THE STREET

Number of Women Visibly
Homeless per 100,000 Women

- 20+
- 10-19
- 6- 9
- 1- 5
- <1
- No Data

HOMELESS SHELTERS

Number of Women
Living in Homeless Shelters
per 100,000 Women

- 80+
- 60-79
- 40-59
- 20-39
- <20

THE HOMELESS IN MAJOR CITIES

Seattle

Portland

Minneapolis

Boston

Cleveland

New York

San Francisco

Denver

Chicago

Philadelphia

Washington D.C.

Kansas City

Norfolk*

Los Angeles

Phoenix

San Diego

San Antonio

New Orleans

Breakdown of the
Homeless Population
(percentage)

Unaccompanied
Youth

Women

Men

Families

* Women and men were counted
as a single group in Norfolk, VA.

128

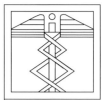
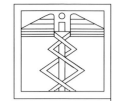

HEALTH

"By health I mean the power to live a full, adult, living, breathing life in close contact with...the earth and the wonders thereof—the sea—the sun."[1]

—Katherine Mansfield

Health care in the United States is a multi-billion dollar industry where men and women, rich and poor receive vastly different types of care. Women must be particularly vigilant when dealing with the medical industry because they are not adequately represented at the policy making levels of clinics, hospitals and medical schools.

Women are an integral part of the health care system of this country. Women deal with the system more than twice as often as men. Women are most often responsible for coordinating health care for children, husbands and often elderly parents or other relatives. But while women (who make up 52% of the population) are 70% of all patients, women make up only 18% of all physicians in the United States, only 5% of all medical school full professors and only 2% of medical school deans. While the current Surgeon General

for the United States is a women, policy makers in the medical field are overwhelmingly male.[2]

Male-biased care seriously affects the health of women. A 1990 *Time* magazine article states that "an information gap...may be endangering millions of American women. A number of treatments now recommended for men and women—from cholesterol-lowering drugs and diets to AIDS therapies and antidepressants—have been studied almost exclusively in men. Little hard evidence exists about their efficacy or safety for women."[3] The fact is, most medical research is done on men and the results are applied to women. This situation is currently changing due, in part, to new guidelines issued in 1990 by the National Institutes of Health (NIH). The NIH is ensuring that women are adequately represented in NIH-funded research with potential relevance to women. The care and treatment women receive are still subject to the findings of years of male-biased medical research. Research on women's health issues such as heart disease, breast cancer, osteoporosis and eating disorders is badly needed.

Trying to achieve society's standard of beauty also affects women's health. Throughout history, women's physical and mental health has been threatened by the pressure to conform to whatever is the current standard of beauty. Victorian women wore corsets that often broke ribs and compressed internal organs. But at no time in our past have advertisements focusing on the "perfect" women been as prevalent as they are today. Ads for hair products, cosmetics, clothes and cars bombard us daily. The models in these ads are presented as "ideal women"; the average woman constantly falls short of the standard presented. The goals are unrealistic and so is comparing the average woman to the models in these ads. The average model weighs 23% less than the average woman.[4] In trying to achieve this "ideal" image, many women resort to a lifetime of dieting. Severely obese women sometimes resort to surgical procedures including liposuction, jaw-wiring and various types of stomach and intestinal surgeries. These procedures, associated with many unpleasant side-effects, are dangerous and are performed almost exclusively on women.[5]

Body image seems to be an issue for the majority of women. The majority of girls of grade school age say that they like the way they look, but by the time they reach high school three out of four girls no longer like themselves as they are. During these years, girls also lose much of their self-esteem, finding that they have to be self-effacing to preserve peace in their relationships. Self-esteem is a problem even as these girls become adults when only 28% of them consider themselves attractive, while 42% of men consider themselves to be handsome.[6]

Women's attempts to attain the "perfect body" have enabled the diet industry to become a big business in this country. Women spend millions of dollars a year on diet programs in order to try to be more like women seen in advertisements. But success in this area is illusive. About 98% of women who diet regain their weight within five years and 90% of them regain more than they lost.[7]

During this century, women have benefited immeasurably from advances in health care. The availability of birth control is one of the greatest advances, giving women the power to control their reproductive lives to a degree unimaginable even 40 years ago. Death from childbirth was a common occurrence at the turn of the century and even in 1950 almost one out of every thousand women (83 deaths per 1,000,000 women) died in childbirth or from ensuing complications. In 1990 the rate had dropped to 2.4 per 1,000,000, less than 3% of the 1950 rate.

But even with the great advances in health care, women must still contend with a medical community that is often insensitive to female patients. Physicians are quicker to attribute women's illnesses to psychological causes than they are for men's. Women are treated more paternalistically and are less likely to have treatments thoroughly explained to them than are men.

Women seeking mental-health care must be doubly vigilant. Training for mental-health professionals is often based on information that inadequately examines women's psychological development as it differs from men's. Female patients are more than twice as likely to have psychoactive drugs prescribed for them than are male patients.[8] The 1990 Census estimated that 40% of the residents in mental institutions were female. The fact that this figure has changed little in the past decade is probably less an indicator of women's improving mental health than it is an indication of the decreasing federal and state funds for institutional mental health care. Of note is that the suicide rate for women (4.8 per 100,000 in 1990) has shown a slight decrease for each of the past two decades, the rate for men (20.4 per 100,000 in 1990) has increased slightly over the same time span.[9]

While life expectancy has increased for both sexes over the past century, women still outlive men. Females born in 1990 can expect to live 78.8 years while males born that year can expect to live only 72 years, almost seven years less than women. A women born in 1990 will live, on the average, 24.2 years longer than one born in 1920. The life expectancy of men has increased only 18.4 years over the same period.[10]

The Center for Disease Control's 1988 report on morbidity and mortality in the United States cites four "behavioral risk factors" that affect life span as occurring more often in men; these behaviors—obesity, sedentary lifestyle, smoking and alcohol abuse—can greatly decrease life expectancy. Among the ten leading causes of death (heart disease, cancer, stroke, accidents, pulmonary disease, pneumonia, diabetes, suicide, chronic liver disease and HIV infection) in the United States in 1990, women's death rates were higher than men's in only three categories (stroke, pneumonia and diabetes). Fifty-seven percent of all deaths that year were from heart disease and cancer. While fewer women died from these diseases than men (95% and 84%, respectively), the proportion of women to men has risen since 1980.[11] In that year 60% of all deaths were attributed to heart disease and cancer, but the proportions of women

to men were lower at 83% and 80%, respectively. So, while these two diseases were accountable for a lower percentage of the overall death rate, women are more likely to die from these diseases than in the past.

Women's health awareness is improving in some areas. As more information becomes available about the health risks involved with smoking and second-hand smoke, fewer women and men are smoking. The percentage of adult women who smoke fell from 33% in 1976 to 27% in 1992. But even with this reduction in the percentage of female smokers, the incidence of lung cancer in women has increased 3% annually since the early 1980s. Lung cancer has surpassed breast cancer as the leading cancer killer of women.[12] The recognition that smoking endangers the health, not only of the smoker, but also of those in the vicinity, has resulted in legislation in many states and on a federal level to prohibit smoking in public spaces. Recently Maryland and Washington became the first states to ban smoking in public and private offices. The news is not all good, however. As tobacco companies lose revenues, they increasingly target young women to replace older, male smokers who have kicked the habit. Consequently, while the rate of new cases of lung cancer among men has remained steady, the number of cases in women has more than doubled since 1980.[13]

Although the percentage of women who smoke has gone down over the past decade, the percentage of women who regularly use alcohol has gone up. Two-thirds of adult women regularly use alcohol, up from 46% a decade ago. Chronic alcohol abuse is particularly devastating for women, who develop alcoholic liver disease after a shorter period of heavy drinking than men and die at a rate 50% to 100% higher than do men.[14] Liver disease ranks as the eighth leading cause of death for women and the tenth leading cause of death for men.

The incidence of AIDS is increasing among women, particularly among minority women. African-American and Hispanic women constitute only about 19% of all women in the nation, yet, in 1991, they represented nearly 73% of women diagnosed as having AIDS. And the recent rate of increase of AIDS for women is greater than for men; between 1988 and 1989, diagnosed cases of AIDS in women increased 29%, compared with 18% in men.[15]

Advances in the methods of birth control and the availability of safe and effective contraceptives have given women a degree of control over their reproductive lives that was unimaginable in the early years of this century. In 1916 when Margaret Sanger opened the United States' first birth control clinic in Brooklyn, New York, it was immediately closed by police and Sanger was arrested and convicted on charges of "maintaining a public nuisance." Nearly 80 years later, birth control is available "over-the-counter" at any drug store. However, Title X funding, the nation's principal funding mechanism for contraceptive services, decreased by two-thirds between 1980 and 1990, thus threatening the availability of family services, especially for the poor.

Probably the single most fiercely debated issue in the arena of women's health is abortion. Until about 1880, abortions were provided in the United States by women trained in the techniques without legal prohibitions. But by 1880, abortion was illegal in the United States except when the mother's life was in danger.[16] This situation finally changed with *Roe v. Wade*, the 1973 Supreme Court decision that a woman has a constitutional right to an abortion. At the point of fetal viability states would be allowed to regulate abortion. In 1989, in *Webster v. Reproductive Health Services*, the Supreme Court ruled that states may place increased restrictions on women's access to abortion. Later court rulings have allowed states to require parental notification before a minor can have an abortion, allowed a mandatory 24-hour waiting period and allowed states to require the distribution of state-authored anti-abortion materials to those seeking abortion.[17]

Such restrictions have contributed to a decline in the number of abortion providers to the point that one-half of all urban counties and 93% of all rural counties have no abortion services.[18] In fact, by 1990 only 17% of U.S. counties had abortion providers.[19] Thus, many women seeking abortions must travel long distances.

These limitations to abortions have been most keenly felt by teenagers and by poor women, those least able to support a child and least likely to be knowledgeable about alternative types of birth control. Lack of public funding often means that low-income women cannot afford abortions and are forced to give birth to children they are economically (and perhaps emotionally) unable to care for, at a much higher cost to society. Being forced to bear unwanted children often eliminates any chance these women may have to escape poverty. Often, the alternative is an illegal abortion, at great risk to their own lives.

Tragically, at a time when we have the most reproductive control of any time in history, the message of how to obtain and properly use contraceptives seems to be getting lost. Annually, more than 56% of pregnancies among women in this country are unintended. Forty-seven percent of these unintended pregnancies occur while women are using contraceptives, which either fail or are used improperly. In more than half of these unintended pregnancies, no contraceptive was used. Between 1982 and 1988, the proportion of unwanted births among women in poverty rose by almost 75%.[20]

THE DAYS OF OUR LIVES

Women live longer than men. The chart, "Life Expectancy Through Time," depicts the life expectancy for women and men between 1920 and 1990. In 1920 women's life expectancy was only one year higher than men's. Relatively high percentages of women at this time were dying in childbirth or complications from childbirth. Gains in medicine improved those statistics and, by 1950, fewer women were dying in childbirth and women were living 5.5 years longer than men. The gap continued to widen between 1960 (when life expectancy for women was 6.5 years longer than men) and 1980 (7.5 years longer), but finally began to close in 1990 when women were expected to live only 6.8 years longer men.[21]

The first map of this chapter, "Life Expectancy, 1979–1981" depicts the average life expectancy at birth of women and the average life expectancy at birth of men as a percentage of women's life expectancy. This is the most current data available by state. Substantial geographic variations exist. For example, Hawaii had the highest life expectancy for women and men at 80.3 and 74.1 years, respectively. Compare this to Louisiana, the state with the lowest life expectancy: 75.9 years for women and 67.6 years for men. Women in Hawaii can expect to live 4.4 years longer than women in Louisiana, while men in Hawaii have a life

expectancy that is 6.5 years higher than men in Louisiana. Three other states, North Dakota, Minnesota and Iowa, join Hawaii as states where women can expect to live about 80 years. Other states having a low average life expectancy for women, along with Louisiana, are Mississippi, Georgia and South Carolina. The disparity of life expectancy rates among states is largely attributed to the racial composition of the state. However, factors such as lifestyle, heredity, living standards, adequacy of health and hospital facilities, and possibly climatic conditions also contribute to life expectancy. As life expectancy among African Americans is not so high as for Whites, states with large African-American populations have lower life expectancy figures. Hand-in-hand with racial composition go poverty levels, so that states with large percentages of their population in poverty have lower life expectancies for their citizens.[22]

In general, no appreciable decrease in the longevity gap has occurred between the highest and lowest ranked states over the previous decade. But two states did show a favorable shift in the rankings. New Mexico moved from 34th to 22nd and Arizona from 31st to 21st. A sharp decline in infant mortality rates in these states along with the influx of large numbers of healthy retirees were responsible for the increase in life expectancy. A few states saw their rankings drop. Oklahoma's ranking fell from 19th to 31st, and Texas and Ohio each lost ten positions dropping to 33rd and 35th, respectively.[23] States with the lowest values for men's life expectancy (as a percentage of women's) were Alaska in the Pacific Northwest, New Mexico and Oklahoma in the West, and seven states in the South.

Lifestyle is an important factor is determining life expectancy and the percentage of women leading a

LIFE EXPECTANCY THROUGH TIME

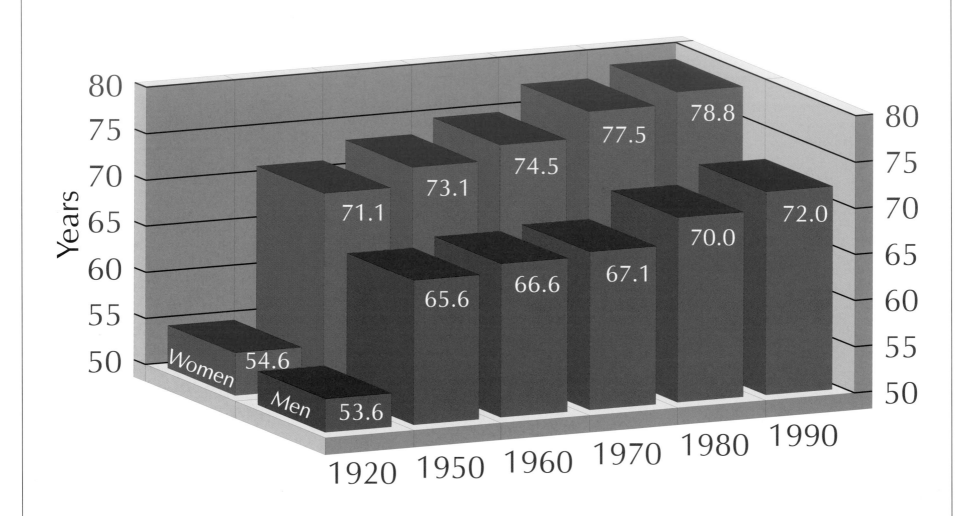

LIFE EXPECTANCY
1979-1981

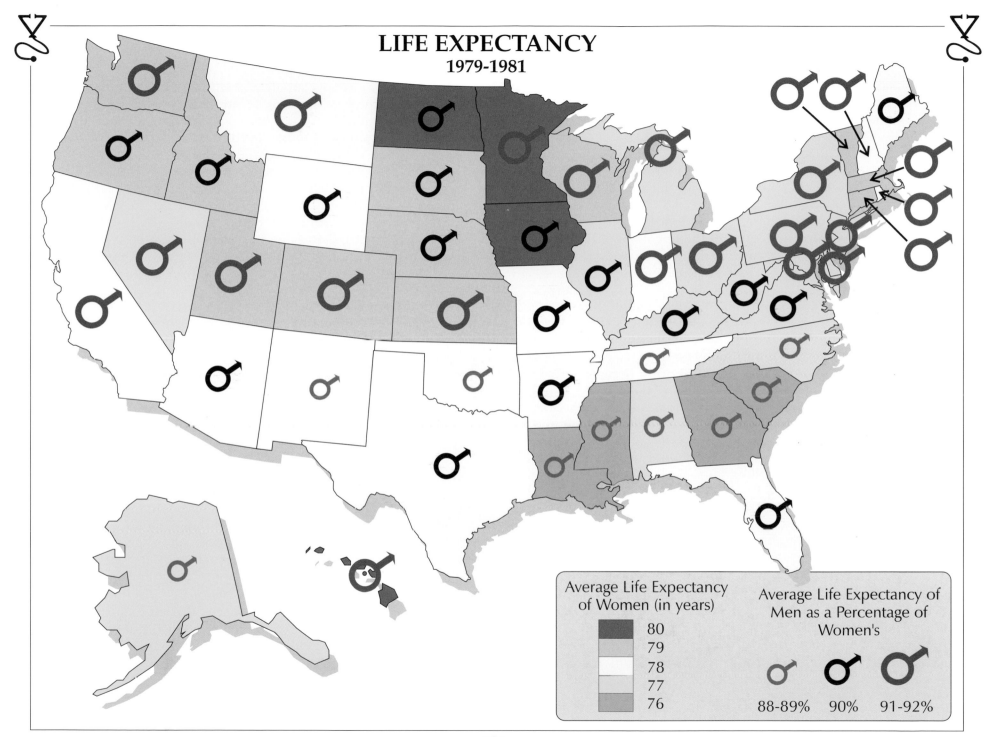

Average Life Expectancy of Women (in years)

- 80
- 79
- 78
- 77
- 76

Average Life Expectancy of Men as a Percentage of Women's

88-89%   90%   91-92%

sedentary lifestyle in a state, as indicated on the map, "Sedentary Lifestyle," affects the life expectancy in the state. A loose correlation exists between states with high percentages of women who lead a sedentary lifestyle and states with relatively low life expectancy. Western states generally had higher proportions of women who exercise and higher life expectancies than did eastern states.

In 21 of the 36 states for which data on obesity are available, more than 20% of the female population was obese. Obesity is loosely defined as weighing 20% more than the standard weight for a person's age, height, sex and race. However, because of variations in frame size, some individuals may weigh 20% above standard weight and not be obese. Rather than becoming too focused on exactly what constitutes the classification of obese, we will focus on the effects of obesity. Obesity is generally associated with a reduced life expectancy, and obese individuals are more likely to suffer from a number of related diseases, among them diabetes, high blood pressure and gallbladder disease. It also exacerbates degenerative diseases of the joints. States with the lowest proportions of obese women were located in New England and the Northeast and in the western half of the United States. Idaho had the lowest percentage of obese women at 12.3% of the female population and Wisconsin had the highest at 30.3%. One possible explanation for Wisconsin's high obesity rate may be its large Germanic population in which high fat German cooking styles are prevalent. The District of Columbia's high rate may be linked to a large poor population whose diet may also be high in calories and fat.

Cholesterol is one of the most frequently discussed topics among those interested in maintaining a healthy lifestyle. More Americans than ever before know their blood cholesterol levels. An elevated cholesterol level is known to be one of the major risk factors for coronary heart disease and reducing this level may help reduce the risk of developing this disease. The maps entitled "Cholesterol" depict the percentage of women aged 18+ who have ever had their cholesterol checked and the percentage of women in that age group who know their cholesterol level. States in and around the Deep South tended to have both low percentages of women who had ever had their level checked (the exception was Florida) and low percentages of women who knew their cholesterol level. Women in California, Washington, Michigan, Wisconsin and Maine were more aware with higher percentages of women who had been checked and who knew the findings.

Coronary heart disease is the number one cause of death of both women and men in the United States. The Framingham Heart Study revealed that not only are heart attacks the leading cause of death for women, but a greater percentage of women who have heart attacks die from them than do men. In the study, 45% of the women with symptomatic heart attacks died within one year, compared to 10% of men.[24] The map, "Death from Heart Disease," uses proportionally sized hearts to represent the rates of deaths from heart disease in each state per 100,000 women. Immediately obvious is that fewer women in the Alaska, Hawaii and the western United States die from this disease than in the east. Nationally, 282 per 100,000 women died from this disease in 1990. State rates varied from a low of 66 per 100,000 in Alaska to a high of 375 per 100,000 in West Virginia. States with low values generally had populations with lower percentages of older women. Only 5% of the female population in Alaska is over age 65,

SEDENTARY LIFESTYLE
(In Selected States)

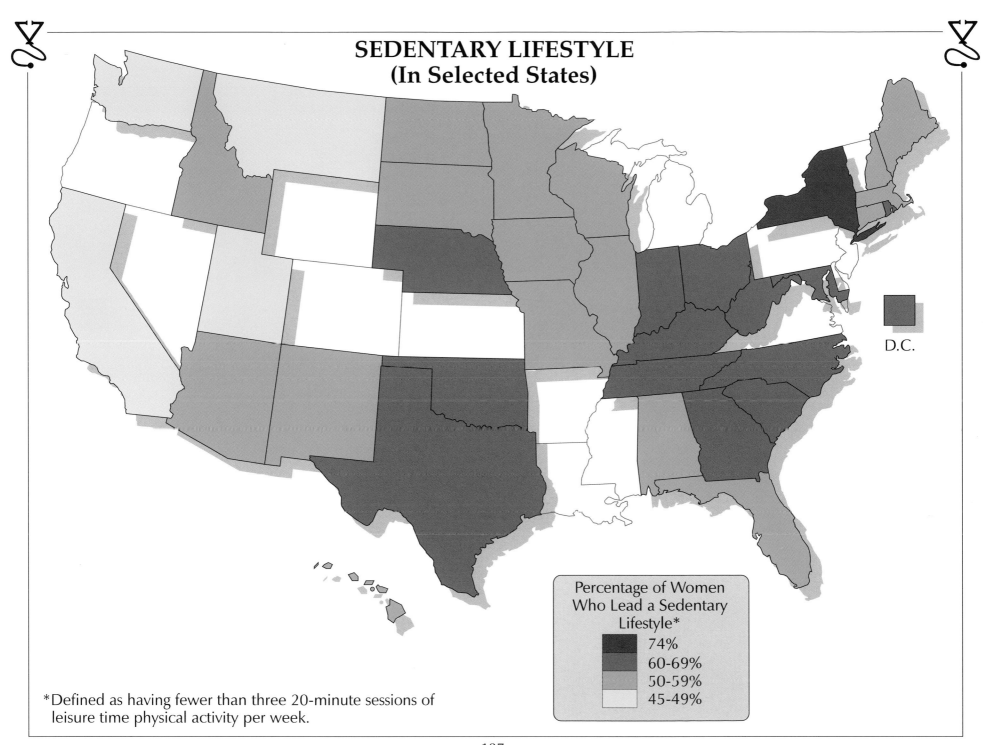

D.C.

Percentage of Women
Who Lead a Sedentary
Lifestyle*

74%
60-69%
50-59%
45-49%

*Defined as having fewer than three 20-minute sessions of
  leisure time physical activity per week.

OBESITY
(In Selected States)

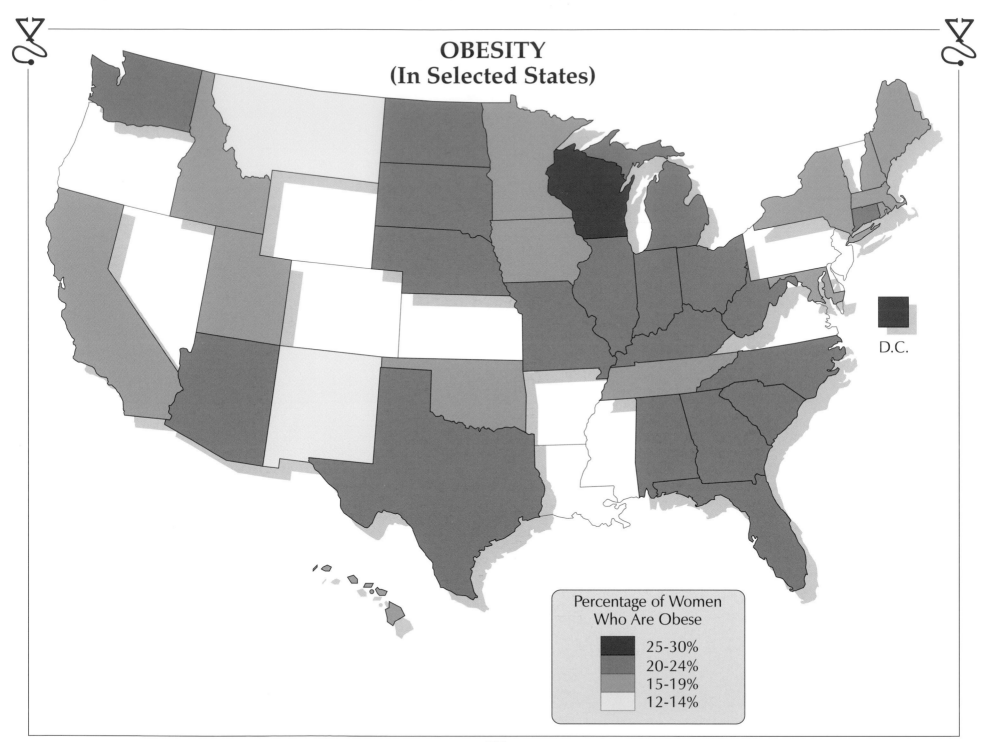

Percentage of Women
Who Are Obese

25-30%

20-24%

15-19%

12-14%

D.C.

CHOLESTEROL
(In Selected States)

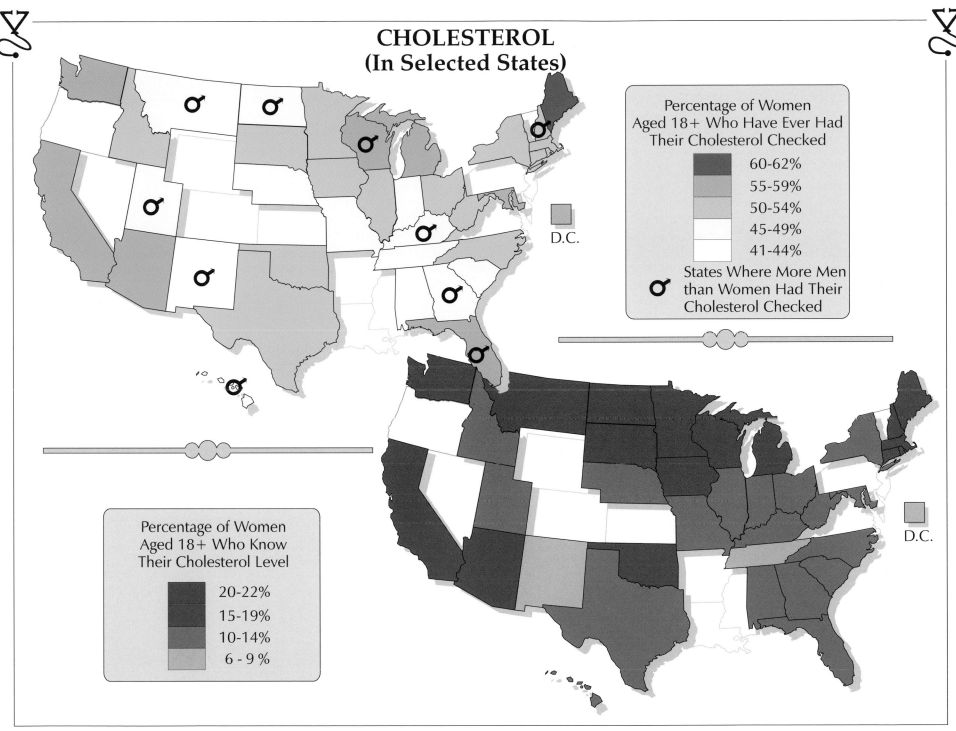

Percentage of Women Aged 18+ Who Have Ever Had Their Cholesterol Checked

- 60-62%
- 55-59%
- 50-54%
- 45-49%
- 41-44%

States Where More Men than Women Had Their Cholesterol Checked

D.C.

Percentage of Women Aged 18+ Who Know Their Cholesterol Level

- 20-22%
- 15-19%
- 10-14%
- 6 - 9 %

D.C.

whereas West Virginia and Pennsylvania, with heart disease death rates of 375 and 372 per 100,000 women, respectively, have between 17% and 18% of the female population over 65. The rates also correlate somewhat with the trends observed for sedentary lifestyle when viewed on a regional, rather than a state to state, basis. In addition, the low rates in Alaska and Hawaii might be due to a diet rich in fish and low in red meat. Such a diet may be common because of the cultural background of the population coupled with the high cost of meat (which must be imported) in these states. The high rates in the Midwest may be linked to a "meat and potatoes" diet consumed by a large portion of the population. In the east, the high rate may be somewhat attributable to higher female stress levels as a greater portion of women pursue careers.

Regional patterns on the map, "Death from Cancer," were strongly defined. Deaths from all types of cancer are represented on this map with New England and the Northeast emerging with the highest rates. Florida, Kentucky, Missouri and Iowa also have cancer death rates of more than 200 per 100,000 women. Alaska, Hawaii and states in a band stretching from Idaho to Texas have relatively low rates. States with rates over 200, with the exception of New Hampshire, tended to have high proportions of older women. States with lower rates had lower proportions of older women, but also had few metropolitan areas and generally had less agricultural activity than neighboring states.

The next two maps, "Death from Breast Cancer" and "Death from Cancer of the Genital Organs," focus on cancers almost totally unique (a small percentage of men do get breast cancer) to women. Breast cancer is the most common cancer among women, accounting for more than one-fourth of all cancers detected in

women.[25] Although the death rate has not significantly changed since the 1930s, there is encouraging news: overwhelming evidence that for women over 50, early detection through mammography screening increases survival.[26] Trends are easy to discern on the breast cancer map, with the highest death rates of 40 to 43 per 100,000 exclusively in the Northeast and Rhode Island. Low rates (18 to 19 per 100,000) appear in Alaska and Hawaii and moderately low rates (20 to 29) extend from California to Texas and into some of the Deep South. When compared to state rates from a decade before, 17 more states have rates above 30 deaths per 100,000 than in 1980.

Roughly the same pattern exists on the map depicting rates of death from cancer of the genital organs, including cervical, uterine and ovarian cancers. While uterine cancer is more common in post-menopausal women, cervical and ovarian cancer are common among younger women. In fact, ovarian cancer is the most common reproductive cancer among women between the ages of 15 and 24.[27] Rates above 15 per 100,000 women appear throughout most of the nation excluding Alaska and Hawaii and a band of states from Idaho through Texas. Again population age is probably a factor in states with the highest values on both of these maps; however, environmental factors may also play a role in urbanized areas, which often suffer from increased air and water pollution.

Fortunately, childbirth is no longer the dangerous ordeal it once was. Maternal mortality rates have decreased dramatically since the 1930s with the greatest improvement occurring during the 1940s when antibiotics were introduced. A 1941 Statistical Bulletin from Metropolitan Life reported that mortality associated with childbirth in the United States was improving. It

DEATH FROM HEART DISEASE

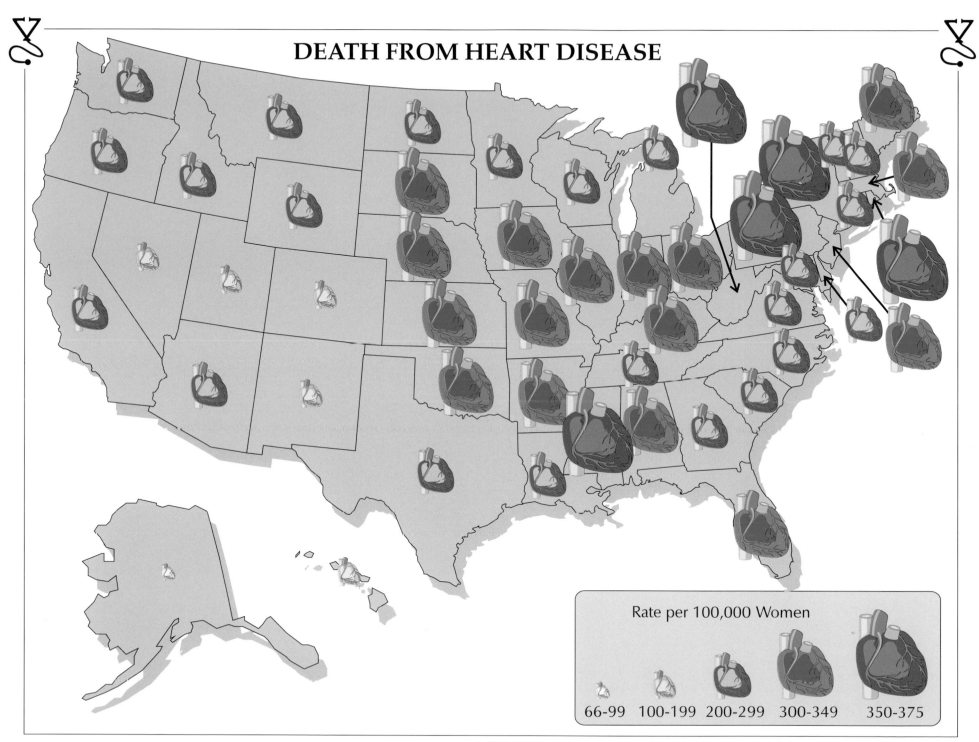

Rate per 100,000 Women

66-99   100-199   200-299   300-349   350-375

DEATH FROM CANCER

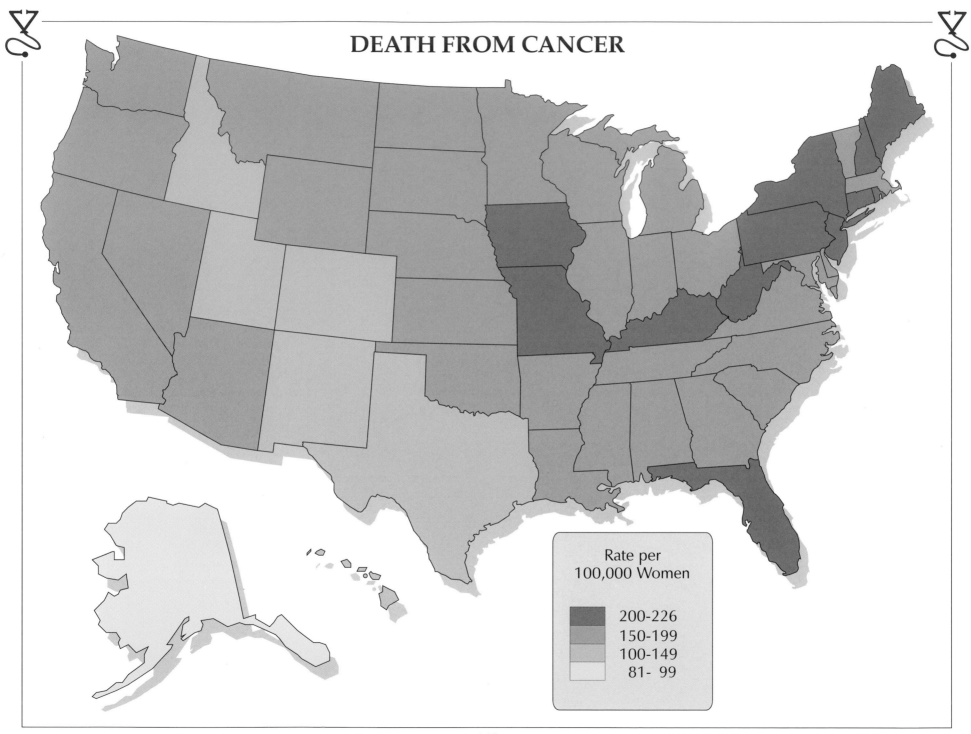

Rate per
100,000 Women

200-226
150-199
100-149
81- 99

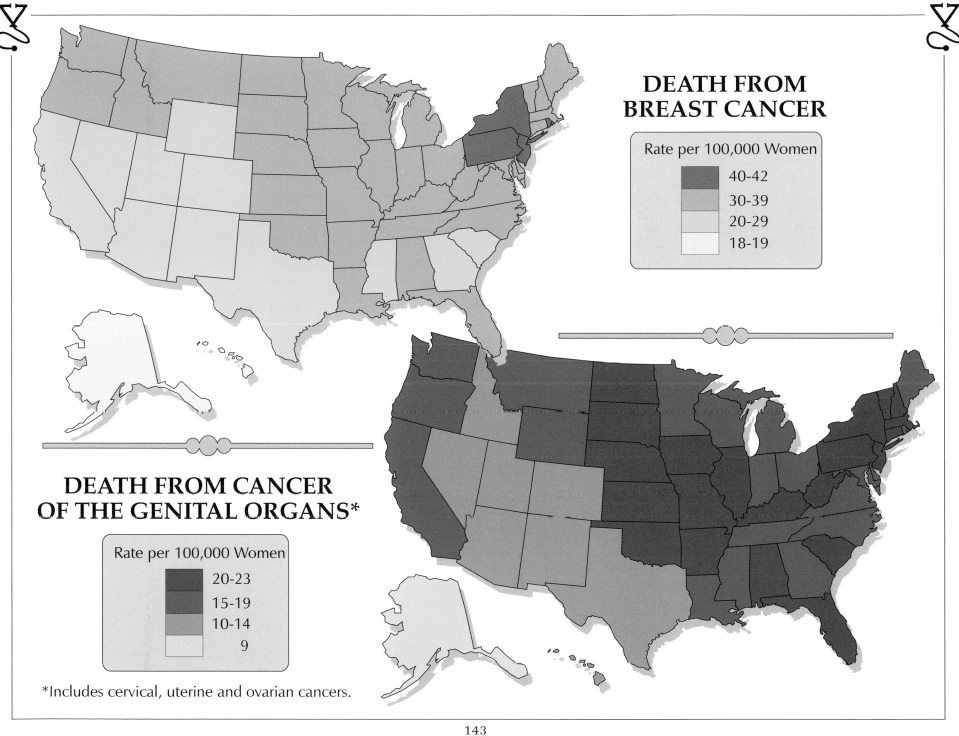

DEATH FROM BREAST CANCER

Rate per 100,000 Women

- 40-42
- 30-39
- 20-29
- 18-19

DEATH FROM CANCER OF THE GENITAL ORGANS*

Rate per 100,000 Women

- 20-23
- 15-19
- 10-14
- 9

*Includes cervical, uterine and ovarian cancers.

states, "In 1939 there were 9,151 deaths from puerperal causes in the U.S.; a decade earlier, the number was over 15,000." By 1986 there were only about 220 deaths from complications due to childbirth.[28] When examining the map, "Death from Pregnancy and Childbirth," no real regional patterns appear. This is not surprising since the rate varies only from one per 1,000,000 to six per 1,000,000. Eight states had rates of zero. The highest rate, six deaths per one million women, occurred in Maryland, probably because data from the District of Columbia were combined with data from Maryland. The high incidence of poverty in the District of Columbia and scarcity of adequate prenatal care among the poor are major contributing factors to this high rate.

Chronic liver disease and cirrhosis are the eighth leading cause of death among women. The consequences of chronic alcohol abuse appear to be more severe for women than they are for men. The development of alcoholic liver disease in women occurs after a shorter period of heavy drinking than it does for men, and female alcoholics die at a rate 50% to 100% higher than do men.[29] Alabama, Florida and New Jersey had the highest rates of death from liver disease as indicated on the map, "Death from Chronic Liver Disease and Cirrhosis." Other regions with high rates are the Northeast, the West, the Deep South and the Northern High Plains. States with low death rates include Alaska and Hawaii and nine other states scattered throughout the country.

The effect of AIDS on women is two-fold. First, women are contracting this virus in ever increasing numbers, and second, women are the most frequent caregivers for those who have AIDS. The chart entitled, "AIDS Through Time," illustrates the progress of the disease among women and men between 1981 and 1991. Historically, women have not had the incidence of AIDS that men have; this is changing, however, as heterosexual transmission is increasing at an alarming rate. Women are almost 18 times more likely to be infected by a male partner than vice versa. Also, women who are diagnosed with AIDS tend to die twice as quickly as men with the virus.[30] For African-American women, the statistics are even worse. In 1988, the rate of AIDS-related deaths among African-American women of reproductive age was almost nine times as high as among White women.[31]

When examining the incidence of AIDS at the state level on the map, "AIDS," it is evident that for women the incidence of AIDS in New York (17.9 per 1,000 women), New Jersey (16.5) and Florida (11.1) is drastically higher than in other parts of the country. The incidence of AIDS is at least three times as high in these states as in the rest of the country. Viewing the map showing the rate of AIDS among men, we see that the high and low values occur in about the same states as they did for women, with the exception of California, which has a high rate for men. The difference between the two maps is a matter of degree, rather than distribution, with the men's rates more that five times as high as the women's. Low rates on both maps occurred throughout the Midwest, Northern High Plains and New England.

Perhaps the most heart wrenching aspect of AIDS is the incidence of the disease in children. While there are widely publicized cases focused on hemophiliac children becoming infected from blood products, the vast majority of HIV+ children became infected prenatally by their HIV+ mothers. Recent studies indicate that nationwide between 7% and 40% of babies born to

DEATH FROM PREGNANCY
AND CHILDBIRTH

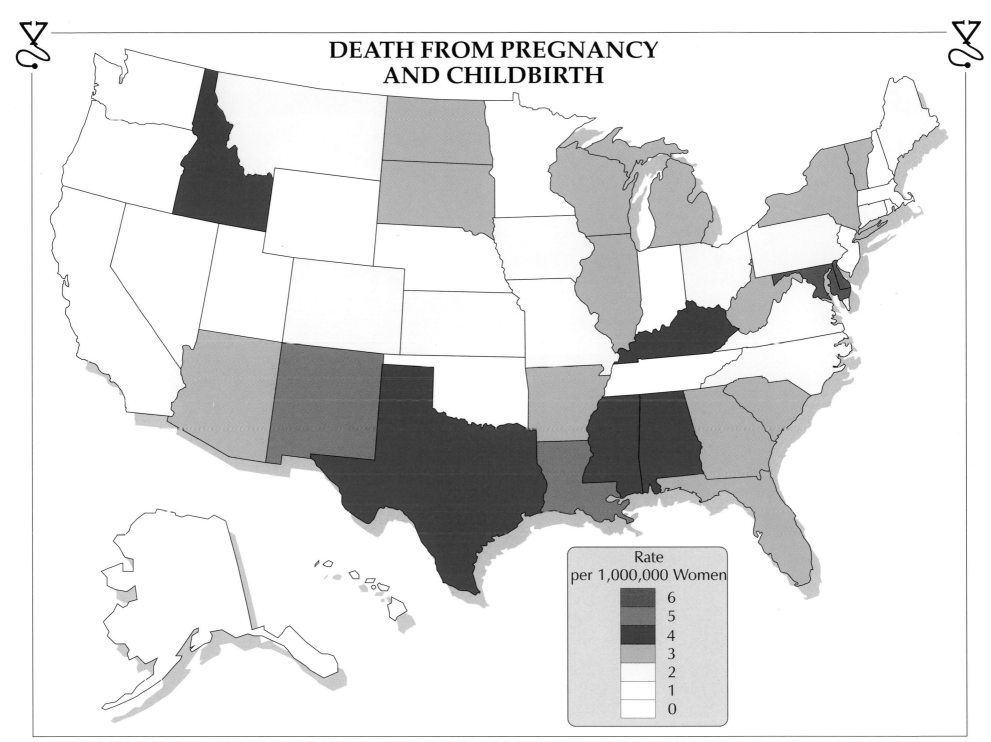

Rate
per 1,000,000 Women

	6
	5
	4
	3
	2
	1
	0

DEATH FROM CHRONIC LIVER DISEASE AND CIRRHOSIS

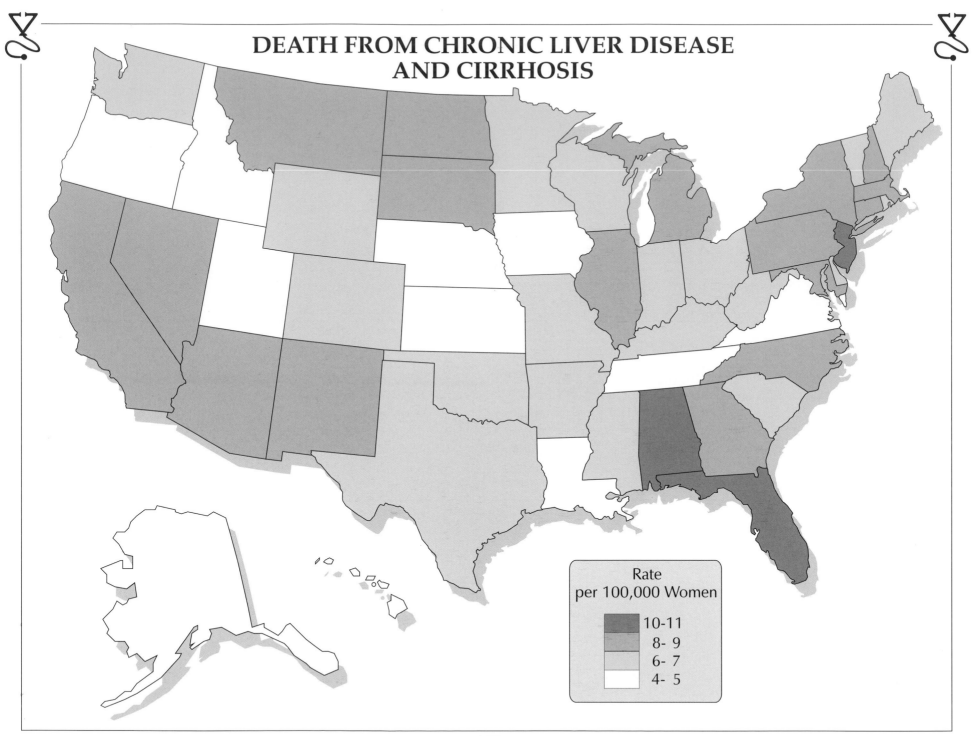

Rate
per 100,000 Women

- 10-11
- 8- 9
- 6- 7
- 4- 5

AIDS THROUGH TIME

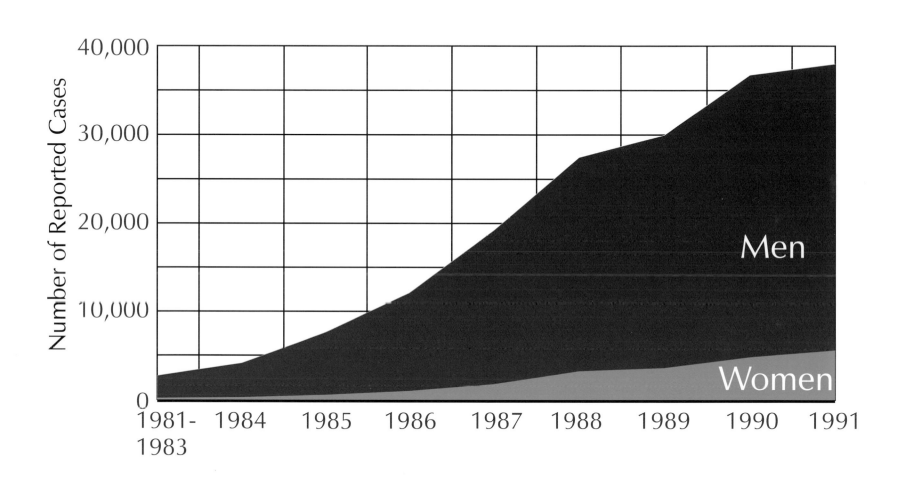

AIDS

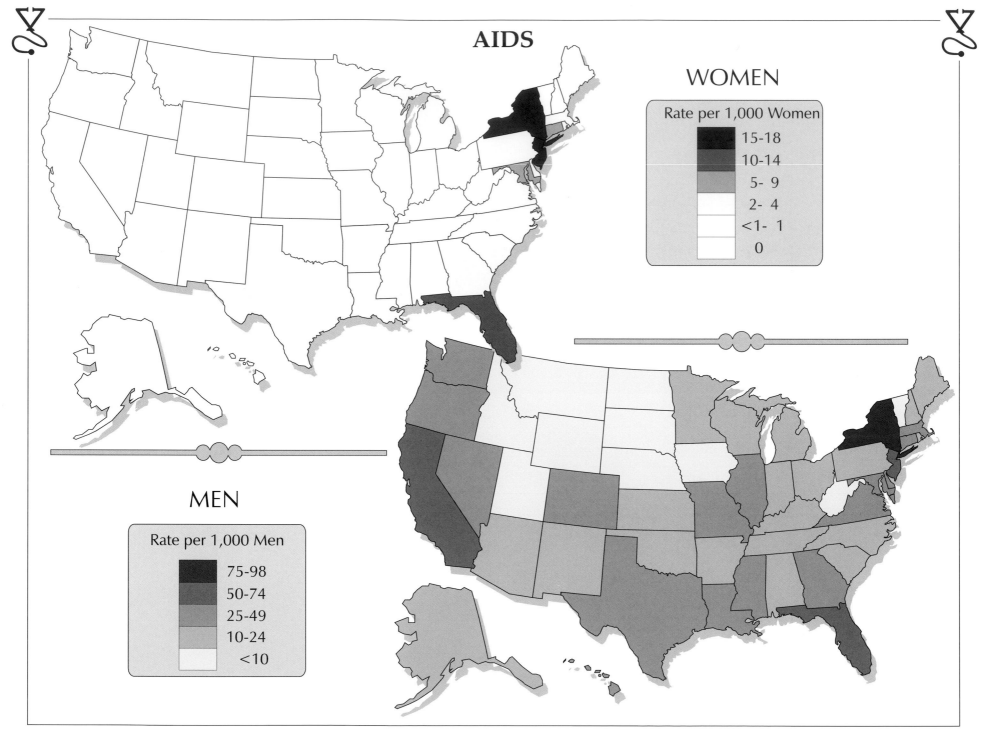

WOMEN

Rate per 1,000 Women

- 15-18
- 10-14
- 5- 9
- 2- 4
- <1- 1
- 0

MEN

Rate per 1,000 Men

- 75-98
- 50-74
- 25-49
- 10-24
- <10

HIV+ women will develop HIV infection. On the positive side, this means that at least 60% will be free of the infection.[32] The two maps on "Children Born with AIDS" examine the number of births to women who are HIV+ per 100,000 live births and the estimated number of babies who are HIV+ per 100,000 live births.

Among the states for which data are available, New York had the highest birth rate to HIV+ women at 628 per 100,000 live births. Seventy-six percent (478 per 100,000 live births) of babies born to these women are HIV infected. States having high proportions of HIV+ mothers and babies are, as would be expected, the same states with higher proportions of women with AIDS. The exceptions are Massachusetts, Connecticut and Delaware; these states have a relatively low incidence of AIDS among women, but high occurrences of HIV+ mothers and babies. So, while the women with AIDS in these states make up a small proportion of the overall population of women, they represent a much larger proportion of mothers and babies who are HIV infected. States having high rates of infected mothers and babies were clustered around the Northeast and Deep South. High rates were also found in Illinois, Michigan and California, all states with major metropolitan areas. States with low rates of infection were located in the nation's interior. Montana had the lowest rate of infection with no HIV+ mothers or babies reported.

Death resulting from injuries received in motor vehicle accidents is an all too common occurrence. Men are three times more likely to die this way than are women. In fact, nationwide, only 32% as many women die in these accidents as do men. Six of the nine states with lowest death rates for women in motor vehicle accidents are located in the Northeast and New England, as portrayed on the map, "Motor Vehicle Deaths." These states, Maine, Massachusetts, Rhode Island, Connecticut, New York, New Jersey, along with Maryland, North Dakota and Hawaii all have death rates for women of between six and nine per 100,000 women. The state with the highest death rate for women was New Mexico with a rate of 20. The "crashed car" symbol associated with each state on the map represents the women's rate as a percentage of men's. In some states, for example New Jersey, even though the death rate for women is relatively low, the proportion of women dying in accidents compared to men is very high. In only seven states is the rate of female fatalities more than 34% of the men's rate.

Seat belt and shoulder harness use greatly reduces traffic fatalities. A Swedish study revealed that fatalities were reduced by 85–90% when a three-point belt system was used as opposed to using no restraint system. Fatalities occurred in cars traveling as slowly as 12 miles per hour when no restraint system was used. Of course these devices only help to prevent injuries and fatalities in a crash. The cause of the crash is an important issue, and alcohol is a factor more than one-third of the time. The maps entitled "Driving While Intoxicated" reveal the percentages of women and of men who have driven while intoxicated. Intoxicated, in the data used for this map, was defined as having driven after drinking too much at least once in the last month. Since this definition is a subjective and not a legal one, the real rate of drunk driving is probably higher than revealed here. A few regional patterns emerge when examining the first map showing the percentage of women who have driven while being intoxicated. Fewer than 1.4% of women in the Deep South reported that they had driven while intoxicated during the last month. High values appear across the northern half of

CHILDREN BORN WITH AIDS
(In Selected States)

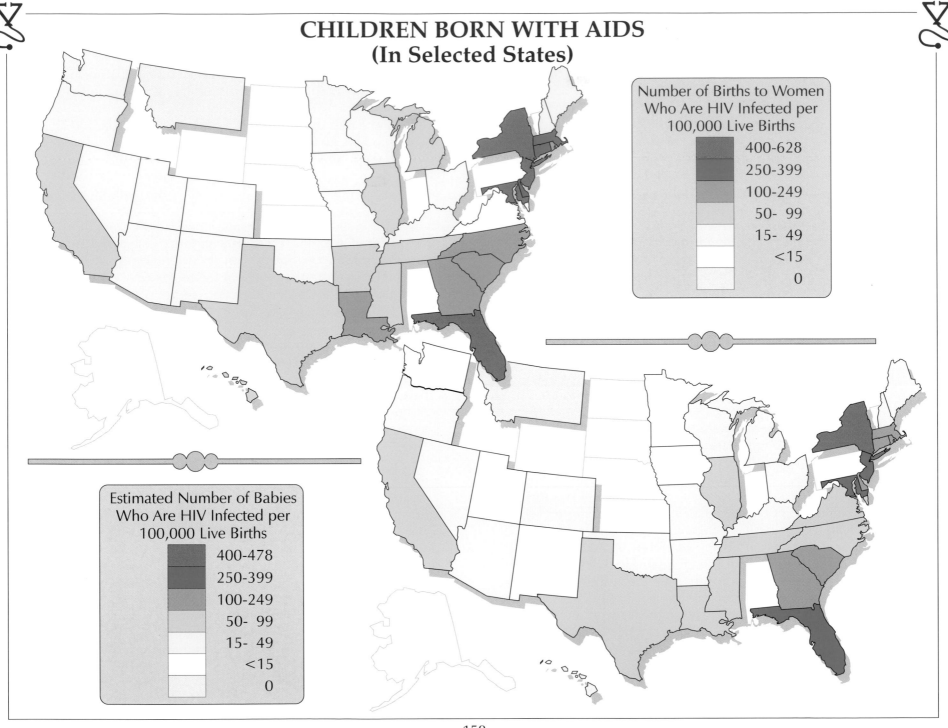

Number of Births to Women Who Are HIV Infected per 100,000 Live Births

- 400-628
- 250-399
- 100-249
- 50- 99
- 15- 49
- <15
- 0

Estimated Number of Babies Who Are HIV Infected per 100,000 Live Births

- 400-478
- 250-399
- 100-249
- 50- 99
- 15- 49
- <15
- 0

MOTOR VEHICLE DEATHS

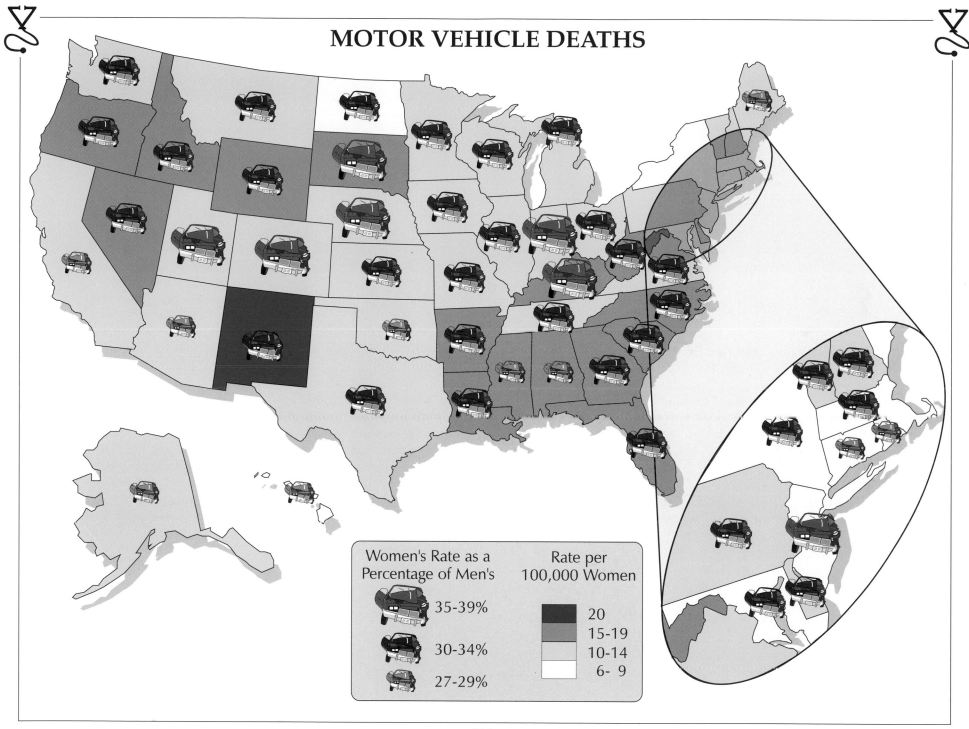

Women's Rate as a Percentage of Men's

- 35-39%
- 30-34%
- 27-29%

Rate per 100,000 Women

- 20
- 15-19
- 10-14
- 6- 9

the United States and in California, New Mexico and Texas. South Dakota and New Mexico topped the nation in the incidence of drunk driving among women. Note that while New Mexico ranked in the highest category for women, it ranked in the lowest for men. The Deep South had a relatively low rate of driving while intoxicated for men as well as for women. Wisconsin ranked highest for men with 11% of the male population admitting to driving while intoxicated.

Throughout history, women have been providing health care for those around them as mothers caring for sick children and family members, as midwives and as nurses. While there were some women physicians in the 19th century, only in the latter part of this century has the field of medicine more widely opened its doors to women wishing to study medicine. Two maps, "Physicians," address the issue of female physicians. The first depicts the number of female physicians per 100,000 women, with rates ranging from a low of 28 in Idaho to a high of 197 in Maryland (includes Washington, D.C.). The average rate for the entire United Stares is 19 per 100,000. Women in the Northeast have greater access to female physicians than other regions of the country.

The second map shows the percentage of physicians who are women. On a national level, 18% of all physicians are women, a figure expected to rise to 25% by the year 2000. State values currently vary from a low of 9% in Wyoming to a high of 23% in Massachusetts and Maryland. In only seven other states (Connecticut, Rhode Island, New York, New Jersey, Maryland, Illinois and New Mexico) were more than 20% of physicians female. Again, the Northeast has among the highest percentages of female physicians. In all states, female physicians are very much in the minority.

STATES OF MIND

Suicide. The mere mention of which makes us shudder. A loved one's suicide often causes intense grief and guilt feelings in those left behind—who may feel as if they could somehow have prevented it. Psychological and sociological factors play a part in the suicide. Social isolation is often regarded as a major causative factor.[33] Suicide is the ninth leading cause of death for women (4.8 per 100,000 women) and the seventh leading cause for men. The rate for men is four times as high as the rate for women. Among young people aged 15 to 24, nearly six times as many men commit suicide as do women. Our final map portraying death rates among adult women is one depicting the suicide rate per 100,000 women in each state. The state of Delaware had the dubious honor of ranking first in the rate of suicide among women. Wyoming was next with eight suicides per 100,000 women. There is a strong east–west division in the data. High values, between six and eight, were observed in ten out of 11 of the continental western states, with Utah being the exception. The eastern states (except Louisiana, Mississippi, Florida and Delaware) exhibit rates between two and five per 100,000 women.

While women represent a smaller percentage of suicides than do men, women make up for a large proportion of those in mental institutions. As mentioned earlier, women must be cautious when seeking psychiatric care. Psychiatrists and psychologists have been trained in a system that often doesn't understand or recognize how much women's psychological development differs from men's. And though the majority of mental health professionals are dedicated and caring

DRIVING WHILE INTOXICATED
(In Selected States)

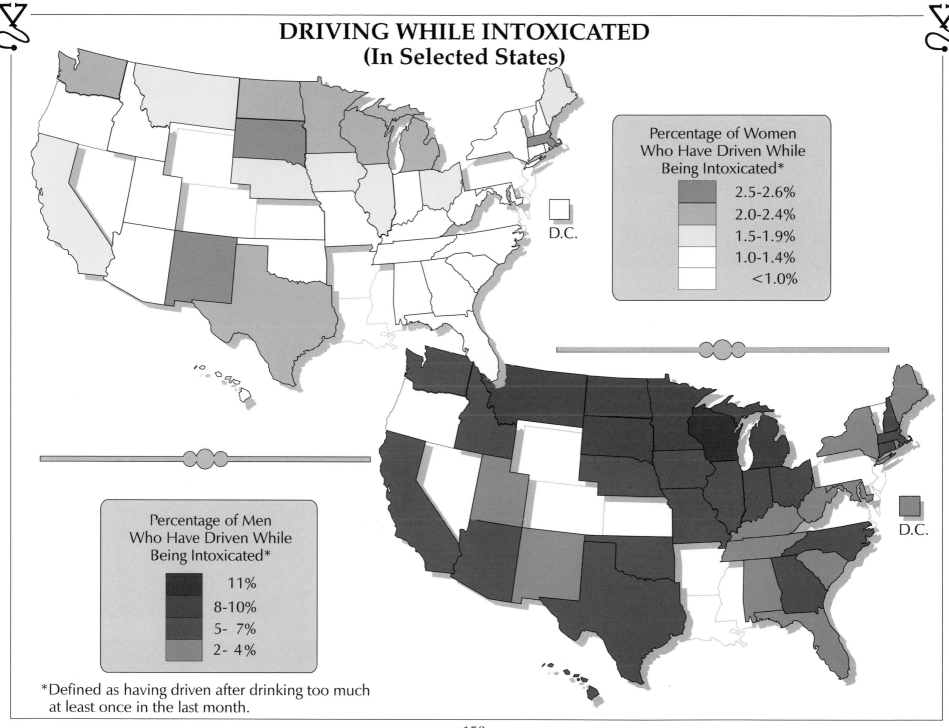

Percentage of Women
Who Have Driven While
Being Intoxicated*

2.5-2.6%
2.0-2.4%
1.5-1.9%
1.0-1.4%
<1.0%

D.C.

Percentage of Men
Who Have Driven While
Being Intoxicated*

11%
8-10%
5- 7%
2- 4%

D.C.

*Defined as having driven after drinking too much
  at least once in the last month.

PHYSICIANS

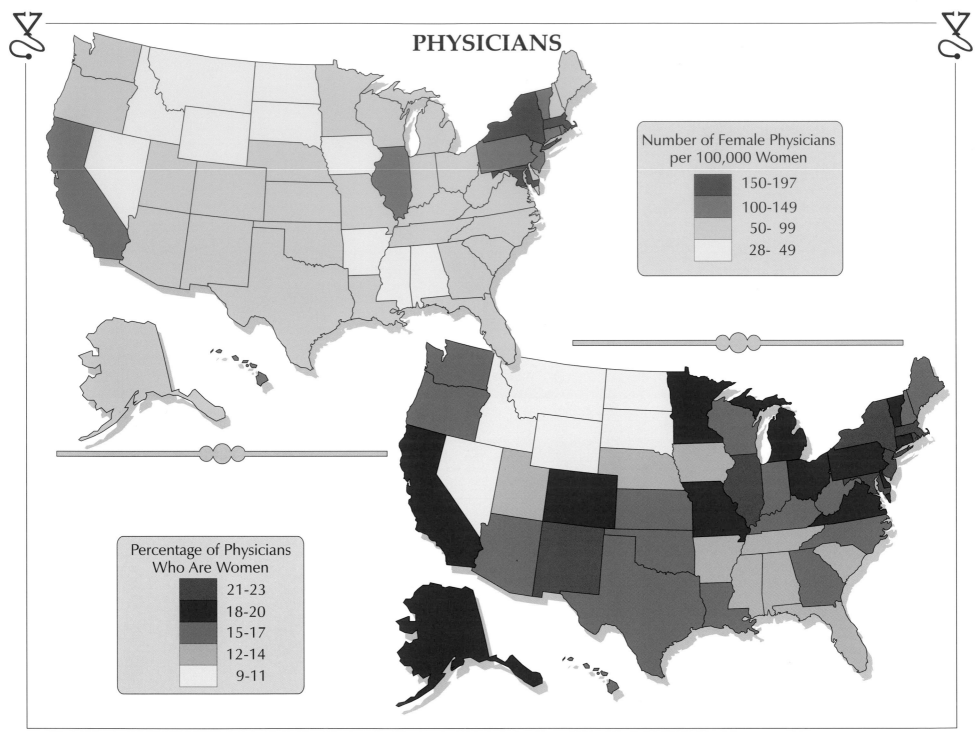

Number of Female Physicians
per 100,000 Women

	150-197
	100-149
	50- 99
	28- 49

Percentage of Physicians
Who Are Women

	21-23
	18-20
	15-17
	12-14
	9-11

SUICIDE

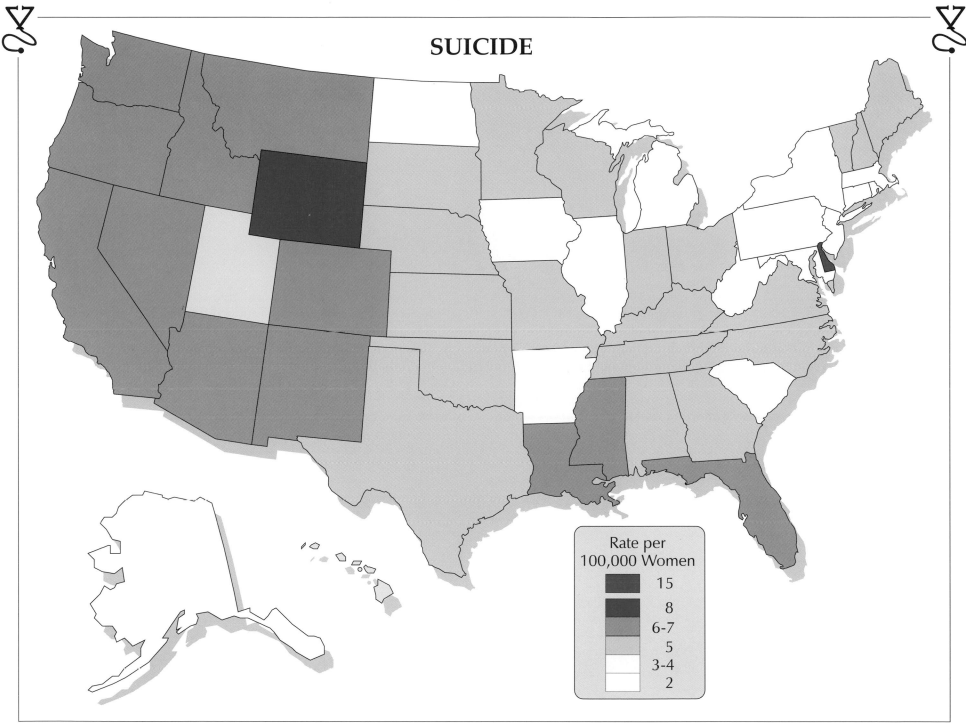

Rate per
100,000 Women

15
8
6-7
5
3-4
2

individuals, women under psychiatric care are more vulnerable to sexual abuse at the hands of unscrupulous practitioners than are men.[34]

Forty percent of the residents of mental institutions in this country are women. The two maps in the illustration "Women in Mental Institutions" depict the number of women living in mental hospitals and the percent of residents who are women. States having the greatest number of women in these institutions tend to be clustered in the east. New York ranks first in number of residents with 94 of every 100,000 women living in a psychiatric care facility. Mississippi ranks second in number of residents with 75 per 100,000 women. The states with the smallest proportion of female residents in institutions are Hawaii and New Mexico, each with 15 residents per 100,000 women. The picture changes at bit when we examine the map depicting the percentage of residents who are women. In only three states, Alaska (59%), New Hampshire (59%) and South Carolina (50%), do women make up half or more than half of the residents in mental institutions. Women make up the smallest percentage of residents, 29%, in Wyoming. Again, eastern states tended to have higher values than western states. While, at first glance, it would be easy to conclude that the higher values in the east could be attributed to the stresses of life and crowded conditions of eastern cities, that would be an oversimplification of the causes. Other factors include the availability of psychiatric care facilities, the proportion of psychiatric care professionals in the population and availability of funding in each state for psychiatric care. Even a community's attitude toward psychiatric care can influence the number of people committed to institutions. The criminal justice system can also be a factor in that some judges are more likely than others to use commitment to an institution for treatment as an alternative to prison sentences.

SUBSTANCE ABUSE

Substance abuse, including use of illegal drugs, smoking and alcohol consumption, is a growing problem in our society. We will confine our examination of this subject to the two legal substances, cigarettes and alcohol, because they are the most common substances abused by women, crossing all racial, religious and socioeconomic lines. The next two maps, "Smoking" and "Heavy Drinking," examine patterns of smoking and heavy drinking among women in the 36 states for which data were available.

Nationwide, an average of 27% of women smoke. On a state level, women in Kentucky were more likely to be smokers (30.7% are smokers) while women in Utah (13.7% are smokers) were least likely to smoke. Smoking appears to be more common in the northeast than in the west or Deep South. Although a number of factors affect whether women become smokers, two factors are obviously at work in the states with the highest and lowest values. Economics plays an important role in Kentucky where tobacco is a major cash crop and taxes on cigarettes are relatively low. Religious beliefs are the primary reason that few women smoke in predominantly Mormon Utah.

While two-thirds of American women regularly use alcohol, the number of women who are heavy drinkers is considerably lower. Heavy drinking is defined here as having more than 60 drinks per month. Heavy drinking is more prevalent in the northeast and in

WOMEN IN MENTAL INSTITUTIONS

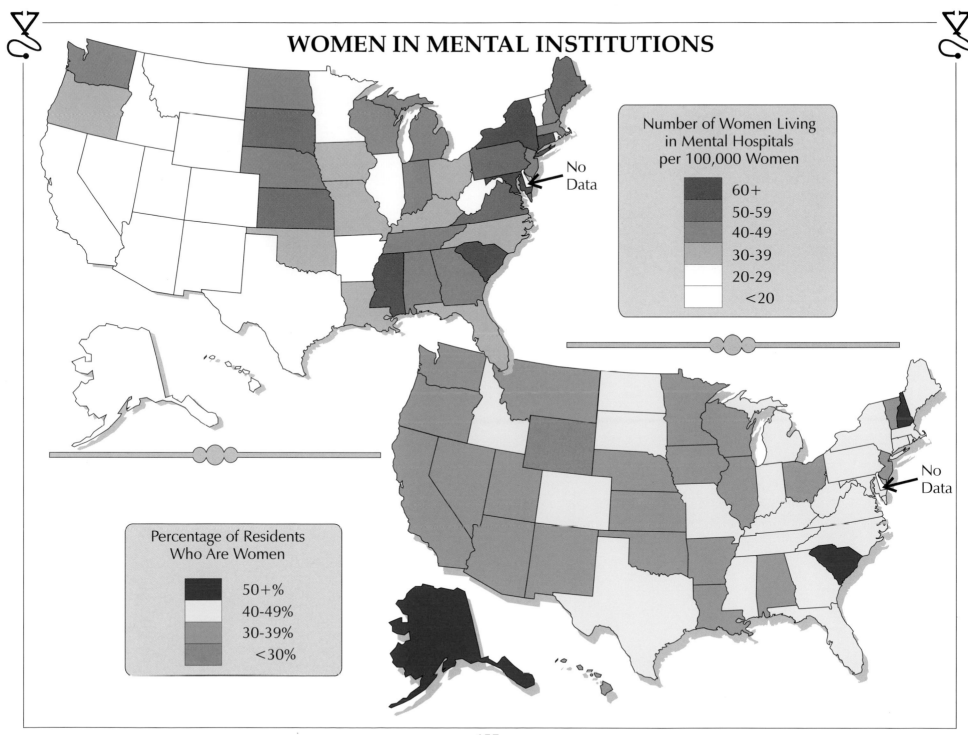

Number of Women Living
in Mental Hospitals
per 100,000 Women

60+
50-59
40-49
30-39
20-29
<20

No Data

Percentage of Residents
Who Are Women

50+%
40-49%
30-39%
<30%

No Data

SMOKING
1988
(In Selected States)

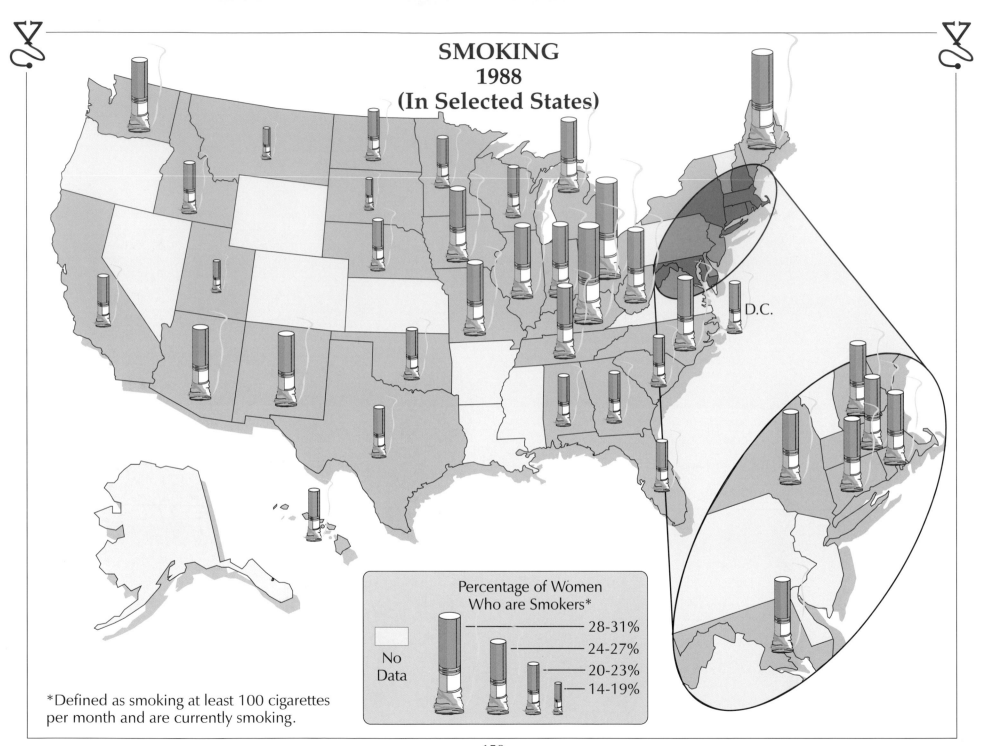

Percentage of Women
Who are Smokers*

28-31%

24-27%

20-23%

14-19%

No
Data

D.C.

*Defined as smoking at least 100 cigarettes
per month and are currently smoking.

HEAVY DRINKING
1988
(In Selected States)

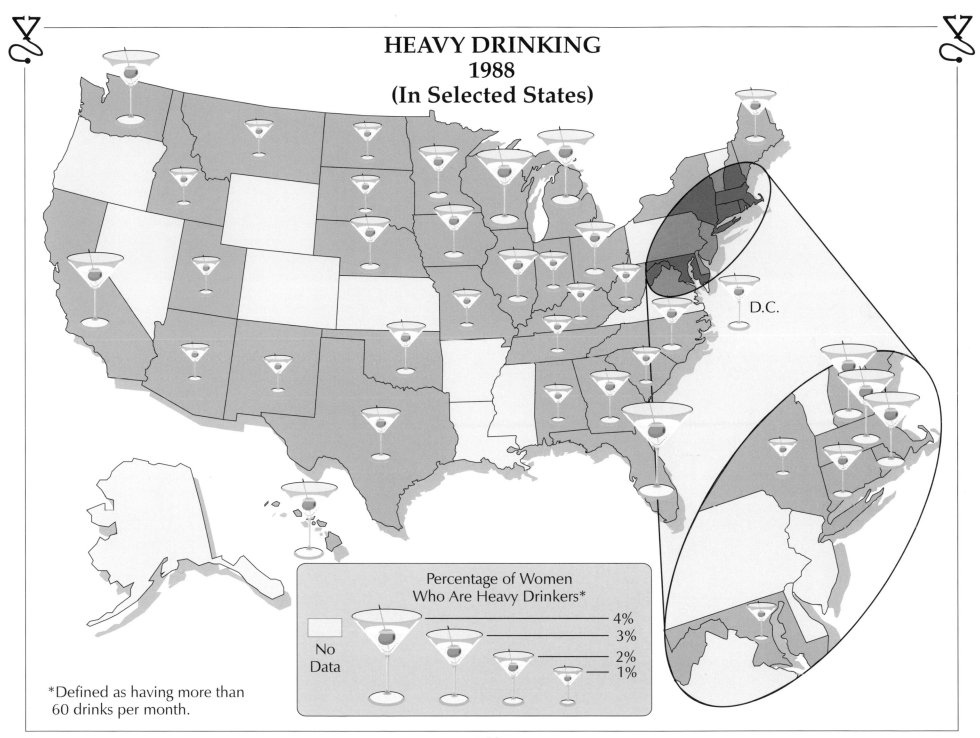

D.C.

Percentage of Women
Who Are Heavy Drinkers*

No
Data

—— 4%
—— 3%
—— 2%
—— 1%

*Defined as having more than
60 drinks per month.

Florida, Hawaii and California. A low incidence of heavy alcohol use was found in the southern states commonly referred to as the Bible Belt. Florida, at 4%, had the largest proportion of women who are heavy drinkers, while less than 1% of the female population in Utah drank heavily.

Caution must be used when drawing conclusions from the map, "Drug and Alcohol Halfway Houses." While one state may have a high percentage of women enrolled in these programs, this may be more a reflection of the availability of treatment than the number of women dependent on drugs or alcohol. Cultural attitudes can also influence the willingness of women to accept treatment for these addictions. The availability of treatment for these women can, however, be perceived as an indicator of a community's willingness to help rather than to ignore these women. But the number of women receiving treatment in a community does not necessarily reflect the number who may still be untreated.

The map does, however, show us that Rhode Island has the highest proportion of women in treatment at 25 per 100,000 women. West Virginia is the lowest at a rate of one per 100,000 women. States on the west coast and in the Northeast and New England, along with Alaska, Minnesota and Florida, had more women in treatment than did other sections of the country.

THE BIRDS AND THE BEES

Although women should not be totally defined by their reproductive systems, reproductive issues are nonetheless of great importance to most women. The maps in this section will examine reproductive issues, primarily issues related to abortion. Infant mortality will also be addressed.

Prior to *Roe v. Wade*, only four states, Alaska, Hawaii, Washington and New York, permitted abortion on demand. The majority of states permitted abortions only if the mother's life was endangered. Since 1973, areas of concern surrounding abortions have included use of public funding to provide abortions, health insurance coverage of abortions, availability of abortions to minors, waiting periods, and spousal and parental notification. Eight maps, entitled "Laws Regulating Abortions," deal with state laws that regulate abortions. The 1989 Supreme Court ruling in *Webster v. Reproductive Health Services* allowed states to restrict access to abortion and a number of states have done just that. Although many of these restrictions are being challenged in the courts, the right to an abortion as outlined in *Roe v. Wade* is under attack. As of this writing, ten states require that husbands be notified or grant consent for married women seeking an abortion. In 1983, only five states required spousal notification or consent. Currently, 36 states require parental consent or state mandated counseling for minors seeking an abortion, compared to only 16 states in 1983. Three states have enacted 24-hour waiting periods, and three states have imposed a "gag rule," which prevents certain health care providers from giving counseling or referrals regarding abortions. Twenty-six states require that women be given state-prepared material that is intended to dissuade them from having an abortion.

All but 15 states prohibit post-viability abortions. Missouri goes so far as to prohibit public employees from participating in the performance of an abortion.

DRUG OR ALCOHOL HALFWAY HOUSES

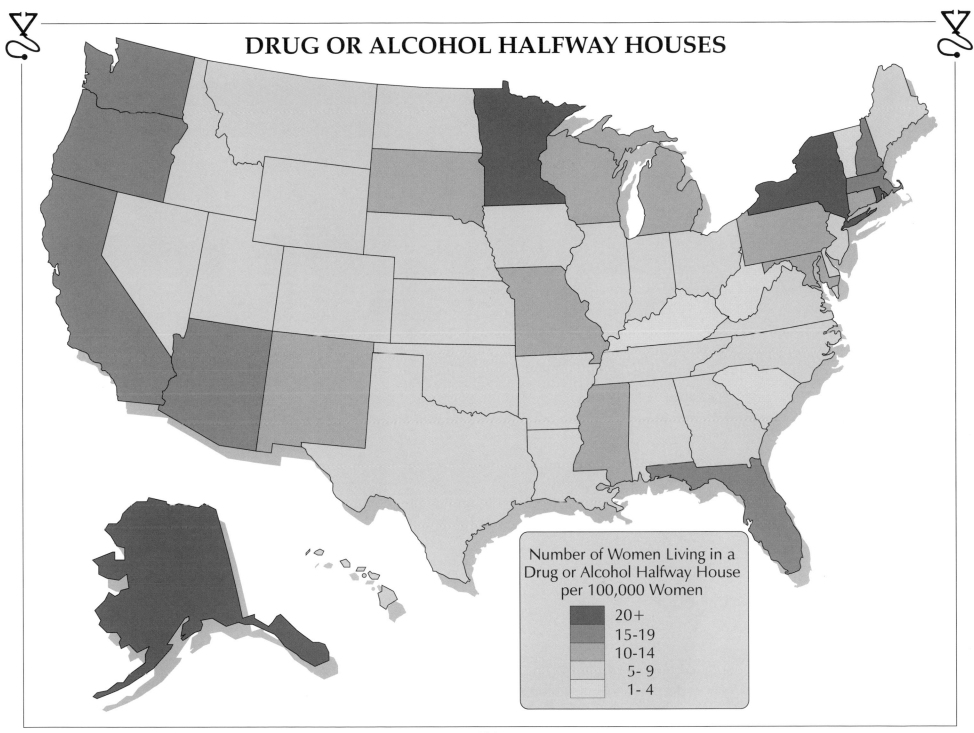

Number of Women Living in a
Drug or Alcohol Halfway House
per 100,000 Women

20+
15-19
10-14
5- 9
1- 4

LAWS REGULATING ABORTIONS

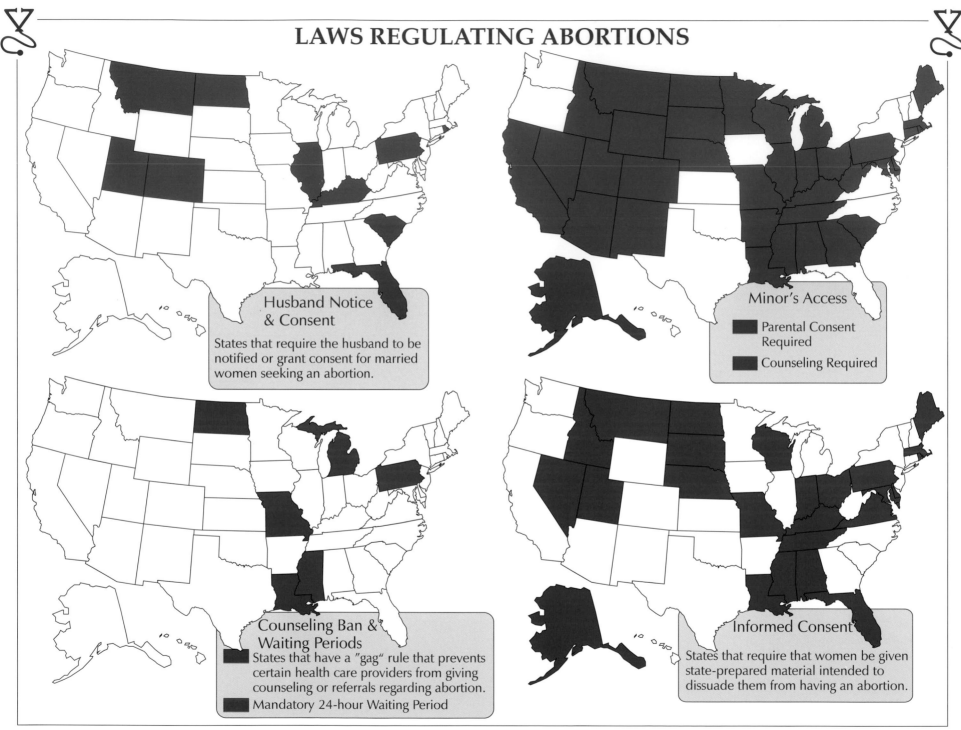

Husband Notice & Consent

States that require the husband to be notified or grant consent for married women seeking an abortion.

Minor's Access

- Parental Consent Required
- Counseling Required

Counseling Ban & Waiting Periods

- States that have a "gag" rule that prevents certain health care providers from giving counseling or referrals regarding abortion.
- Mandatory 24-hour Waiting Period

Informed Consent

States that require that women be given state-prepared material intended to dissuade them from having an abortion.

162

LAWS REGULATING ABORTIONS

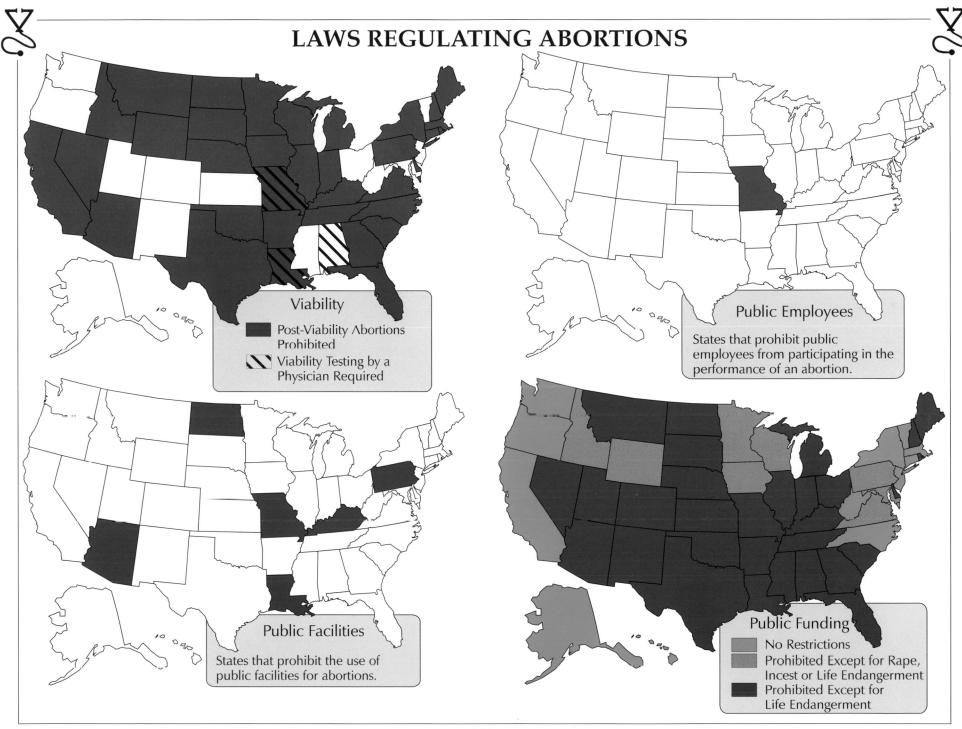

Viability

- Post-Viability Abortions Prohibited
- Viability Testing by a Physician Required

Public Employees

States that prohibit public employees from participating in the performance of an abortion.

Public Facilities

States that prohibit the use of public facilities for abortions.

Public Funding

- No Restrictions
- Prohibited Except for Rape, Incest or Life Endangerment
- Prohibited Except for Life Endangerment

The states of Arizona, North Dakota, Missouri, Louisiana, Kentucky and Pennsylvania prohibit the use of public facilities for abortions. The final map on this subject examines the use of public funds for abortions, revealing that in 38 states, public funds cannot be used for abortions unless the mother's life is endangered. The Hyde Amendment, passed in 1976, prohibited the use of federal Medicaid funds for the abortions of indigent women. While the Hyde Amendment did not affect state laws, these 38 states have their own policies that severely restrict the use of state money for abortions. Eight of these states, however, will allow abortions in cases of incest or rape. Only 12 states had no restrictions on the use of public funds for abortions.

The next three maps, entitled "Public Funding," indicate the total federal and state expenditures per 1,000 women of reproductive age for contraceptives, sterilizations and abortions. While expenditures for contraceptives are fairly high in most states, ranging from one dollar to around 15 dollars per woman, public funds are less available for sterilization and are virtually nonexistent for abortions. In states providing non-restrictive, publicly funded abortions, funding is provided on a state level.

States having the highest abortion rates, as shown on the map, "Abortion Rate, 1988" are also, with the exception of Nevada, states that provide non-restricted, publicly funded abortions. Nevada's rate is probably high, despite of the lack of public funds, because prostitution is legal in the state. The District of Columbia had the highest abortion rate of any region with 1,248 abortions per 1,000 live births. New York was the state with the highest rate, 629, while the lowest rate, 81, was found in South Dakota. West Virginia also has a low abortion rate even though the state's restriction is

limited to parental consent for minors. Nationwide, there were 201 abortions per 1,000 live births. Almost 3% of women between the ages of 15 and 44 obtained an abortion in 1988.[35] Rates would probably be higher in many states if abortion services were more available and affordable.

Since the 1973 Supreme Court decision in *Roe v. Wade*, all but three states, South Dakota, Kansas and New York, and the District of Columbia, have shown increases in their rates of abortion (see map, "Change in the Abortion Rate 1973–1988"). These statistics include abortions provided to in state and out-of-state residents. The states having the greatest increases since 1973 were Nevada with an increase of 446 more abortions per 1,000 live births and New Jersey where there were 440 more abortions per 1,000 live births in 1988 than in 1973. With the exception of Nevada, eastern states tended to have larger increases than the rest of the country.[36,37]

For women seeking abortions, especially poor women, two considerations are paramount: the availability of funding and the accessibility of an abortion facility. These are often what decide whether she can obtain an abortion or not. Funding has been drastically cut since the passage of the Hyde Amendment, and the number of abortion providers decreased dramatically in the years since 1985. The map, "Change in the Number of Abortion Providers from 1985 to 1988," indicates the states that have shown increases and decreases during that time. Only nine states have increased the number of abortion providers, while 37 states have shown a decrease in the number of providers. Much of the decrease can be attributed to the loss of federal and state funding for abortions; in addition, the escalating violence surrounding abortion

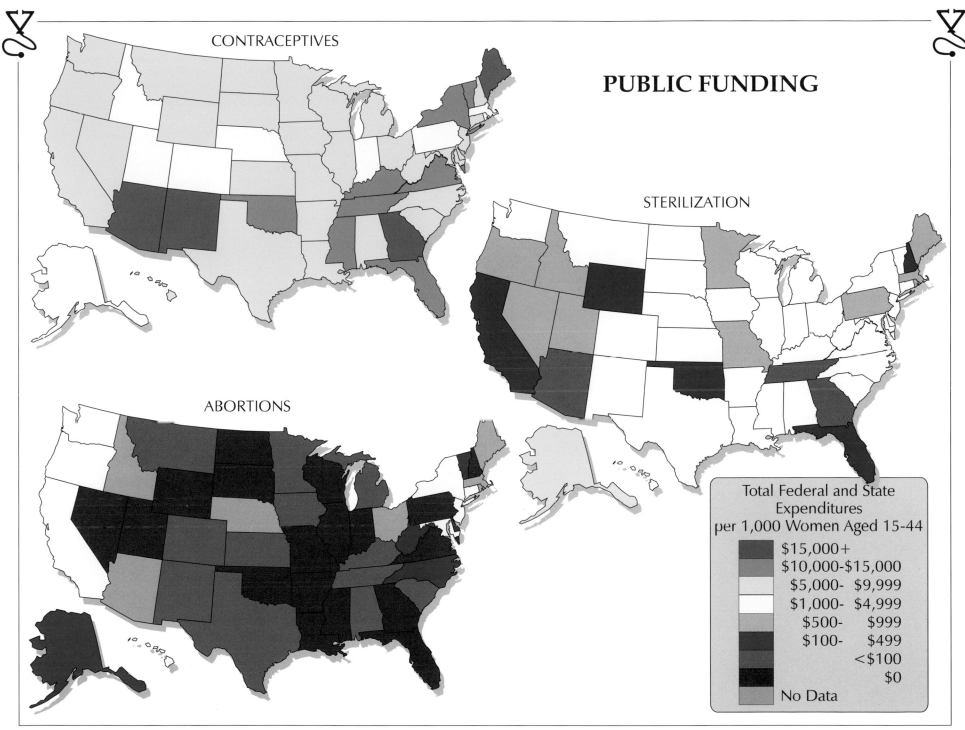

PUBLIC FUNDING

CONTRACEPTIVES

STERILIZATION

ABORTIONS

Total Federal and State
Expenditures
per 1,000 Women Aged 15-44

$15,000+
$10,000-$15,000
$5,000- $9,999
$1,000- $4,999
$500- $999
$100- $499
<$100
$0
No Data

ABORTION RATE
1988

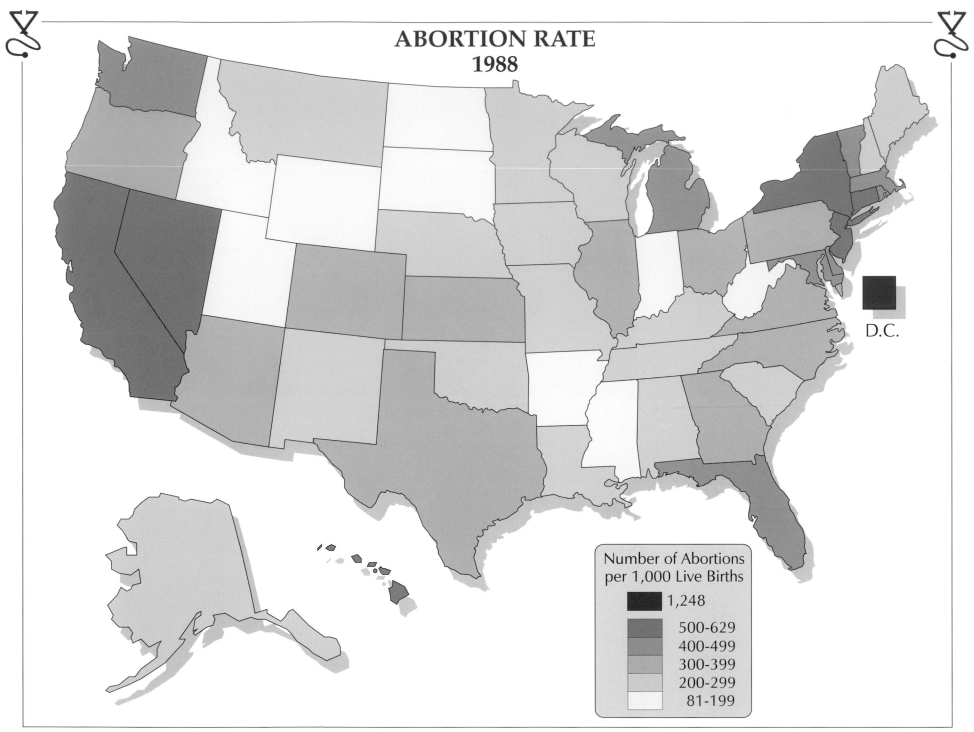

D.C.

Number of Abortions per 1,000 Live Births

- 1,248
- 500-629
- 400-499
- 300-399
- 200-299
- 81-199

CHANGE IN THE ABORTION RATE
1973-1988

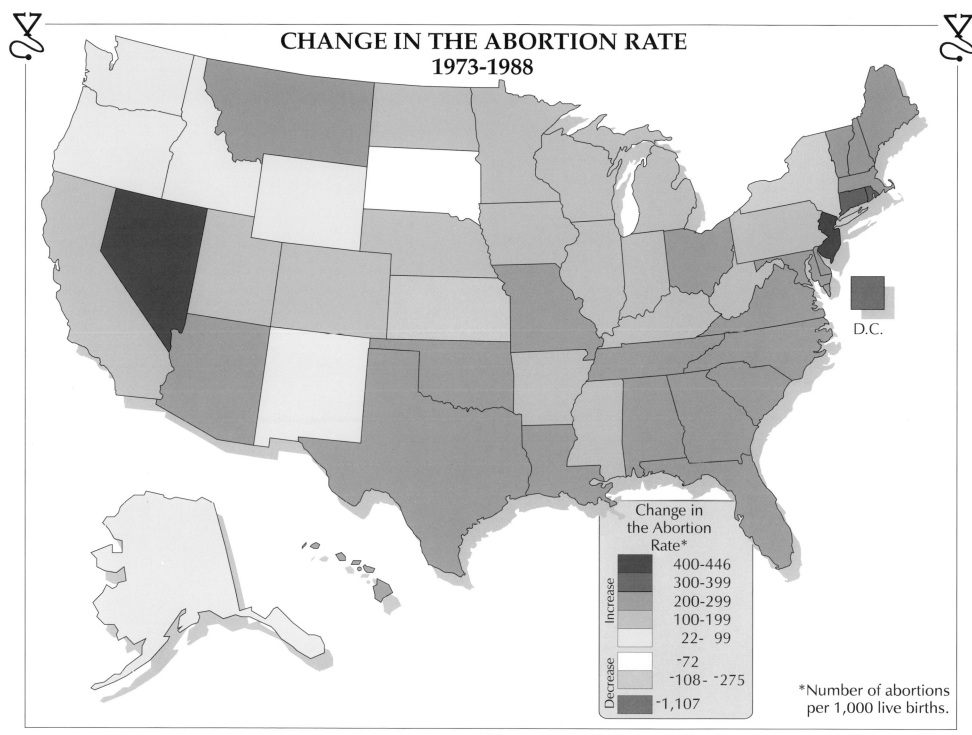

Change in the Abortion Rate*

Increase

400-446
300-399
200-299
100-199
22- 99

Decrease

-72
-108 - -275
-1,107

D.C.

*Number of abortions per 1,000 live births.

CHANGE IN THE NUMBER OF ABORTION PROVIDERS FROM 1985 TO 1988

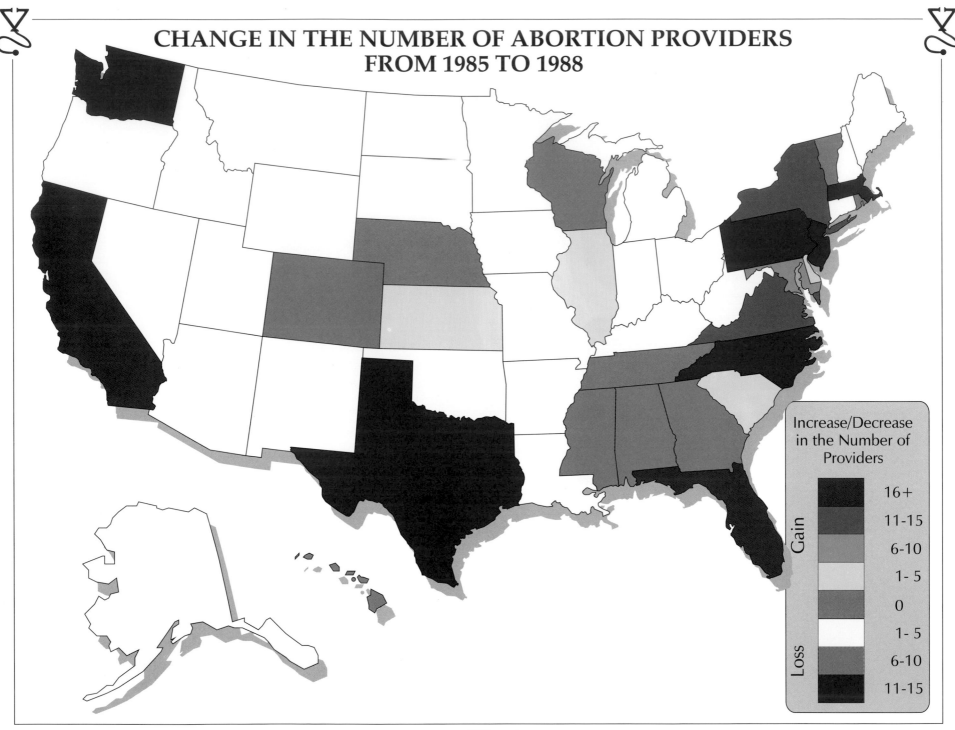

Increase/Decrease in the Number of Providers

Gain

16+
11-15
6-10
1- 5
0
1- 5
6-10
11-15

Loss

providers in many areas has probably influenced some providers to "throw in the towel," deciding that the risk to both the providers and the patients is too great.

Residents of states having few abortion providers and laws requiring 24-hour waiting periods and parental consent, for example, may choose to go elsewhere to have an abortion. In "Place of Abortions vs. State of Residence," the percentage of residents obtaining abortions out-of-state and the percentage of abortions provided to out-of-state residents are indicated by state. More than 10% of the abortions in 17 states were provided to out-of-state residents. More than 45% of the abortions provided in North Dakota and the District of Columbia involved out-of-state residents. This is surprising for North Dakota, which has some of the most restrictive abortion laws. Out-of-state abortions were obtained by more than 45% of the women obtaining abortions in both South Dakota and Wyoming.

A baby's birth weight is often directly related to the health of the mother. Mothers who have had adequate pre-natal care and good nutrition during their pregnancies are more likely to have babies of average weight. Women in poverty often have had little or no pre-natal services and lack the wherewithal to obtain nutritious (and expensive) food and supplements. Thus, the babies they bear are more likely to be of low birth weight, less than 5.5 pounds, than babies of women not in poverty. The two maps entitled "Low Birth Weight 1987–1989" depict the percentage of live births with low birth weight and the percentage of live births with low birth weight among White and African-American women. The highest rates of low birth weight babies occurred in the Deep South. Low rates were found in New England, the upper Midwestern states, the Northern High Plains and the Pacific Northwest. African-

American women were almost three times as likely to have low birth weight babies than were White women.

Sadly, for every 1,000 live births in the United States, ten babies die within the first year. The map, "Infant Mortality," depicts the infant mortality rate per 1,000 live births. The highest rate occurred in the District of Columbia with 23 infants dying per 1,000 live births. New England had among the lowest rates, between seven and eight, in its four most northern states. Low rates were also found in Nevada, Utah, North Dakota, Nebraska, Minnesota and Iowa. The Deep South has the highest regional infant mortality, with rates ranging from 11 to 13. Other states with high infant mortality rates are Montana, Illinois, Michigan, New York and Delaware. Poverty directly affects infant mortality rates, and states having high rates generally have large numbers of women living below the poverty line.

A shocking picture is revealed when infant mortality rates are examined by race, as shown on the group of maps entitled, "Infant Mortality by Race." White infants have the best chance of survival in the United States. The infant mortality rate in 1988 for White children ranged from five to 10 deaths per 1,000 live births. The highest rates appeared in the Deep South, the Northeast, and two other states, Montana and South Dakota. In no state was the rate more that ten per 1,000. The infant mortality rate for African-American infants (17.6) was twice that for White infants (8.5).[38] The largest differences in the rates between White and African-American babies occurred in the Northeast, where the rate of infant mortality of African-American infants was 10.2 points higher than for White babies. The Rocky Mountain states show the least difference in mortality rates. Oklahoma had the lowest infant mortality rate for African-American babies—14 out of every 1,000 babies die within their first year of life. This rate is 40% higher than the highest state mortality rate for White infants. The same pattern exists for other minorities except in the western states. Again the infant mortality rate for other minorities was about twice as high as for White infants. Ironically, the District of Columbia, our nation's capital, had the highest infant mortality rate for all races.

PLACE OF ABORTION VS. STATE OF RESIDENCE

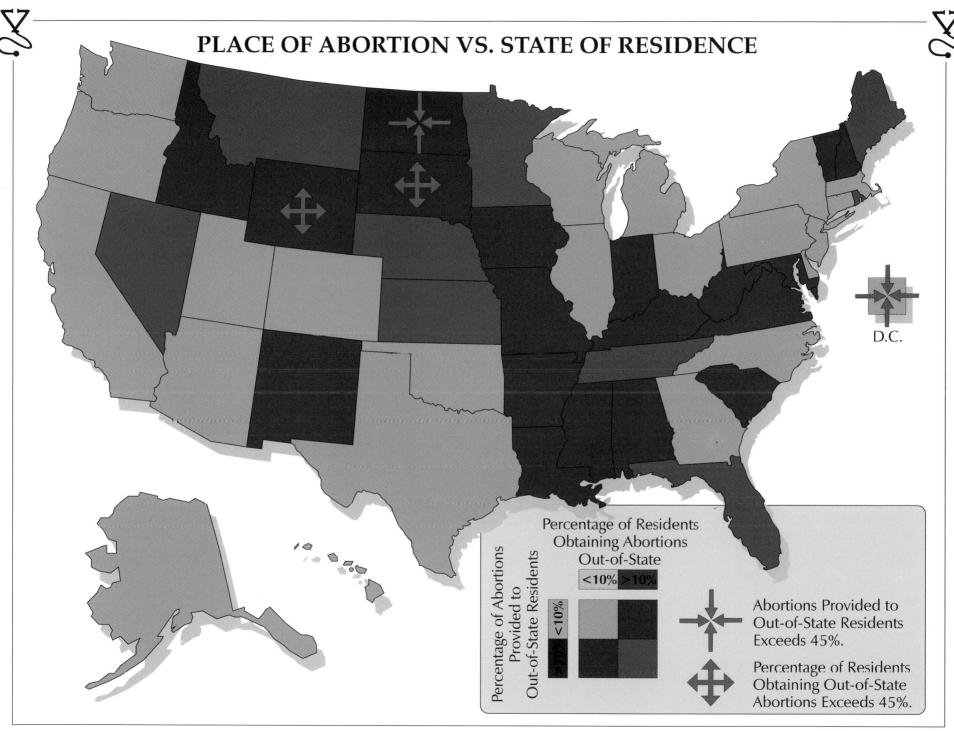

Percentage of Residents Obtaining Abortions Out-of-State

<10% >10%

Percentage of Abortions Provided to Out-of-State Residents

<10%

>10%

D.C.

Abortions Provided to Out-of-State Residents Exceeds 45%.

Percentage of Residents Obtaining Out-of-State Abortions Exceeds 45%.

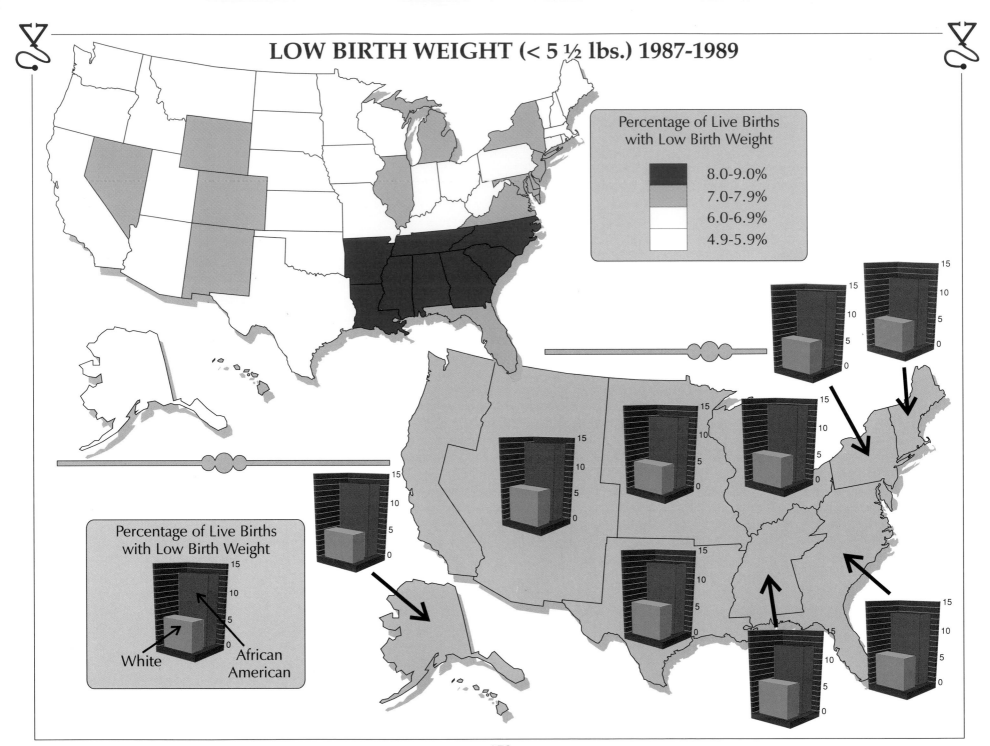

Percentage of Live Births with Low Birth Weight

	8.0-9.0%
	7.0-7.9%
	6.0-6.9%
	4.9-5.9%

Percentage of Live Births with Low Birth Weight

White

African American

INFANT MORTALITY

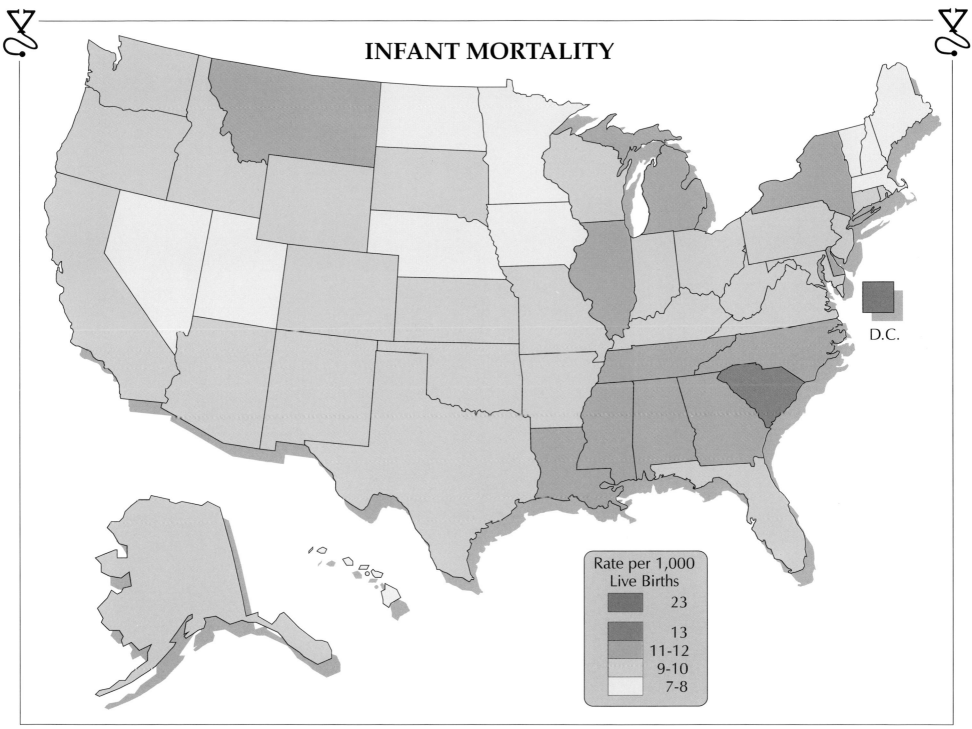

D.C.

Rate per 1,000
Live Births

23

13

11-12

9-10

7-8

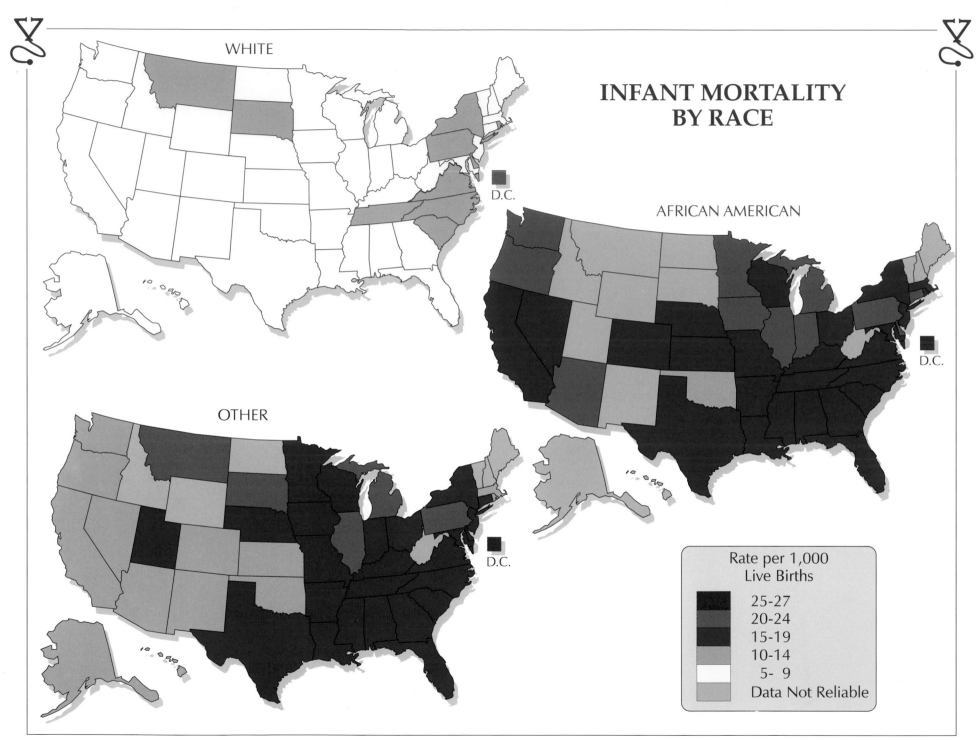

WHITE

INFANT MORTALITY BY RACE

D.C.

AFRICAN AMERICAN

D.C.

OTHER

D.C.

Rate per 1,000
Live Births

25-27
20-24
15-19
10-14
5- 9
Data Not Reliable

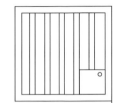

CRIME

"Crime remains one of people's most pressing concerns and government's greatest challenge."[1]

—New York Governor Mario M. Cuomo

Crime casts its shadow over all of our lives. Recent surveys show that crime has replaced health care issues as the number one concern of Americans. Daily we are bombarded by news reports of murder, theft, rape and family abuse. Women are all too often involved in these events.

Women's involvement in crime can be viewed from three different perspectives: as the victims of crime, as the perpetrators of crime or as the criminal justice professionals dealing with the aftermath of crime.

The only involvement most women will ever have with crime is as victims. Women are the perpetrators of crime much less frequently than men—less than 25% of crimes are committed by women. Women accounted for 22% of murder victims in 1991, but only 7% of murder offenders.[2] And as criminal justice professionals, women encounter the same barriers to advancement as women in other careers.

Why are women less likely than men to be criminal offenders? This question has puzzled criminologists for more than 100 years. Explanations vary in complexity and usually reflect the individual criminologist's attitudes toward women. A simple explanation may be that women have been socialized to give rather than take and to be nurturing rather than aggressive.[3] They are also taught to solve problems verbally rather than physically and may therefore be less likely to resort to violence.

Women have, historically, made up a very small percentage of those arrested or incarcerated for crimes. There is some evidence that this was due to the "chivalry" factor, a reluctance of law enforcement officials to arrest and incarcerate women. Greater equality for women has had an effect, however, and many women who would not have been arrested or punished for a crime a generation ago are now feeling the full weight of the law. Georgette Bennett, author of *Crimewarps, The Future of Crime in America*, believes that the current female "crime wave" is, in part, a result of the greater willingness of society to treat women as criminals.[4]

Patterns of male and female criminal activity can be examined using the *FBI Uniform Crime Statistics*, published annually. These statistics should be viewed with caution, however, as they focus on the number of arrests each year rather than on the number of persons arrested. A habitual criminal may be arrested several times during a year or a person might be arrested and not convicted. These statistics give no indication of unreported crimes. But even with their limitations, these statistics are probably the best indicators of criminal activity available.

The FBI collects and maintains statistical information on 29 different categories of crime. These include violent crimes against persons (murder, forcible rape, robbery and aggravated assault), property crimes (burglary, larceny, motor vehicle theft and arson) and crimes such as fraud, forgery, vandalism and sexual offenses. Also included are so-called "victimless" crimes, of which prostitution, gambling and runaway activity are examples.

Female arrests exceeded male arrests in only two categories, prostitution and runaways, with women making up 66% and 57% of arrests respectively. Women compose between one-third and one-half of the arrests in three other categories: forgery and counterfeiting (35%), embezzlement (39%) and fraud (43%). Overall, women accounted for 12% of arrests for violent crimes and 25% of arrests for property crimes.

While all crime statistics involving women are of interest, our maps focus on statistics for crimes and issues of interest to the greatest number of women.

These crimes include abuse, rape and homicide. Maps concerning women convicted of federal crimes, women in correctional facilities and women as correctional officers are also included.

It is interesting to examine the types of criminal activity engaged in by men and women. Eighty-one percent of the persons arrested for crimes in 1991 were men; 88% of violent crime arrests and 75% of property crime arrests were men. Men were most often arrested for driving under the influence, accounting for 13% of all male arrests. The crime for which women were most often arrested was larceny-theft, accounting for 78% of arrests of women for Index crimes (includes both violent and property crimes) and 19% of all female arrests. In the ten year period from 1982 to 1991, male arrests rose 15% and female arrests rose 36%.

Puritan New England relied on the church to maintain social order. As society grew more secular and the church was removed from public authority, a new institution was needed to impose moral discipline and isolate offenders from the population at large.[5] The institution that has evolved in the United States since that time is a system of municipal and county jails and state and federal correctional facilities. Initially, the goal of these facilities was to protect society from the offender and to punish criminals in the hope that punishment would serve as a deterrent. Later, efforts were directed toward rehabilitation and reform. Rising crime statistics are ample evidence that neither approach is particularly effective.

Prisoners of both sexes in the 19th century lived in unspeakable squalor. Brutal treatment by guards was commonplace. As bad as the situation was for men, it was worse for women. As prisons had been built with men in mind, there were no facilities for women. A woman prisoner was likely to be housed in a small, dirty, unventilated building within the prison walls. Chaplains, physicians and teachers rarely sought them out as their location outside the main body of inmates was inconvenient. In addition, a woman inmate was frequently sexually assaulted and otherwise terrorized by both guards and male inmates. Because society believed she should be locked up and forgotten, improvement in women prisoners' conditions was slow in coming. Furthermore, the number of women in prisons was low and a woman incarcerated was considered to be fallen, depraved and unredeemable.

Only after 1873 were separate facilities for women (and staffed by women) begun to be built. This also marked the beginning of new careers for women in the criminal justice system. Women who had previously been involved in the temperance and abolitionist movements focused their attention on the need for prison reform for women. They argued that women would be better suited than men to redeem fallen women and that it could best be done in an all-female institution. But even though the establishment of female institutions meant an immediate improvement in the treatment of female prisoners, barriers to equal treatment remained. These inequalities have changed little in the past century. Because the number of women in prison remains relatively small compared to the number of men, states usually operate only one prison for women. Most states find it too expensive to allow women the same options in education and job training. Women in female-only institutions generally have more limited access to medical and legal resources than do male prisoners.

Would female prisoners be better off in a coed institution than in a single-sex prison? The arguments for

and against are compelling. Women in a coed institution would have access to job training for traditionally male blue-collar jobs. These jobs that would be higher paying than the training women receive in most all-female facilities. Other arguments for coed facilities focus more on the humanizing effect women might have on the men in an all-male institution, but not on the needs of the women.

On the other side, many of the women currently residing in prisons have backgrounds of abuse; incarceration in a mostly male facility would only increase their risk of being further victimized. Interestingly enough, women in an all-female prison would be likely to receive some of the same benefits as women in single-sex educational settings receive. They could have a chance to gain self-confidence in themselves and their abilities without the overbearing presence of male offenders, who tend to regard women as sex objects.

Women's most likely role in crime is, unfortunately, as victim. The pattern of their victimization, however, is different from men's. Men are more frequently the victims of all crimes than are women. In 1990, the rate of male victimization was 105 of every 1,000 men. The rate for women was more than 20 points lower at 82.6 per 1,000 women. This means that men were victimized 1.3 times as often as women. The victimization of men was more pronounced for violent crime with the male rate 1.7 times higher than the female rate. Robbery and assault rates for men were dramatically higher than for women. Men were robbed and assaulted almost two times more frequently than women in that year. Only for rape and personal larceny (purse snatching) were the victimization rates of women higher.[6]

We focus here on women as victims on the three most common areas of female victimization: murder, abuse and rape. Twenty-two percent of murder victims in 1991 were women and nine out of ten of them were murdered by males. Among female murder victims in 1991, 28% were slain by their husbands or boyfriends as compared to only 4% of male victims who were murdered by wives or girlfriends. Only 13% of male murder victims were killed by women.[7]

The problem of spousal abuse is not new, but the women's movement did help to bring it to public attention. Every 18 seconds an incident of wife abuse takes place in this country; this abuse crosses all socioeconomic and racial boundaries. Men who batter their wives were likely to have been raised in homes where either they were abused or they watched their mothers being abused. Many women who endure this abuse themselves come from homes where intimidation and battering were the accepted pattern of relationships between men and women.[8] Domestic violence has been condoned throughout history because women were largely viewed as property and bound by marriage vows and society to obey their husbands. What took place in the privacy of a home was generally not regarded as a matter of concern for police. But domestic violence does affect society in general and police in particular. Domestic violence calls are regarded by police as among the most volatile situations they encounter, resulting in the highest number of assaults upon police officers.[9]

The crime of which women are the most fearful is rape. Much evidence supports this fear. Between 1960 and 1990 the rate of forcible rape per 100,000 people rose from 9.6 to 41.2. Every six minutes a woman is forcibly raped in the United States, and one in three American women is sexually assaulted during her lifetime. A 1987 *Ms.* magazine survey found that 84% of those raped knew their attacker and that 57% of rapes happened on dates. Nine out of ten rapes occur between members of the same racial group.[10]

Rape, as a crime, is classified as either forcible or statutory. The FBI defines forcible rape as "the carnal knowledge of a female forcibly and against her will." Statistics on forcible rape also include attempts to commit rape by force or threat of force. An increasing number of states recognize forced oral or anal sex, and penetration by an object as rape, as well as the rape of men. Statutory rape refers to intercourse with a female who is below the age of consent or with a person unable to comprehend the consequences of sexual intercourse, such as a mentally retarded adult.

Statistics on rape are far from accurate. Large numbers of rapes go unreported. The FBI estimates that only one in three rapes is reported, but other estimates go as high as one in 12. Rapes go unreported for a variety of reasons. Many times a women believes that enough evidence is not available to convict and that it will come down to "her word against his." Often women don't want to go through the ordeal of a trial in which their own reputations will undoubtedly be called into question. The odds of conviction are not good, only 20% to 30% in most states.[11] Many women don't want friends or relatives to know they have been raped because of the stigma that is sometimes attached to being a victim of sexual assault. Additionally, many women don't realize that the forced sex they have endured is rape. One nationwide survey, whose questions did not use the word "rape," revealed that one in four women admitted that an incident meeting the legal definition of rape had happened to them.[12]

Rape within a marriage has long been an accepted form of aggression. A number of states have statutes exempting husbands from being charged with spousal rape. But by 1985, ten states had completely abolished the marital rape exemption, thus according married women the same legal recourse after rape by their husbands as available to other victims of rape.

Prior to the feminist movement in the 1970s, rape victims were generally blamed for their victimization. The prevailing belief was that somehow the rape victim must have done something, such as wear provocative clothing or "led a man on," to provoke the attack. Fortunately, the assessment of the nature of rape has changed, and rape is now revealed to be a crime of violence in which forced sexual intercourse is used to inflict harm and humiliation upon an individual. The inclusion of sexual intercourse in the rape act is a means by which a rapist can accomplish the infliction of physical and psychological harm as a way of venting anger and feeling empowered. And while the overwhelming majority of rape victims are female, the rate of rape among men in 1990 was 20 per 100,000. Rape is now seen as an expression of hate, and victims are not to blame.

This understanding of the nature of rape has led to some improvements in the way rape victims are treated by the criminal justice system. Most states currently have rape shield laws that limit the degree to which the victim's sexual history can be used as a subject of inquiry in court. Many police departments, particularly in larger cities, have personnel trained to be sensitive to the victim. Rape crisis centers exist (though many have been closed because of lack of funding) to help counsel victims. A relatively new evidence collection kit, available in some hospitals and rape crisis centers, can drastically improve the chance for a conviction.

Accompanying the discussion of rape victims, it is useful to examine attitudes that perpetuate or condone rape. Many theorists believe that male sexual socialization is crucial to understanding why rape occurs. One study in 1981 found 35% of several groups of male college students admitted there was some likelihood they would rape a women if they were certain they could get away with it.[13] Another study of 432 high school males revealed that half of them believed it was acceptable to hold a girl down and force her to have sex when she gets the male excited or first consents to sex, but then changes her mind.[14] In a more recent survey of Rhode Island ninth graders, one-fourth of the boys and, astoundingly, one-sixth of the girls said that if a man spent money on a woman, he was entitled to force her to have sex. Indeed, men who initiate the date, drive and pay all expenses are more likely to be sexually aggressive than men who don't.[15] These attitudes among our nation's young men may help to explain why the United States has the highest rate of rape in the world, a rate at least ten times higher than in most of Europe.

A growing sensitivity to the needs of female crime victims is largely a result of the introduction of female personnel into the criminal justice system. The groundwork for women in all areas of criminal justice was laid by the women who, after the establishment of all-female prisons in the 1870s, became correctional officers and superintendents. The opening of these facilities created nontraditional career opportunities for women in what had been an exclusively male system. But although these women did the same jobs as men, they received lower salaries than men and were virtually excluded from positions of high authority in the correctional system. This began to change with the women's movement of the late 1960s. The 1964 Civil

Rights Act outlawed discrimination based on race and sex and gave women the legal basis they needed to demand more equal treatment, but they were strongly opposed by both male staff and male inmates. It was not until after 1972, when the Equal Employment Opportunity Commission was given jurisdiction over government employment, that real gains were made in terms of increased employment opportunities for women in correctional facilities. By 1990, 18% of all correctional officers and 11% of supervisors were women, many of them serving in all male institutions. African-American women have made the greatest strides and by 1983 constituted almost a third of all female correctional officers.[16]

WOMEN AS VICTIMS

A number of factors contribute to the number of women living in shelters for abused women, as displayed on the map, "Abused Women." While we could conclude that states with low proportions of women in shelters for abused women have a lower incidence of abuse of women, this is probably not the case. A community's concern for abused women and its willingness to make a financial commitment to the operation of shelters for victims of abuse obviously greatly affects the number of women who are sheltered. So while communities with higher rates of women being sheltered may have a greater incidence of wife abuse, they may also be communities that give the protection of women a high priority. Religious and cultural factors also influence the number of women residing in shelters. Areas with traditionally high religious affilia-

tions, for instance the Bible Belt, might have a lower incidence of spousal abuse, or more likely a lower incidence of reported spousal abuse. Women in these regions may be less likely to reveal that they are in an abusive relationship because religious teachings place men at the physical and spiritual head of the family and make the wife subordinate to him. In addition, some cultures may be more at risk for spousal abuse because of the stresses its members face. The majority of the states with a large proportion of Native Americans, Alaska, Montana, Wyoming and New Mexico, have higher rates of women in shelters. This could indicate that the Native American culture is more tolerant of abuse, but more likely is the fact that the grinding poverty and high unemployment rates among Native Americans create a more stressful environment in which abuse is more likely to occur.

As stated earlier, rape is a crime that often goes unreported and, as a result, rape statistics depicted on the next maps are lower than the actual number of occurrences. However, recently more women have been coming forward to report rapes. Therefore, it is difficult to attribute the rise of rape rates entirely to an increase in the actual number of offenses. A portion of the increase is attributable to more women reporting the crime to police. Despite this, the rape rate in the United States is disturbingly high. The chart "Rape Rate Through Time" shows the steady increase of rapes since 1960. During the 1970s the incidence of rape increased dramatically and a similar trend appears to be starting in the 1990s.

The distribution of rape rates is depicted on the maps "Rape Rate" and "Rape Rate in Major Cities." The map "Rape Rate," showing the five states (Alaska, Delaware, Michigan, Nevada and Washington) that represent the

ABUSED WOMEN

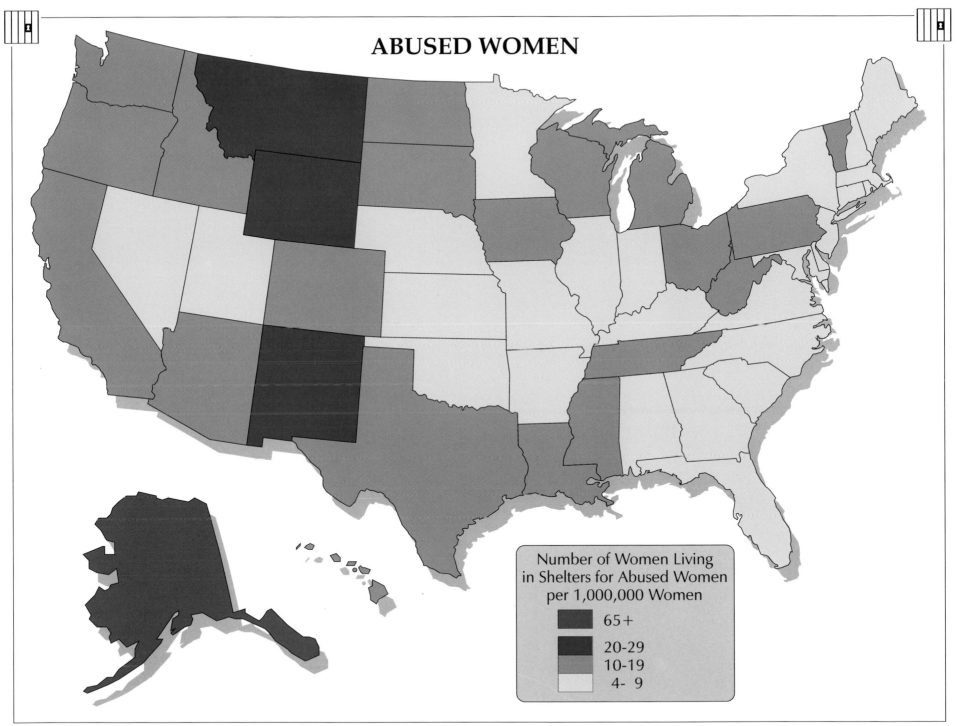

Number of Women Living
in Shelters for Abused Women
per 1,000,000 Women

- 65+
- 20-29
- 10-19
- 4- 9

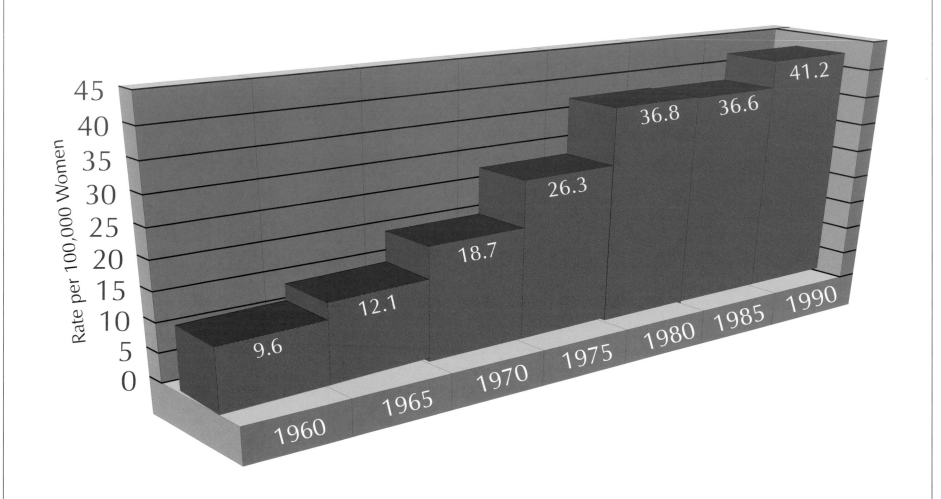

high end of rape rates in the United States, does not exhibit a pattern of distribution. Nor is a pattern discernible for the low end—represented by three states (Iowa, Maine and North Dakota). The remainder of the states exhibit a southwest to northeast pattern.

On "Rape Rate in Major Cities," the number of rapes reported per 100,000 women in selected metropolitan areas is depicted using circles of various sizes, the larger the circle, the higher the rate of reported rapes. Although the incidence of reported rapes is highest in metropolitan areas, they have shown the smallest change over the past ten years.[17] These rates are surprising, with cities generally perceived to have high crime rates, such as New York and the District of Columbia, actually having very low rates of reported rapes. In the District of Columbia, the city with the lowest rate of reported rapes, 66 of 100,000 women reported being raped. New York's rate was only slightly higher at 74 per 100,000. A Midwestern city, Minneapolis, had the highest incidence of reported rapes with 392 per 100,000 women. Cleveland (at 340) and Atlanta (at 309) also had very high rates of reported rapes. The rates in metropolitan areas of California were all low, less than 150 per 100,000.

According to FBI statistics, more than half of the forcible rapes reported to police in 1991 were cleared by arrest or exceptional means. Rape charges are sometimes cleared by plea bargains that reduce the charge of rape to lesser offenses, such as breaking and entering or aggravated assault. The rape clearance rate relates only to arrests, not final convictions. The map, "Rape Clearance Rate," indicates the percentage of reported rapes cleared by arrest in each state. The clearance rates in rural counties were slightly higher that in cities and suburban areas. Wisconsin had the highest clearance

rate at 63% with the Mid-Atlantic states also having high rates. The state with the lowest clearance rate was Illinois at 11%.

Between 1982 and 1991 the percentage of minors (persons under the age of 18) arrested for forcible rape rose 24% as compared to an 18% rise in adult arrests. The map, "Minors Arrested for Rape," depicts the percentage of persons arrested for rape who were under the age of 18. Illinois had, by far, the highest percentage with minors constituting 38% of those persons arrested for rape. The next closest state was Utah at 27%. In Idaho, the state with the lowest value, only 4% of those arrested for rape were minors. In three other states, Vermont, Massachusetts and Arkansas, minors composed less than 10% of arrests for rape. Variations in rape laws make state to state comparisons difficult, especially when considering statutory rape, so caution must be used when drawing conclusions from this data.

Marital rape laws, as illustrated by state on our map of the same name, are usually complex and vary greatly among states. Some states have statutes that seem to contradict each other and, as these statutes are both confusing and lengthy, we urge those interested to examine the individual state statutes. In three states, South Dakota, Illinois and Alabama, marital rape exemption laws were in effect that made it unlikely that a wife could charge her husband with rape. Twenty-five states have limited marital rape exemption laws in effect where the marital exemption is abolished in cases where a couple is legally separated, are living apart, and/or legal separation, divorce or annulment proceedings have been initiated. In ten states, Oregon, Nebraska, Kansas, Wisconsin, Florida, New York, Vermont, Massachusetts, Rhode Island and Maryland,

RAPE RATE

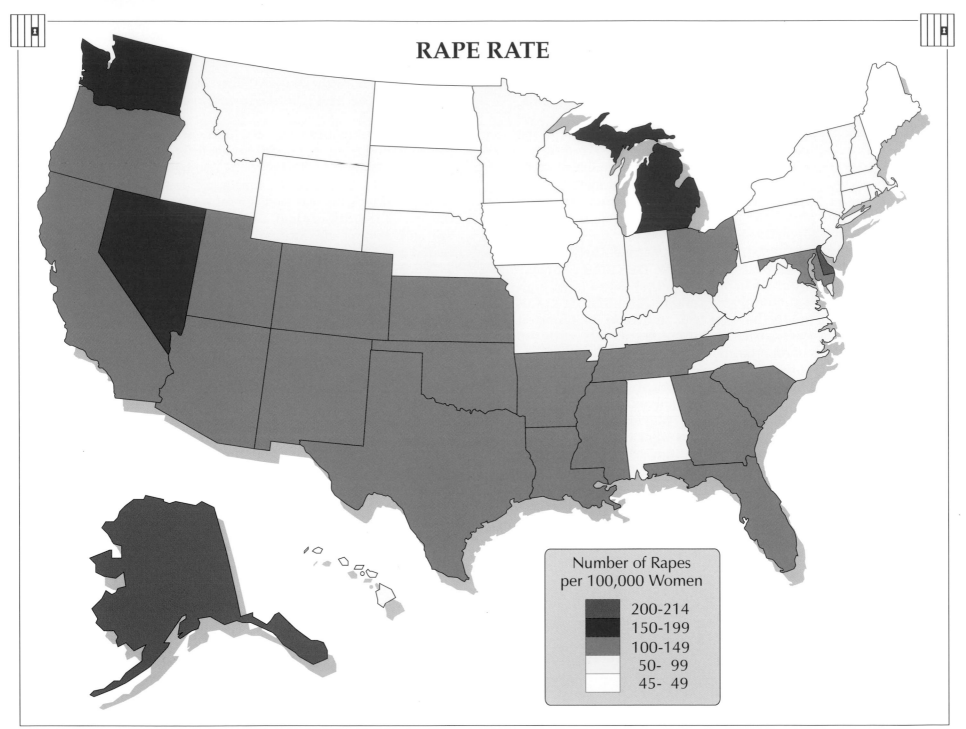

Number of Rapes
per 100,000 Women

- 200-214
- 150-199
- 100-149
- 50- 99
- 45- 49

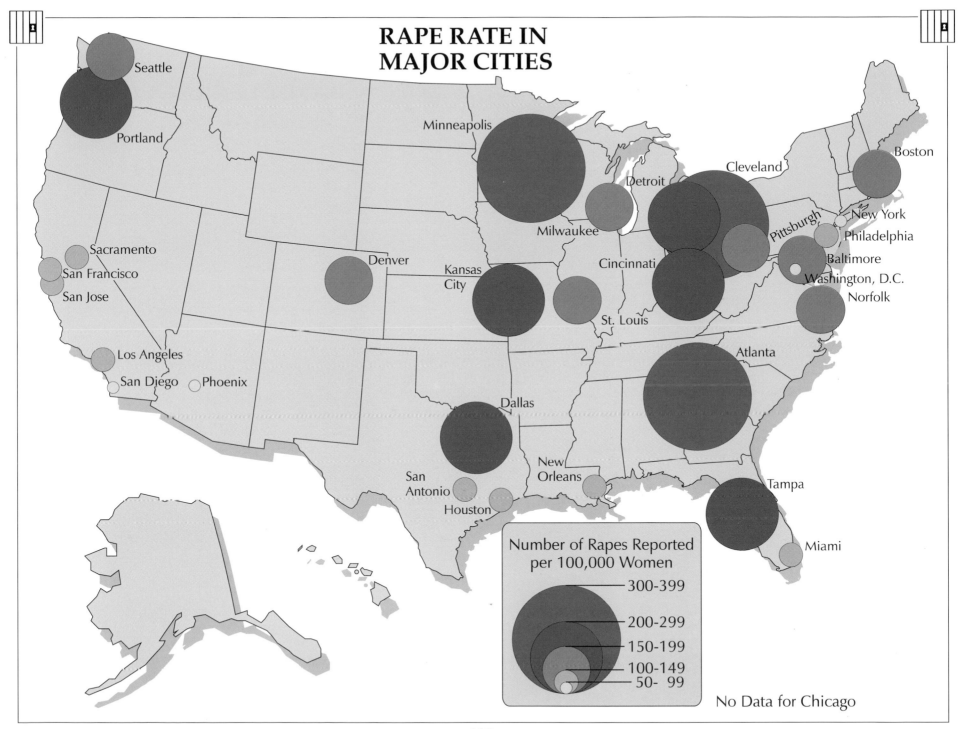

RAPE RATE IN
MAJOR CITIES

Seattle

Portland

Minneapolis

Detroit

Cleveland

Boston

Milwaukee

Pittsburgh

New York

Sacramento

Cincinnati

Philadelphia

San Francisco

Denver

Kansas City

Baltimore

San Jose

Washington, D.C.

St. Louis

Norfolk

Los Angeles

San Diego

Phoenix

Atlanta

Dallas

San Antonio

New Orleans

Tampa

Houston

Miami

Number of Rapes Reported
per 100,000 Women

300-399

200-299

150-199

100-149

50- 99

No Data for Chicago

185

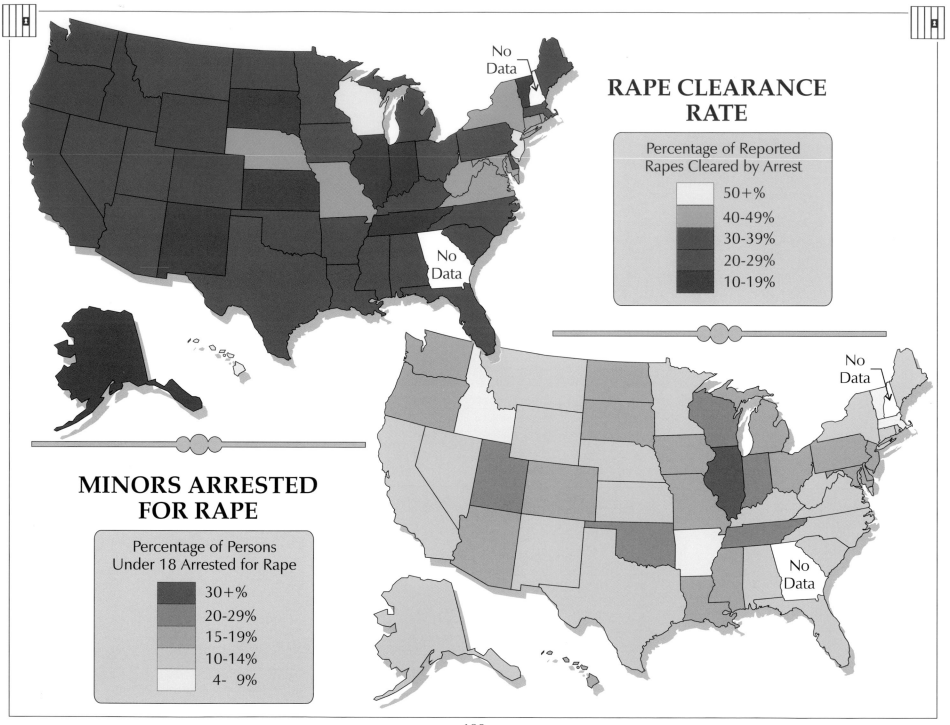

RAPE CLEARANCE RATE

Percentage of Reported Rapes Cleared by Arrest

- 50+%
- 40-49%
- 30-39%
- 20-29%
- 10-19%

No Data

No Data

MINORS ARRESTED FOR RAPE

Percentage of Persons Under 18 Arrested for Rape

- 30+%
- 20-29%
- 15-19%
- 10-14%
- 4- 9%

No Data

No Data

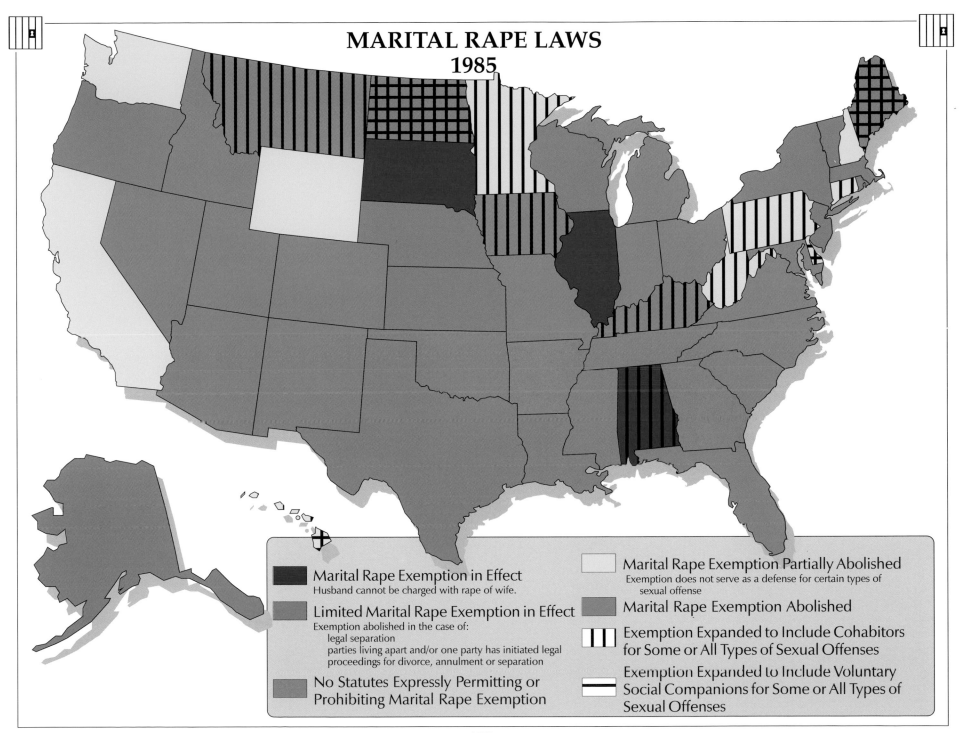

MARITAL RAPE LAWS
1985

Marital Rape Exemption in Effect
Husband cannot be charged with rape of wife.

Limited Marital Rape Exemption in Effect
Exemption abolished in the case of:
legal separation
parties living apart and/or one party has initiated legal
proceedings for divorce, annulment or separation

**No Statutes Expressly Permitting or
Prohibiting Marital Rape Exemption**

Marital Rape Exemption Partially Abolished
Exemption does not serve as a defense for certain types of
sexual offense

Marital Rape Exemption Abolished

**Exemption Expanded to Include Cohabitors
for Some or All Types of Sexual Offenses**

**Exemption Expanded to Include Voluntary
Social Companions for Some or All Types of
Sexual Offenses**

the marital rape exemption has been abolished and a wife can bring rape charges against her husband, even if they are living under the same roof.

In 1991, four out of every 100,000 women in the United States were homicide victims. Of the female murder victims that year, 66% were White, 25% were African American and 8% were of other races. As is illustrated on the map, "Homicide," the region with the highest homicide rate for women is the south. Regions with the lowest rates are found in the Midwest (excluding Michigan), the Northeast and New England. The states with the highest homicide rate for women were Georgia and Maryland (which includes rates for the District of Columbia) where seven per 100,000 women were murdered in 1991. The lowest rates were found in Iowa and Vermont, where only one woman per 100,000 was a homicide victim that year. In nine states more than half of female murder victims were African American; White women made up half of the victims in 38 states. In Alaska and Hawaii other races, probably Native American and Asian Americans, respectively, made up half of the murder victims.

UP THE RIVER

Women are perpetrators of crime as well as its victims. The remaining maps in this chapter concern the conviction and incarceration of women. The first map, "Women Convicted of Federal Crimes—1985," depicts the rate per 100,000 women of women who are convicted of a federal crime. The second map shows the percentage of all those convicted of federal crimes who are women. Both the conviction rate and the percent-

age of women convicted are very low. In only two states, Hawaii (with a rate of 12) and Maryland (including the District of Columbia with a rate of 10) did the number of women convicted exceed ten per 100,000 women. Thirty-three states had rates below seven per 100,000 women. New Hampshire, Vermont and Wisconsin had the extremely low rate of one per 100,000. Indeed, the rate for the nation as a whole was only four per 100,000.

The second map reveals distinct regional boundaries for the percentages of women convicted of federal crimes. Men are convicted of the bulk of federal crimes, more than 70% in all states. New England, most of the Northern High Plains and most of the Southwest had low proportions of convicted female federal offenders. High values were found in the Pacific Northwest (except Alaska) and much of the North Central region. Hawaii ranked highest again with 29% of the state's convicted federal offenders being female. In Vermont, a low 5% of federal crime convictions were of women.

The graph "Percentage of Homicides Committed by Women" shows that the percentage of murders committed by women has exhibited a gradual drop since the mid-1970s.

The population of prisons in the United States is almost exclusively male. The maps entitled "Prison Population" show the rate per 100,000 women of women in prisons and the percentage of all prison inmates who are women. As expected, these maps and the maps depicting women convicted of federal crimes are similar. New England and the Midwest have low rates for women in prison. The West has the nation's highest rate; at 192 per 100,000 women, Nevada had the highest rate of women in prison. The lowest rate was found

HOMICIDE

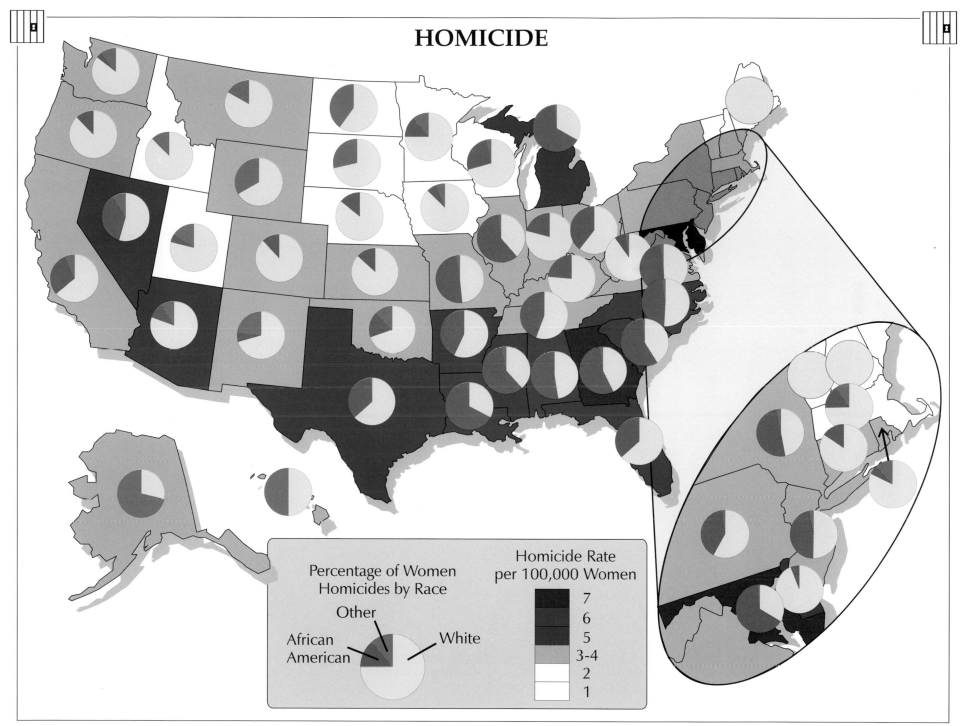

Percentage of Women
Homicides by Race

Other

African
American

White

Homicide Rate
per 100,000 Women

7
6
5
3-4
2
1

WOMEN CONVICTED OF FEDERAL CRIMES
1985

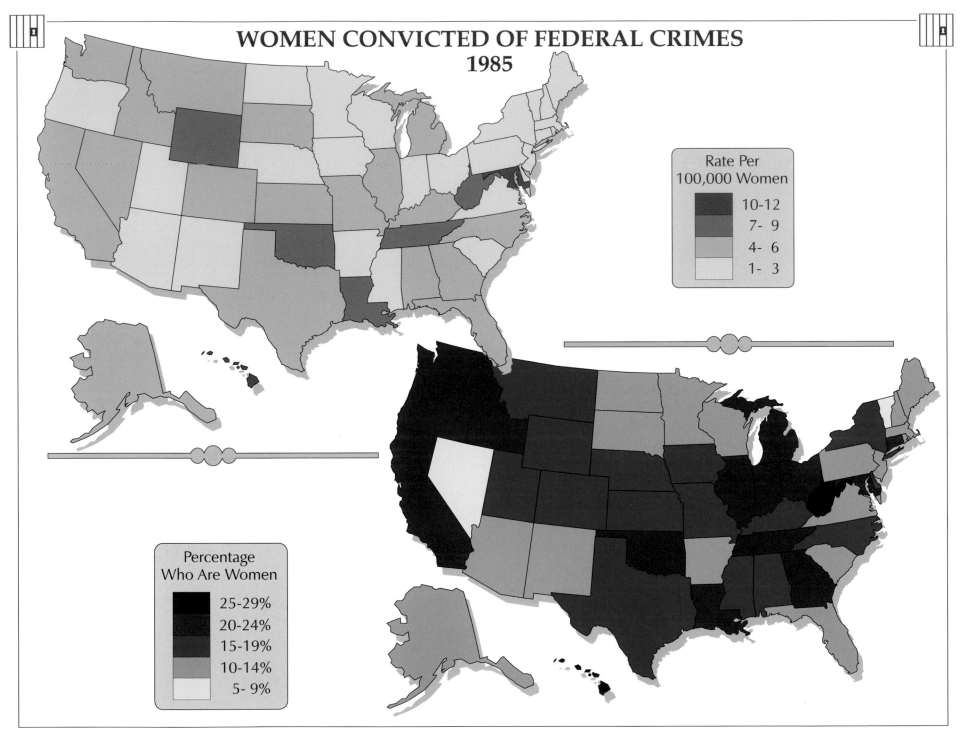

Rate Per
100,000 Women

10-12
7- 9
4- 6
1- 3

Percentage
Who Are Women

25-29%
20-24%
15-19%
10-14%
5- 9%

PERCENTAGE OF
HOMICIDES COMMITTED BY WOMEN

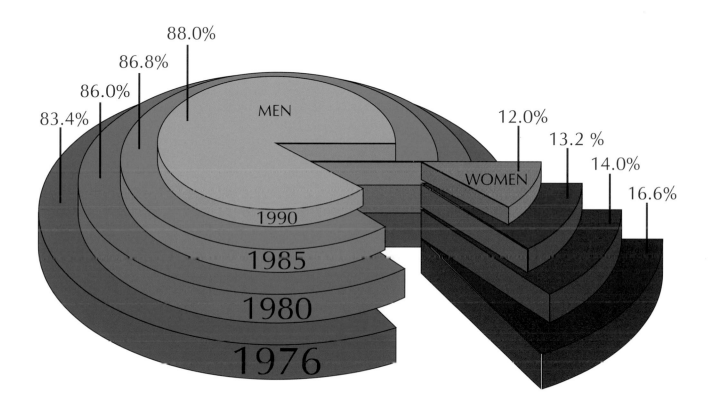

in West Virginia where only 17 out of 100,000 women are in state or federal prisons. The map showing percentages of the prison population who are female reveals that Vermont has the prison population with the lowest proportion of women, at 2%. Most of New England and the Deep South (with the exception of Florida) have female prison populations of less than 10%. Florida has the highest percentage of female inmates at 28%. In the western half of the country more than 10% of the populations of state and federal correctional facilities are female.

A quick glance at the map "Racial Distribution of the Prison Population" reveals that the female prison population in eastern states is predominantly African American, while in the western states, it is predominantly White. This is a reflection of the general population of the United States. The concentration of African Americans is greater in the east. Native Americans make up a very small proportion of the prison population except in the states of Alaska, Montana, North Dakota and South Dakota. In Hawaii, Asian American women make up the largest segment of female inmates.

Female juvenile offenders are a very small but growing proportion of the population in secure holdings. Juveniles are generally held in facilities exclusively for juveniles, with the hope that they can be protected from more hardened adult criminals and rehabilitated. However, many states are now trying juvenile offenders, particularly those accused of murder, as adults. Those convicted as adults are increasingly going to prisons instead of juvenile facilities. The first map on this topic, "Juvenile Offenders Under Supervision," illustrates the number of female juvenile offenders in secure holdings per 100,000 women aged 10–18. Most

states held fewer than 75 per 100,000 women of this age. Five states had rates higher than 75, with North Carolina topping the list with 444 per 100,000 juvenile women being held. North Carolina's rate was two and a half times higher than the next highest state, Wyoming. Just as in the adult prison population, juvenile women represent a smaller percentage of the total number of juveniles residing in institutions than juvenile men. But while for adult prisoners only two states (Florida and Kentucky) had inmate populations that were more than 20% female, juvenile offenders in four states (Illinois, Montana, North Carolina and Wyoming) were more than 20% female. The state with the highest percentage of female juvenile offenders was Wyoming where almost half (48%) of juvenile offenders were women. Minnesota had the lowest percentage of female juvenile offenders at 2%.

As illustrated on the map, "Women's Correctional Institutions," ten states had no female-only prisons as of 1992. These states house their female inmates in coed or out-of-state facilities. Twelve states have more than one institution exclusively for women inmates. The map uses graduated circles to display inmate populations at each facility. Green circles represent prisons whose populations are within the prison's capacity; red circles indicate prisons whose capacity has been exceeded. Twenty of the 57 state facilities (35%) are overcrowded. The nation's largest female correctional facilities are located in California and Texas, each with more than 1,000 inmates. Apart from these two states, the largest institutions are located in the eastern United States.

Security arrangements for female offenders are classified as maximum, medium and minimum security. Ideally, the offender is assigned to the level most

PRISON POPULATION

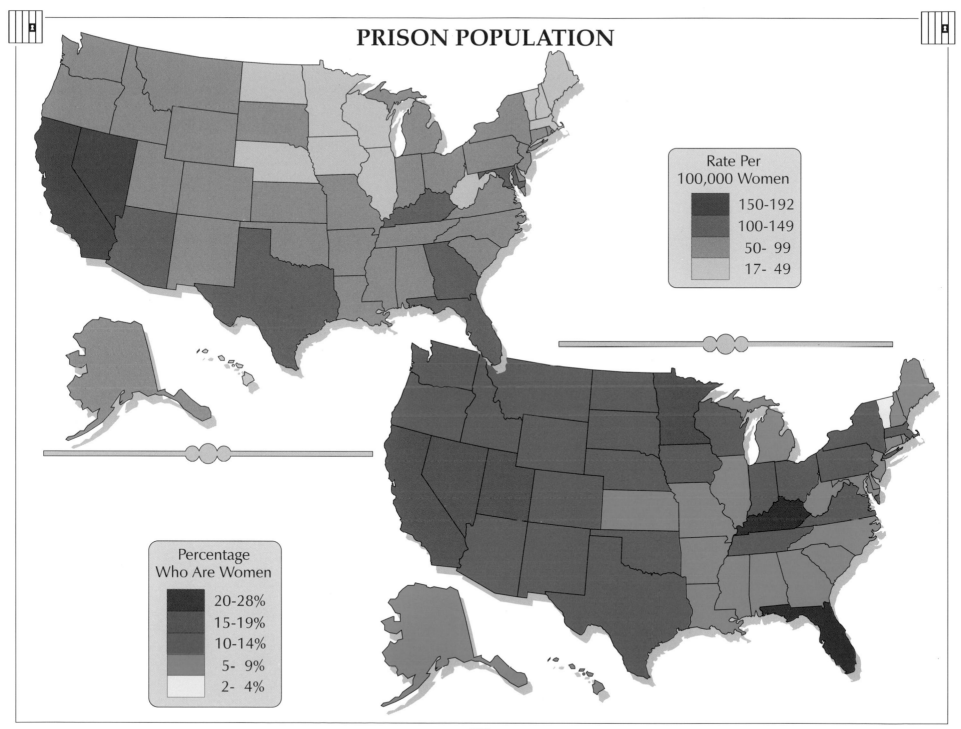

Rate Per
100,000 Women
- 150-192
- 100-149
- 50- 99
- 17- 49

Percentage
Who Are Women
- 20-28%
- 15-19%
- 10-14%
- 5- 9%
- 2- 4%

RACIAL DISTRIBUTION OF THE PRISON POPULATION

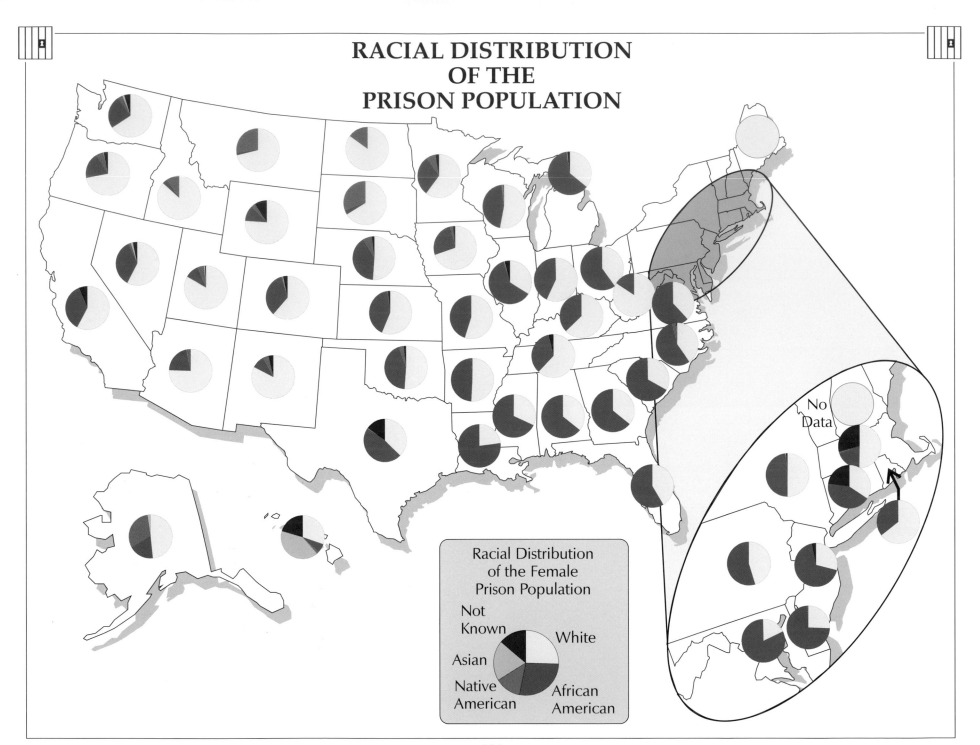

Racial Distribution of the Female Prison Population

Not Known

White

Asian

Native American

African American

No Data

JUVENILE OFFENDERS UNDER SUPERVISION

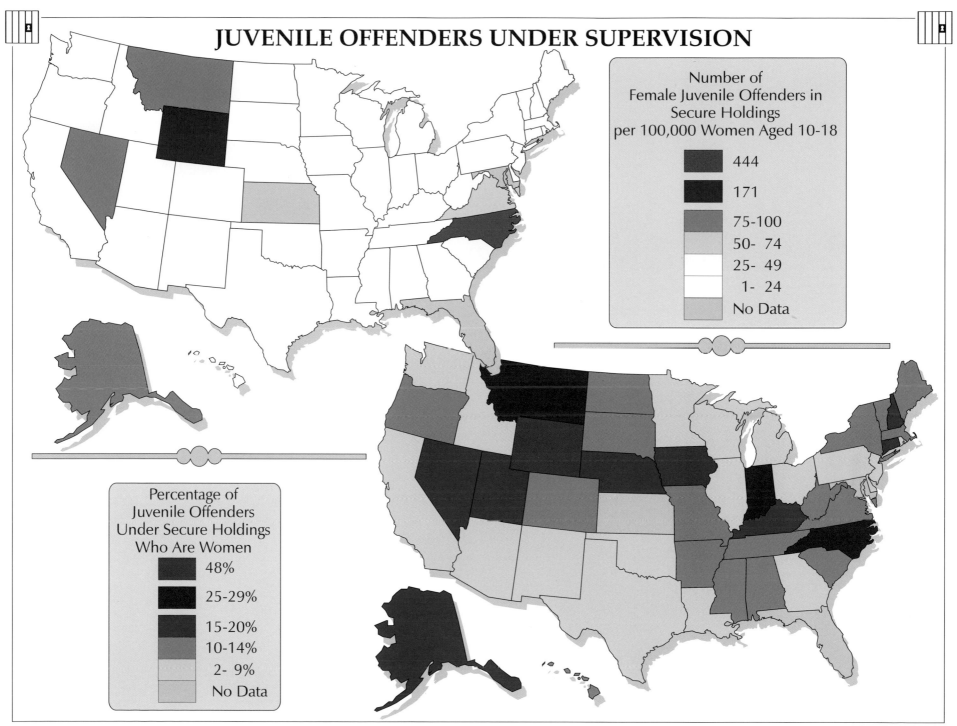

Number of
Female Juvenile Offenders in
Secure Holdings
per 100,000 Women Aged 10-18

- 444
- 171
- 75-100
- 50- 74
- 25- 49
- 1- 24
- No Data

Percentage of
Juvenile Offenders
Under Secure Holdings
Who Are Women

- 48%
- 25-29%
- 15-20%
- 10-14%
- 2- 9%
- No Data

WOMEN'S CORRECTIONAL INSTITUTIONS*

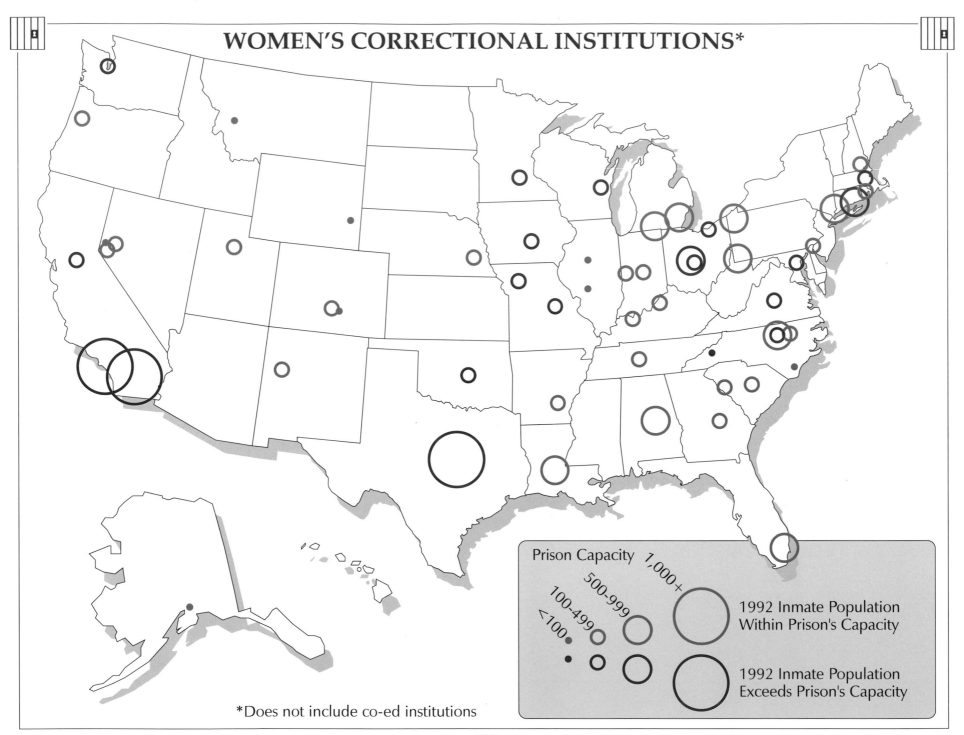

Prison Capacity

1,000+

500-999

100-499

<100

1992 Inmate Population Within Prison's Capacity

1992 Inmate Population Exceeds Prison's Capacity

*Does not include co-ed institutions

appropriate to her offense; criminals considered the most serious threat to others are housed in maximum security facilities. Those deemed less dangerous might be confined at medium- or minimum-security levels.

For some states, however, the data reflected on the map "Security Arrangements" are more an indication of available space in prisons than of appropriate assignments of offenders. The map uses pie charts to indicate the proportion of a state's female prison population in each of the three security levels. Women in maximum security facilities generally made up the smallest percentage of inmates in states, with the exception of Arkansas where 53% of the women incarcerated were under maximum security. Two states had all their female prison population under a single type of security. All female inmates in Louisiana were in medium-security facilities and all in New Jersey were under minimum security. Maximum-security arrangements were more plentiful in the nation's midsection, while minimum security facilities were more common in the east.

Debates about the appropriateness of capital punishment have continued for centuries. At the end of 1992, the death penalty was in force in all but 14 states in the United States. The maps, "Women on Death Row," depicts four types of data: first, the number of White and African-American women on death row at the end of 1992; second, states that have had at least one woman on death row between 1972 and 1992; third, the percentage of persons serving life sentences that are women; and fourth, which states had death penalties in force. At the end of 1992 there were 20 White women and 12 African-American women living on

death row in the nation's prisons. These women were concentrated in southern prisons. North Carolina had the greatest number of women on death row, with five women awaiting execution.

About 4% of prisoners serving life sentences in this country are women. Arkansas had the highest proportion of women serving life sentences, at 8%, as compared to men. Six states, Hawaii, Maine, Montana, North Dakota, Vermont and Wyoming had no women imprisoned for life. Of those six states only Montana has a death penalty in force.

The final two maps in this chapter deal with female correctional officers. The first map depicts the percentage of all correctional officers who are women, and the second shows the percentage of supervisors who are women. The line of states starting with Michigan and going south to the Gulf, along with a dozen other states scattered throughout the country, have correctional officer staffs that are more that 20% female. In one state, Mississippi, more that 44% of correctional officers are female. Six states, North Dakota, Iowa, New York, Rhode Island, Connecticut and North Carolina, have staffs that are less than 10% female. Women in supervisory positions are even scarcer than female correctional officers. South Dakota has the highest proportion of female supervisors at 43%, nearly twice as high as the next state. Two states, West Virginia and Massachusetts, had no female correctional supervisors. It is interesting to note that states with a high percentage of female correctional officers often do not have a high percentage of female supervisors. Only Indiana and Oregon have high percentages of both female correctional offices and supervisors.

SECURITY ARRANGEMENTS
1993

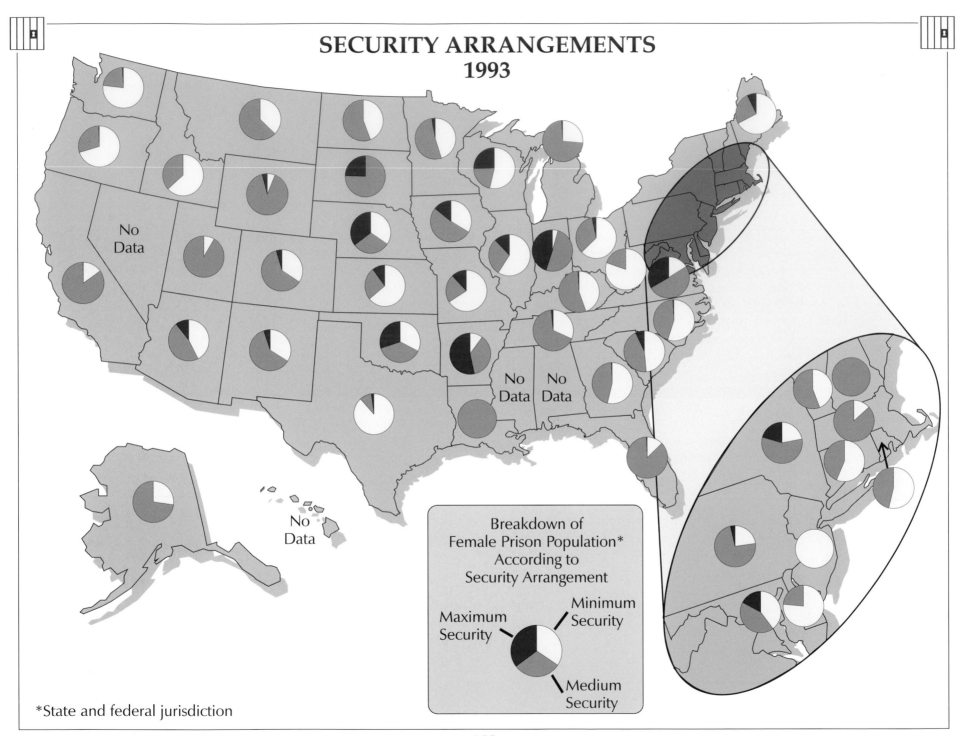

No Data

No Data

No Data

No Data

No Data

Breakdown of
Female Prison Population*
According to
Security Arrangement

Maximum
Security

Minimum
Security

Medium
Security

*State and federal jurisdiction

WOMEN ON DEATH ROW

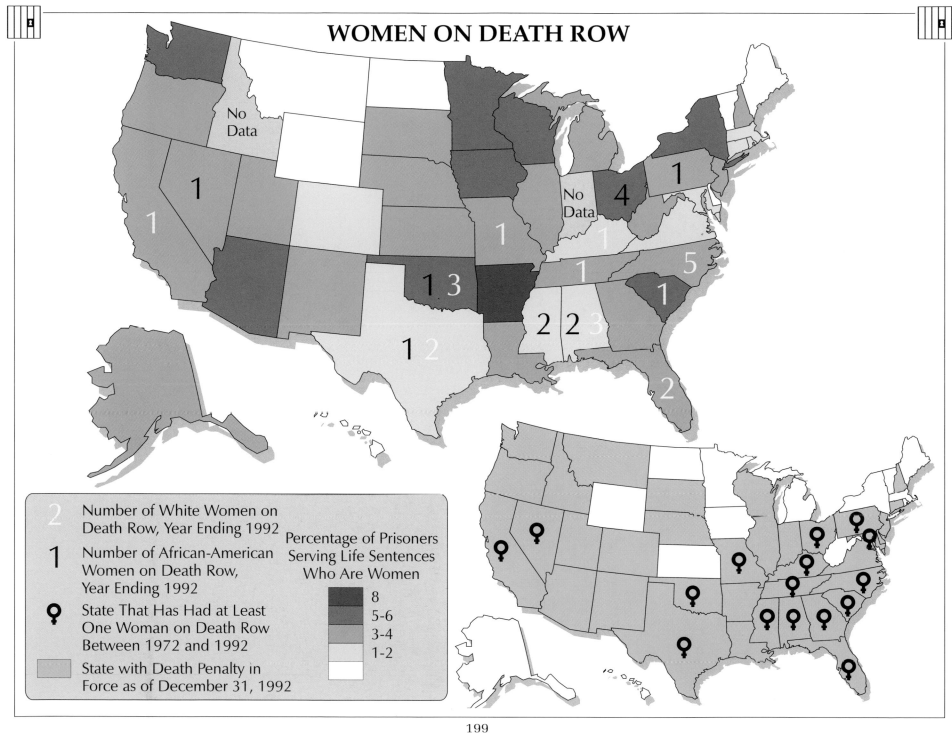

Legend:

2 — Number of White Women on Death Row, Year Ending 1992

1 — Number of African-American Women on Death Row, Year Ending 1992

♀ — State That Has Had at Least One Woman on Death Row Between 1972 and 1992

▢ — State with Death Penalty in Force as of December 31, 1992

Percentage of Prisoners Serving Life Sentences Who Are Women

- 8
- 5-6
- 3-4
- 1-2

CORRECTIONAL OFFICERS IN ADULT SYSTEMS

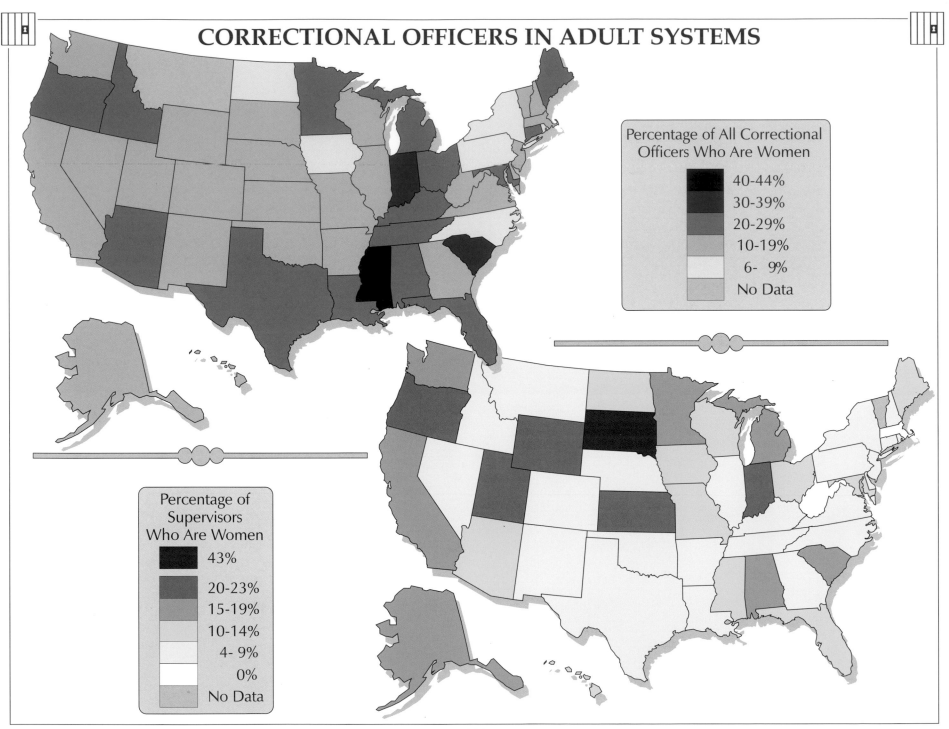

Percentage of All Correctional Officers Who Are Women
- 40-44%
- 30-39%
- 20-29%
- 10-19%
- 6- 9%
- No Data

Percentage of Supervisors Who Are Women
- 43%
- 20-23%
- 15-19%
- 10-14%
- 4- 9%
- 0%
- No Data

POLITICS

"How will our nation be different when women are fully equal citizens and officeholders?"[1]

—from Preface to *Running As a Woman*

Until 1920 the United States of America was not a democracy. While this statement might, at first glance, appear inflammatory, the truth is that no society can be considered a true democracy until all its citizens are allowed a voice in its government. Prior to 1920 and the ratification of the 19th Amendment to the Constitution, one-half of the adult population of this country was not allowed to vote. Women, in most states, had no legal right to cast a ballot.

For generations, women had been left out of the political process. Politics, with its reputation for shady and unscrupulous dealings, was considered unsuitable for women, and men were reluctant to allow women the chance to obtain the power that voting could provide. There was a group of women, however, that was not content with their limited sphere of influence. Their interests went farther than the realm of home and family. These women, led by such individuals as Elizabeth Cady Stanton, Susan B. Anthony and Lucy Stone,

made the achievement of political equality their primary goal. Many of these women had been active in the abolitionist movement and were disillusioned when, at the end of the Civil War, African-American men were given the vote but women remained excluded. In 1869 two organizations, the National Woman Suffrage Association and the American Woman Suffrage Association, were founded with the declared objective of obtaining the vote for women. In 1913 they were joined by the National Women's Party and mounted an immense campaign to secure the vote for women.

Prior to winning the right to vote, suffragists believed, or at least hoped, that once women became voters, government would be irrevocably changed. But the passage of a law doesn't immediately change behavior, and the generations women spent being taught that politics and running the country were best left to men made women slow to seize this new opportunity for change. In the 1920 elections only about one-third of the eligible women, as compared to two-thirds of the eligible men, voted.

After winning the right to vote in 1920, the movement for women's equality did not really gain national attention again until the early 1960s. The Civil Rights movement, along with the publication of Betty Friedan's *The Feminine Mystique*, brought public awareness of women's issues to a new level. A number of organizations were founded at that time to promote equality for women, among them the National Organization for Women, the National Women's Political Caucus and the Women's Equity Action League.

Fortunately, succeeding generations of women are learning to recognize their political power and exercise their right to vote. Women of voting age outnumber men of voting age by nine million. Sixty-eight percent of eligible women are registered to vote, compared to 65% of men, and the women vote more than men do. In 1988, 58% of women voted while only 56% of men did.[2]

But women are still excluded from the upper reaches of government, particularly the Senate, the House of Representatives and the White House. Prior to the elections of November 1992, women represented a mere 2% of the United States Senate and about 6% of the House of Representatives.

But in 1991 one event changed the future of women in politics. President George Bush nominated Clarence Thomas to the United States Supreme Court. Soon afterward Anita Hill, an Oklahoma University law professor, gave closed-door testimony to the Senate Judiciary Committee accusing Thomas of sexual harassment.

The Judiciary Committee chose not to pursue Professor Hill's charges. Infuriated, the women on Capitol Hill marched to the Senate to demand an investigation. For several days in October the nation was riveted to the television as the confirmation hearings and the testimony of Professor Hill progressed. Women (and many men) all across America were enraged at the ferocity directed toward Professor Hill by the all-male, all-White members of the Senate Judiciary Committee. These hearings created a never-before-seen awareness about the absence of women in the Senate. The direct result of the indignation surrounding this event was that more women than ever decided to run for public office. Carol Moseley-Braun, who, in 1992, became the first African-American women to be elected to the United States Senate, said of the Thomas–Hill hearings: "I would not have run for the Senate had the Senate not gone on television."[3]

Four women were elected to the U.S. Senate in 1992, bringing the total number of female senators to six. The number of women in the House of Representatives increased by nearly 70% from 29 to 48. Several circumstances contributed to the wave of women elected to Congress and to other state and local offices. After the 1990 Census, reapportionment created and/or changed the representation of many districts. A predominant feeling existed among voters to "throw out" incumbents. The outcome of these events was that the number of open seats, positions without an incumbent officeholder, was four times higher in 1992 than in the previous election year, 1990. Twenty percent of the seats in Congress were open in 1992.[4]

Prior to the election of 1968, women voted less often than men and no attempt had been made to study why or for whom they voted. By the 1980s some evidence showed that women voted differently from men and a new term, "gender gap," was coined to describe this behavior. One of the first to understand and to target women voters was Shirley Chisholm of New York, the first African-American woman to serve in Congress. During her first campaign in 1968, her opponent began to campaign in Brooklyn calling Chisholm "a bossy female, a would-be matriarch." When one of her staff realized that there were two and a half times as many women registered in the district as men, Chisholm appealed to these women and won.

The battle continues to be uphill for women in politics. The two main factors inhibiting the progress of women in the political arena are the low rate of turnover in office and the high reelection rate of incumbents. More than 90% of the candidates who run for reelection in the House of Representatives are successful. Women experience difficulty getting a foothold in the predominantly male political machine. Women stand a much better chance in local and state elections—the route taken by most of the current female members of Congress. In the past, the majority of congresswomen were there serving out the term of a decreased husband. Women often enter the realm of politics on the local level, campaigning on issues that directly affect them and their families. Because of deep-rooted concern, women politicians are the ones who have brought issues such as child support enforcement, day care, pension reform, equal credit and domestic violence to the political forefront.

Scholars of the political process hope to gain insight on woman as politicians by studying the women who run for and serve in political office. The methods these women use to cope with a historically male dominated political machine and the strategies they use to achieve their goals are of interest to all current and future female politicians. However, many of the questions concerning the differences women make in politics must remain unanswered until more women occupy positions of power.

THE RIGHT TO VOTE

The 19th Amendment to the Constitution, ratified in 1920, states as follows: (1) The right of citizens of the United States to vote shall not be denied or abridged by the United States or by any state on account of sex; and (2) Congress shall have power to enforce this article by appropriate legislation.

We open this section with the map, "The Right to Vote." Examining this map reveals regional attitudes toward women's rights. Prior to ratification, politicians of individual states considered how the inclusion of women in the voting population would help or hinder the party in power. A few western states allowed women to vote, while they were still only territories. Many believed that allowing women to vote provided extra leverage to those groups favoring statehood. Other special interest groups, the liquor industry, for example, attempted to block women's suffrage for economic reasons, fearing that if women were allowed to vote, prohibition laws would be enacted. When the prospect of women as voters furthered the interest of the party in power, suffrage was supported; when suffrage was seen as a threat to the party, it was discouraged.

Ten states, all located in the southeastern section of the country, had failed to ratify the 19th Amendment by the time it took full effect. Full suffrage had already been granted to women in 15 states prior to the passage

THE RIGHT TO VOTE

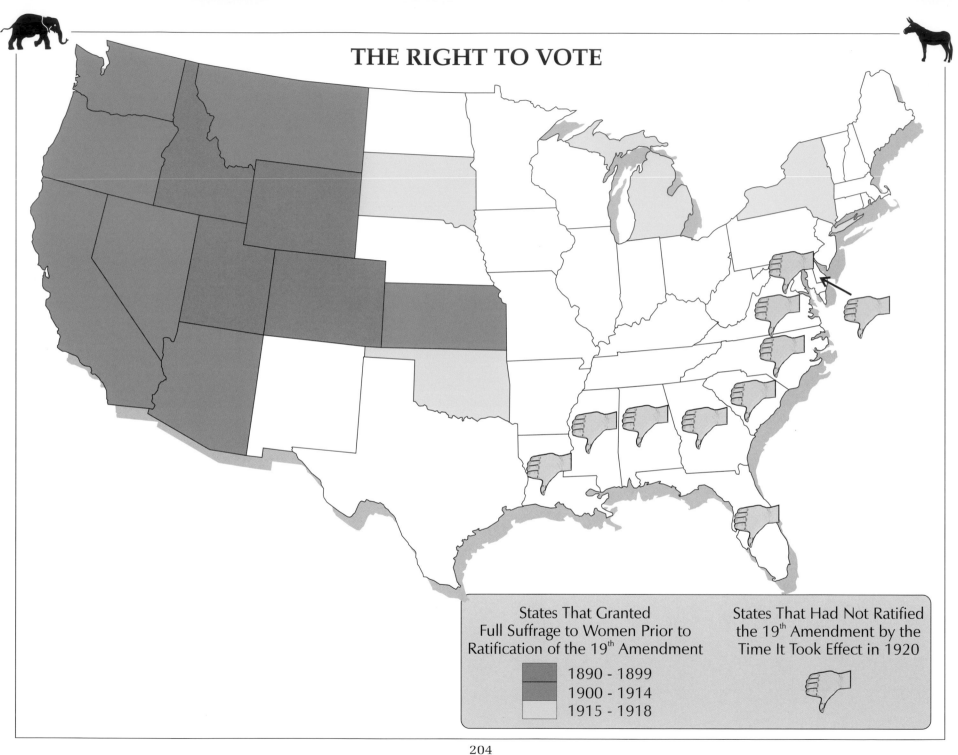

States That Granted
Full Suffrage to Women Prior to
Ratification of the 19th Amendment

- 1890 - 1899
- 1900 - 1914
- 1915 - 1918

States That Had Not Ratified
the 19th Amendment by the
Time It Took Effect in 1920

of the 19th Amendment. As mentioned earlier, suffrage was granted to women in many western states before it was achieved on a national level.

The dates in the map's legend refer to the time suffrage was achieved for states. In four states, suffrage was actually achieved while the state was a territory. The territory of Wyoming was the first to provide for women's suffrage in 1869 and incorporated it into its constitution in 1889. Three other territories, Utah in 1870, Washington in 1883 and Alaska in 1912, provided for women's suffrage prior to admission into the union. However, in two territories, Utah and Washington, women's suffrage was later repealed, not to be restored until 1896 and 1910, respectively, when each became a state.

THE PARTIES

The national party committees formulate platforms on a variety of issues and are instrumental in promoting candidates for political office. Both parties have been slow to accept women and have been guilty of backing female candidates only as "sacrificial lambs" against opponents who were deemed unbeatable by male candidates. Qualified and experienced female potential candidates have frequently been passed over in favor of men with no political experience. Women's success in the 1992 elections has initiated a degree of change in both parties' attitude toward women candidates and the future seems more promising in terms of obtaining party support for women.

The map, "Democratic and Republican Committees—1991," illustrates the number of female committee members for each party by state. The map shows that women are better represented in the Democratic party. The Republican Party Committee had only one woman member per state in all but seven states and the District of Columbia, which had only two women members. By contrast, female representation in the national Democratic Committee varied from two to nine members per state. Nine states had four or more women members on the Democratic National Committee, seven of which were in the eastern half of the country. Only five states, Montana, Kansas, Mississippi, New Hampshire and Rhode Island, and the District of Columbia had the same number of Democratic and Republican female members.

THE UPHILL BATTLE

For women with political ambitions, the battle has been uphill since the birth of the nation in 1776. In the first 200 years of this nation's existence, men outnumbered women 156 to 1 in the United States Senate, 110 to 1 in the United States House of Representatives, and 101 to 1 in the president's cabinet.[5] In the past 20 years, however, particularly on the state level, we have begun to see real changes in the percentages of women serving in elected offices as depicted on the chart "Women in Politics." Between 1971 and 1991, the percentage of state legislators who were women rose from 5% to 18%. Women mayors remained a small percentage of all mayors during that time, but the percentage did rise slowly from 3% in 1971 to 6% in 1991. A greater rate of growth can be seen among United States congresswomen who represented less than 1% of all members of Congress in 1971 and increased to 17% by 1991.

DEMOCRATIC AND REPUBLICAN COMMITTEES
1991

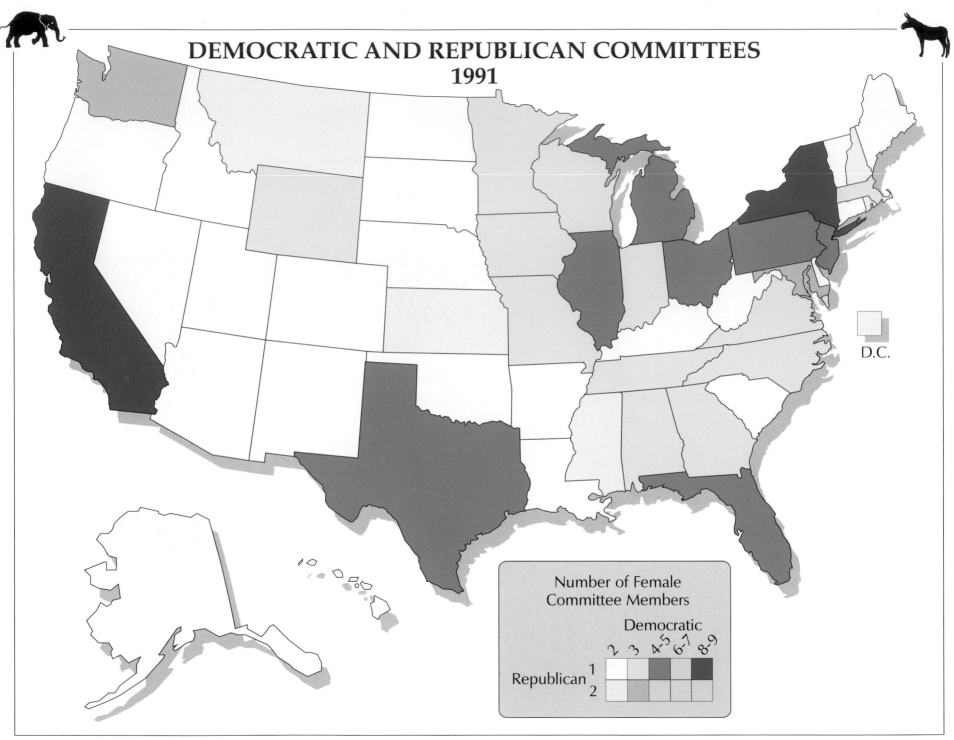

D.C.

Number of Female
Committee Members

Democratic

2 3 4-5 6-7 8-9

Republican 1
2

WOMEN IN POLITICS

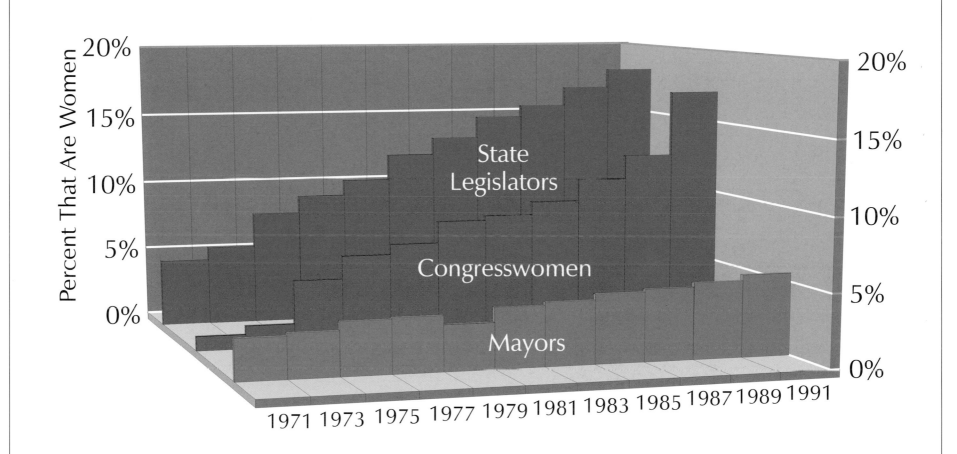

The map, "Women as Candidates," shows, for the November 1990 state legislative elections, the number of female candidates per 100,000 women and the percentage of those candidates who were elected. Three states, Louisiana, Mississippi and New Jersey, had no state legislative elections that year. Women as candidates fared well all over the country. In all but nine states with elections that year more than half of the women running in state elections won. While it is encouraging to see so many winning at the polls, this map may be a bit misleading if used to judge women's progress as candidates. A good example is Virginia. The map indicates that 100% of woman running for the state legislature were elected. While this is true, there was only one woman running for legislative office that year, meaning that Virginia had only 0.48 female legislators per 100,000 women in the state. That is among the nation's lowest rates of representation of women. New Hampshire had an amazing 204 women running for legislative office that year, with 137 winning their races.

WOMEN IN THE STATEHOUSE

The next two maps, "State Legislatures," focus on women lawmakers at the state level after the elections of 1991. Arizona, at 34%, had the highest percentage of female legislators. Five other states, Colorado, Washington, Vermont, New Hampshire and Maine, all had legislatures that were more than 30% female. Women were not so well represented in the legislatures of six states, all located in the southern United States. Kentucky, Oklahoma, Arkansas, Louisiana, Mississippi and Alabama had legislatures whose female members accounted for less than 10% of the elected lawmakers. Louisiana, at 2%, had the dubious honor of having the lowest proportion of women legislators. Again, states in the western half of the nation and most of New England had legislatures with the greatest proportion of women.

Perhaps a better indicator of how well women are represented is the number of female legislators per 100,000 women in the population. Wyoming and three New England states, Maine, New Hampshire and Vermont, were the only states where the rate of female legislators was more than ten per 100,000 women. The Northern High Plains states of North Dakota, South Dakota and Montana, along with Idaho and Alaska had the next highest rate of female representation—between 5 and 9 per 100,000. In 21 states, located mostly in the eastern United States (with the exception of California, Texas and Oklahoma), fewer than one per 100,000 women were state legislators. Women appear to be better represented in states with lower population densities and least represented in states with higher population densities. In one state, Arizona, the speaker of the house was a women and in three states, Nevada, Michigan and Florida, a woman was president of the senate.

THE RIGHT TO CHOOSE

More than 250 pieces of legislation on abortion were introduced in state legislatures around the country in 1990 as a result of the 1989 Supreme Court decision allowing states greater regulation of abortions. Less than 10% of these proposals actually became laws. Both political parties agree that abortion rights are becoming

WOMEN AS CANDIDATES
November 1990 State Elections

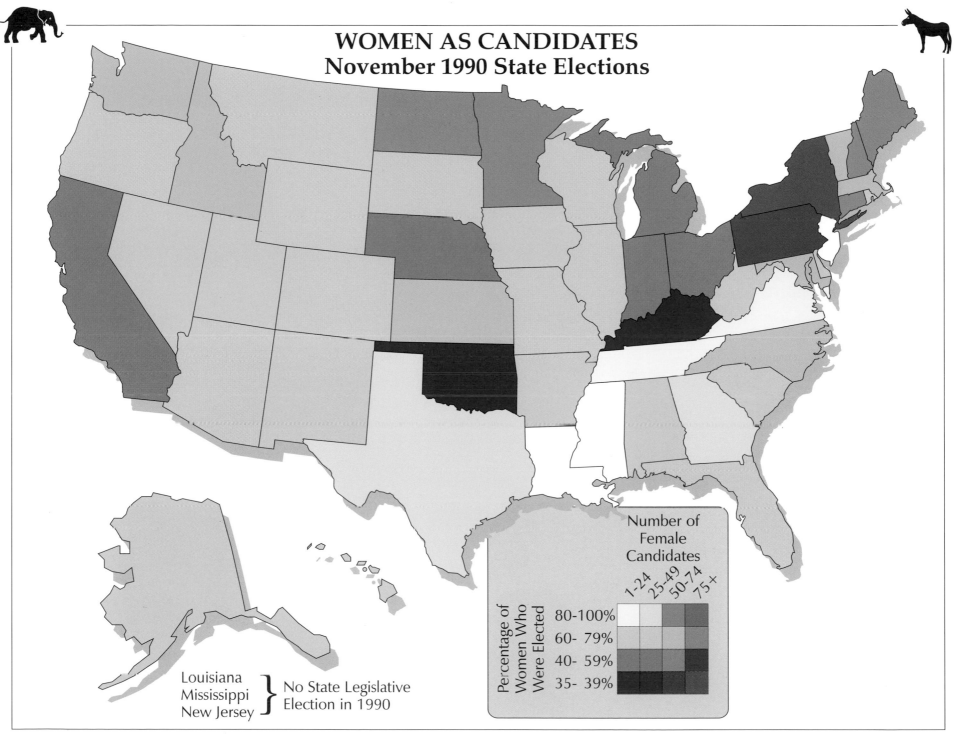

Louisiana
Mississippi
New Jersey } No State Legislative Election in 1990

Number of Female Candidates

	1-24	25-49	50-74	75+
80-100%				
60- 79%				
40- 59%				
35- 39%				

Percentage of Women Who Were Elected

STATE LEGISLATURES
1991

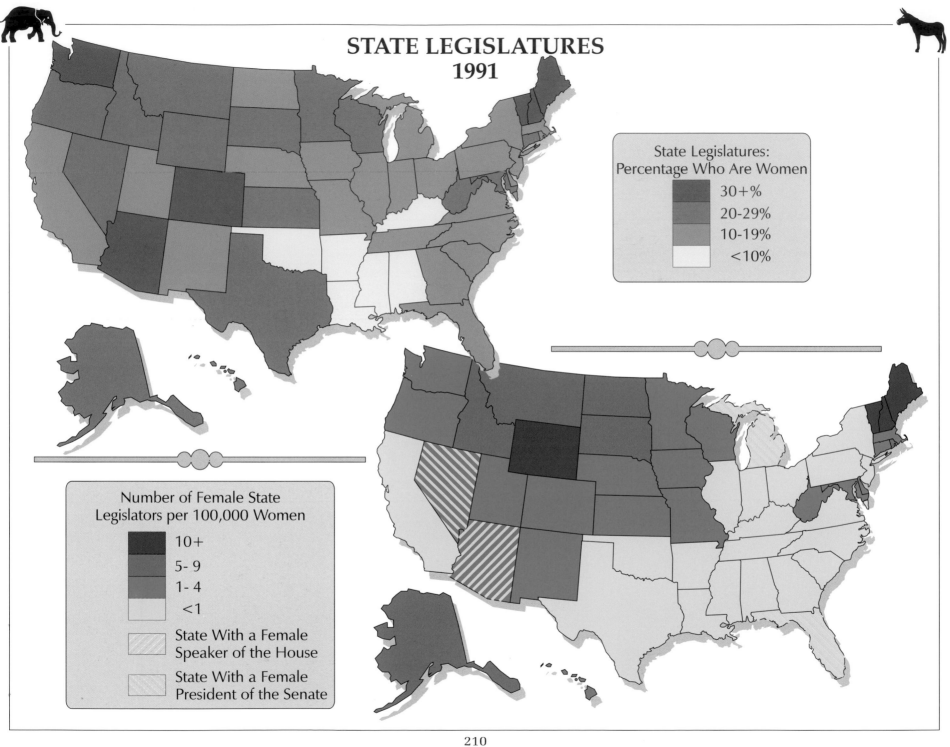

State Legislatures:
Percentage Who Are Women

- 30+%
- 20-29%
- 10-19%
- <10%

Number of Female State
Legislators per 100,000 Women

- 10+
- 5- 9
- 1- 4
- <1

State With a Female
Speaker of the House

State With a Female
President of the Senate

an increasingly important issue for younger women, who are concerned that their right to terminate a pregnancy may be in danger.

The next map, "Positions of Legislatures and Governors on Keeping Abortion Legal," examines the positions of the three branches of government (Nebraska does not have a bicameral legislature) in each state. Triangles in each state are trisected to represent the governor's position (upper section of triangle), the senate's position (left section), and the house/assembly's position (right section). If a branch is likely to vote "yes" on the issue of keeping abortion legal, the section is shaded green; if the vote is likely to be "no," the section is shaded red; if a section is shaded brown it indicates a legislative body that is closely divided on the issue. In 26 states all three branches of government agree on the issue of abortion with 15 states being in favor of keeping abortion legal under the conditions of *Roe v. Wade* and 11 states in favor of placing serious limitations on abortion. That leaves 24 states in which the governing bodies are divided on the issue. States that are pro-choice are concentrated along the eastern seaboard and in the far West. The position of a state's governor is especially critical. With the power of the veto he or she can block any legislation, pro or con, involving abortion. This occurred in New Hampshire when the governor vetoed a bill liberalizing abortion laws that had been passed by both legislative bodies.

THE FEDERAL GOVERNMENT

The total number of women representatives who had served in the U.S. Congress up to the 102nd Congress is

shown on the map "Congress Past—The House of Representatives." The time frame of the map begins in 1919, even though Jeannette Rankin of Wyoming, the first woman to be elected in her own right, entered Congress in 1917. In the first 20 years or so after suffrage, most women serving in Congress (about two-thirds) had been appointed by their governors to finish the terms of their deceased husbands.[6] The symbols are color coded to indicate when the female representative first entered Congress. The number of female representatives varied from 21 for the first period (1919–1933) to 46 for the fourth period (1971–1991). It was more common for coastal states to have female representatives, although Illinois sent at least two female representatives to Congress during each of the time periods examined. New York had the most women in the House, 14, during these four periods, with six serving prior to 1953. California is next with ten past congresswomen, only three of whom served before the 83rd Congress in 1953. Eleven states had no female representatives from 1919 to 1991.

The next map, "Congress Past—The Senate," depicts the number of women sent to the United States Senate prior to the 1992 elections. The four time periods are the same as on the previous map. Prior to the 1992 elections, only 16 women had served in the United States Senate, representing only 12 different states. Four states, Louisiana, Alabama, South Dakota and Nebraska had two female senators.

The map, "The 103rd Congress," depicts female representation in both the Senate and the House of Representatives for the 103rd Congress. Four women were elected to the Senate in 1992 bringing to six the total number of women senators. Five of the six women serving in the Senate are Democrats, and one, Carol

POSITIONS OF LEGISLATURES AND GOVERNORS ON KEEPING ABORTION LEGAL

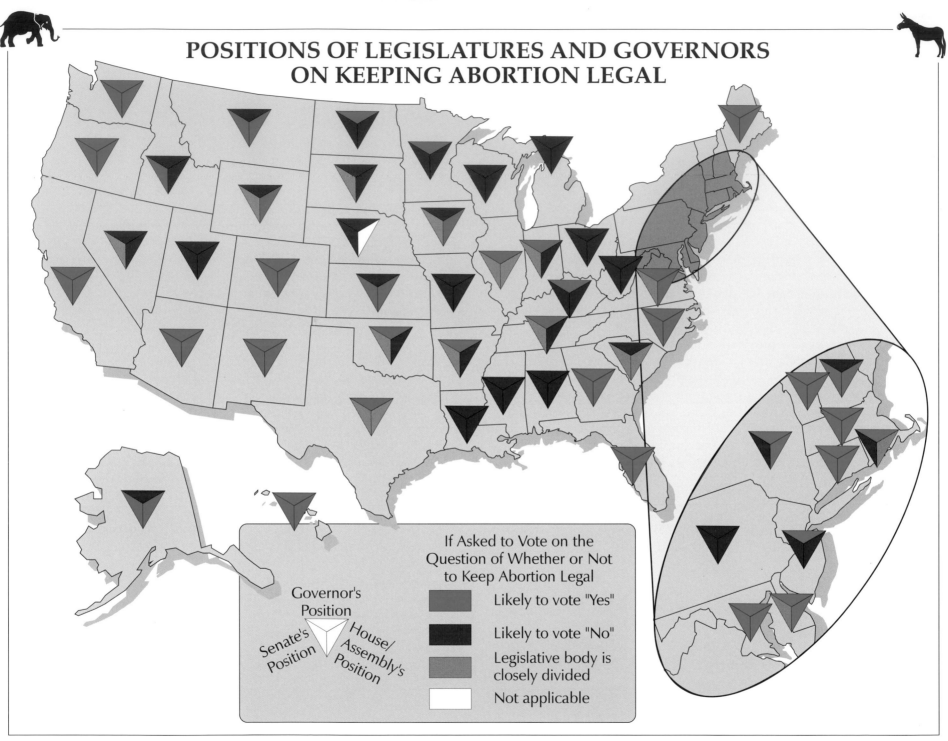

If Asked to Vote on the Question of Whether or Not to Keep Abortion Legal

Likely to vote "Yes"

Likely to vote "No"

Legislative body is closely divided

Not applicable

Governor's Position

Senate's Position

House/ Assembly's Position

CONGRESS PAST
THE HOUSE OF REPRESENTATIVES

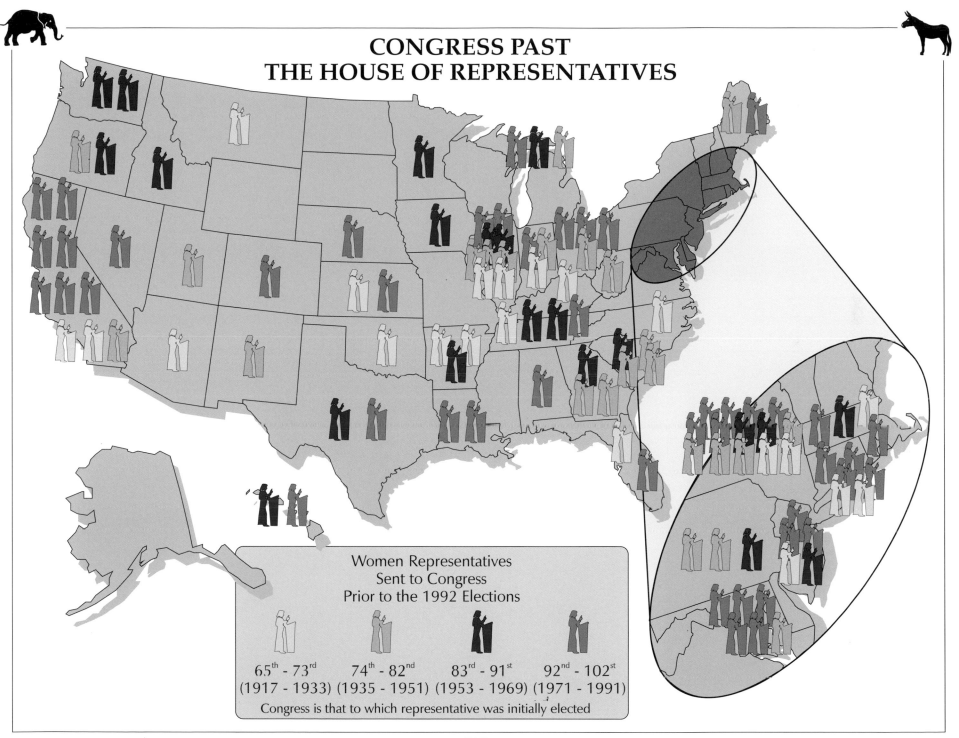

Women Representatives
Sent to Congress
Prior to the 1992 Elections

65th - 73rd   74th - 82nd   83rd - 91st   92nd - 102st
(1917 - 1933) (1935 - 1951) (1953 - 1969) (1971 - 1991)

Congress is that to which representative was initially elected

CONGRESS PAST
THE SENATE

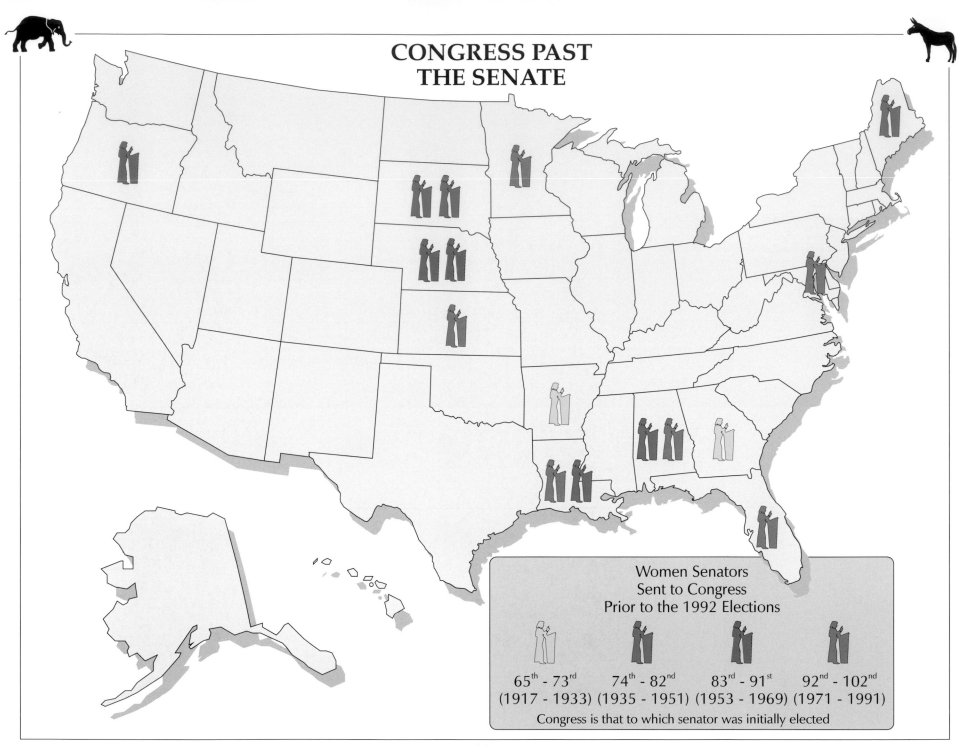

Women Senators
Sent to Congress
Prior to the 1992 Elections

65th - 73rd   74th - 82nd   83rd - 91st   92nd - 102nd
(1917 - 1933) (1935 - 1951) (1953 - 1969) (1971 - 1991)

Congress is that to which senator was initially elected

THE 103rd CONGRESS
1993

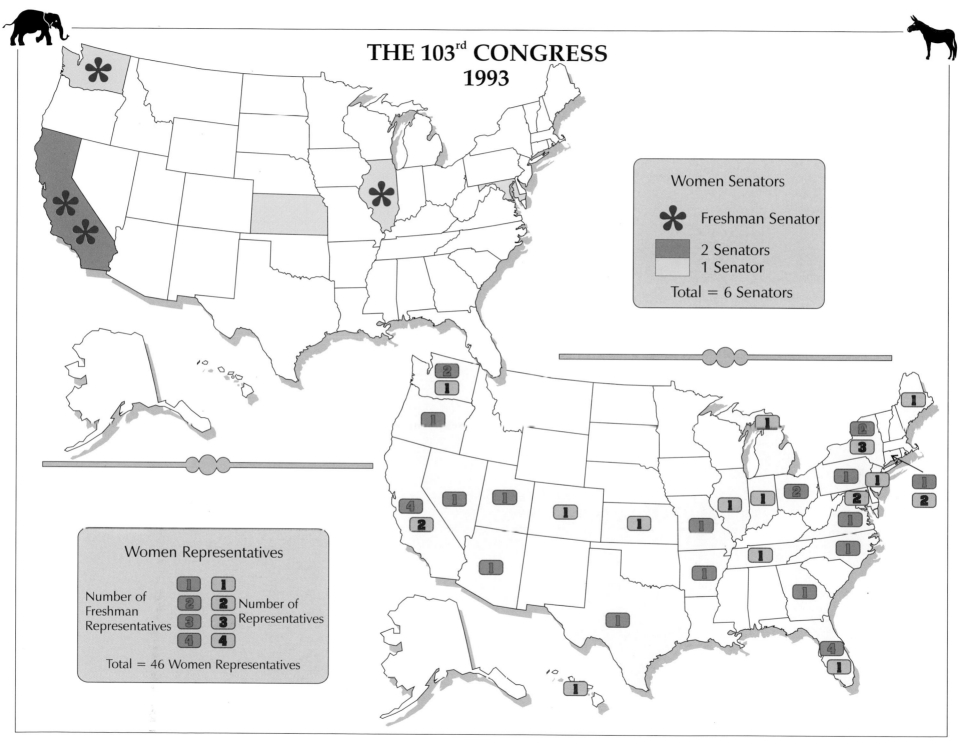

Women Senators

✻   Freshman Senator

▮   2 Senators

▯   1 Senator

Total = 6 Senators

Women Representatives

Number of Freshman Representatives	Number of Representatives
1	1
2	2
3	3
4	4

Total = 46 Women Representatives

Moseley-Braun, is the first African-American women elected to the Senate. Nancy Kassebaum, the lone Republican among the Senate women, was first elected in 1978 and was the first woman to be elected to the Senate without having been preceded by her spouse.[7]

Forty-six women are currently representing their states in the House of Representatives. Seven states, Washington, California, Florida, Maryland, Ohio, Connecticut and New York, have more than one congresswoman. The map indicates that states in the north-central section of the United States have no female representatives in Congress. Among the freshman congresswomen in the House, there are a number of "firsts." The first African-American women to represent Georgia and North Carolina, Cynthia McKinney and Eva Clayton, were elected to the House. Virginia elected its first woman, Leslie L. Byrne. Nydia Velazquez, the first Puerto Rican congresswoman, was elected in New York City, and Los Angeles sent Lucille Roybal-Allard, the first Mexican American.[8]

THE EXECUTIVE OFFICE

Women have a tough time gaining any elected office, but those who campaign for mayor are even more scrutinized than women campaigning for state offices. Voters see the office of mayor as having the most potential for affecting their daily lives. How will local tax money be spent? Are the streets safe at night? Is money available for repairing roads? In the position of mayor, voters expect proven fiscal and managerial skills. These skills are usually learned in business. As women-owned businesses become more common and women

gain experience in business, more cities should begin to see women being elected as mayors.

In 1991, 151 cities with populations over 30,000 had woman as mayors. The map, "Mayors—1991," indicates the size and location of these cities. Women were the mayors of only three cities (San Diego, Dallas and Houston) of more than a million people and of five cities (Washington, D.C., El Paso, San Antonio, San Jose and Fairfax, VA) with populations between half a million and a million. Several regions of the country stand out as having very few women mayors. States in the southern, north central and mountain regions have very few women mayors. However, remember when viewing this distribution that many of the states with few women in executive office have very few cities with more than 30,000 people. Montana, North Dakota, South Dakota, Nebraska and Maine are examples. States having large numbers of women mayors, for example California, Michigan, Texas and New Jersey, have populations that are clustered around major urban areas.

Women governors have been rare and those elected in their own right even rarer. The first woman to achieve this office on her own merits was Ella Grasso, who in 1974 was elected governor of Connecticut. In addition to the 4 women now serving as governors, Christine Todd Whitman of New Jersey, Barbara Roberts of Oregon, Joan Kinney of Kansas and Ann Richards of Texas, only five other women have been elected on their own merits: Connecticut's Ella Grasso, Washington's Dixie Lee Ray, Kentucky's Martha Layne Collins, Vermont's Madeleine Kunin and Nebraska's Kay Orr.[9] Other women elected as governors were elected in place of their husbands. Nellie Taylor Ross of Wyoming was elected in 1925 to take over for her

MAYORS
1991

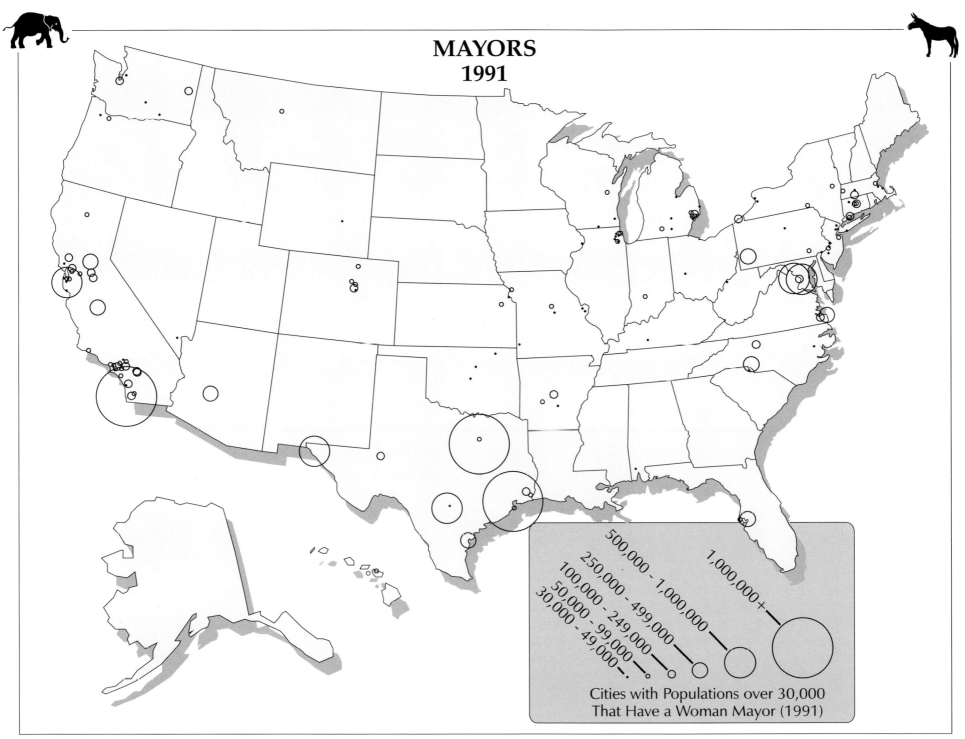

500,000 - 1,000,000
250,000 - 499,000
100,000 - 249,000
50,000 - 99,000
30,000 - 49,000
1,000,000+

Cities with Populations over 30,000
That Have a Woman Mayor (1991)

GOVERNORS

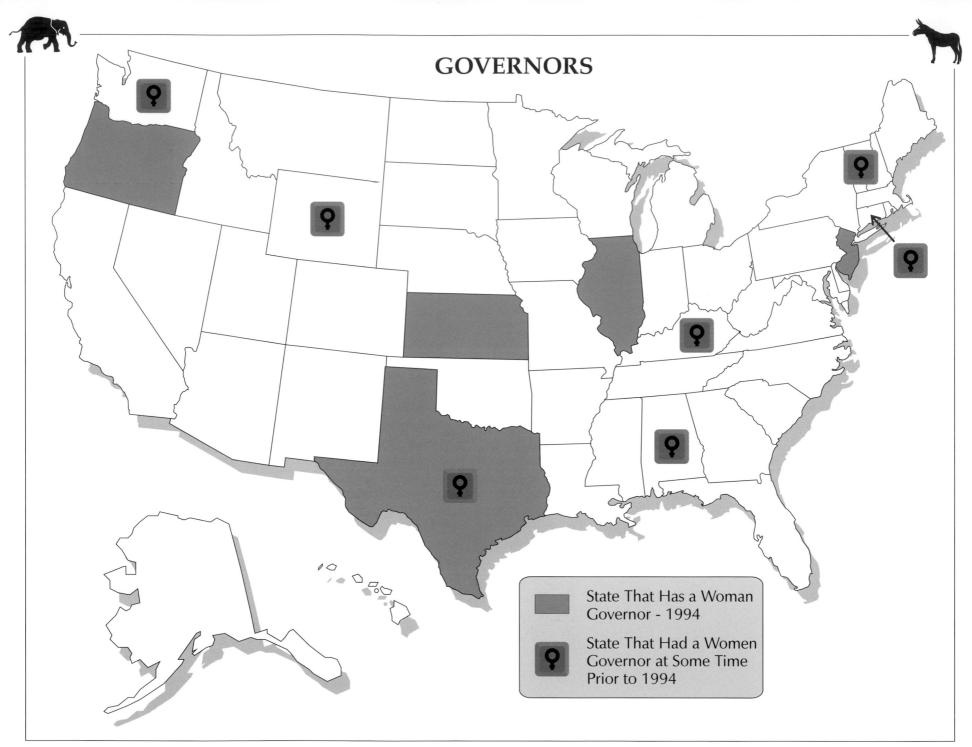

State That Has a Woman Governor - 1994

State That Had a Women Governor at Some Time Prior to 1994

husband when he died in office. Texas elected Miriam Ferguson of the infamous "Ma" and "Pa" Ferguson in 1925 and again in 1933 in place of her husband, who had been impeached while serving as governor in 1917. Lurleen Wallace of Alabama was elected in 1967 when her husband, George Wallace, could not succeed himself as governor.

The success of women in attaining other state offices can be observed on the map "State Officials." States with women in the offices of Lieutenant Governor, Secretary of State, Treasurer and Attorney General are depicted by various hatch patterns. In 1992, seven states (Connecticut, Michigan, Wisconsin, Minnesota, Iowa, Nebraska and Nevada) had a woman serving as lieutenant governor. Women occupied the office of secretary of state in 14 states. Ten states had a woman as state treasurer. Women were the attorneys general of only four states. Women were not represented in any of the positions in 26 states, most noticeably in the Deep South and New England.

In 1933, Franklin D. Roosevelt appointed Frances Perkins as his Secretary of Labor, the first women to serve in the cabinet. Perkins was one of only two members of FDR's cabinet to serve throughout his four terms. She resigned two months after Roosevelt's death in office in 1945. Two of her major accomplishments were her work with the Social Security Act and the Fair Labor Standards Act. She also pushed for a minimum wage and unemployment compensation. The map, "Women Cabinet Appointees," shows the name, position and birthplace of women who have served in Presidential cabinets. Since the tenure of Frances Perkins, only 12 other women have served as cabinet members, although a few have served in more than one position. During the Carter administration, Patricia Roberts Harris served as Secretary of Housing and Urban Development and later as the Secretary of Health, Education and Welfare. The only woman to serve in two different administrations was Elizabeth Dole who served as the Secretary of Transportation during the Reagan administration and as Secretary of Labor for President Bush. The Clinton administration has three women in cabinet positions. Donna Shalala serves as Secretary of Health and Human Services, Janet Reno serves as Attorney General and Hazel O'Leary is the Secretary of Energy. None of these positions had previously been held by a woman.

The First Lady of the United States is most commonly the wife of the president. However, if the president is not married, any other woman of his choice may hold that position. John Tyler, for example, designated his daughter-in-law and James Buchanan his niece as first lady. The map of first ladies shows the birthplaces only of those who were married to the president while he was in office. Dots indicating the birthplaces of the first ladies are also color coded, indicating the time period in which they served. Note how birthplaces moved west as the country matured and the center of population shifted accordingly. Most first ladies were born east of the Mississippi and one, Louise Adams, was born in England.

STATE OFFICIALS

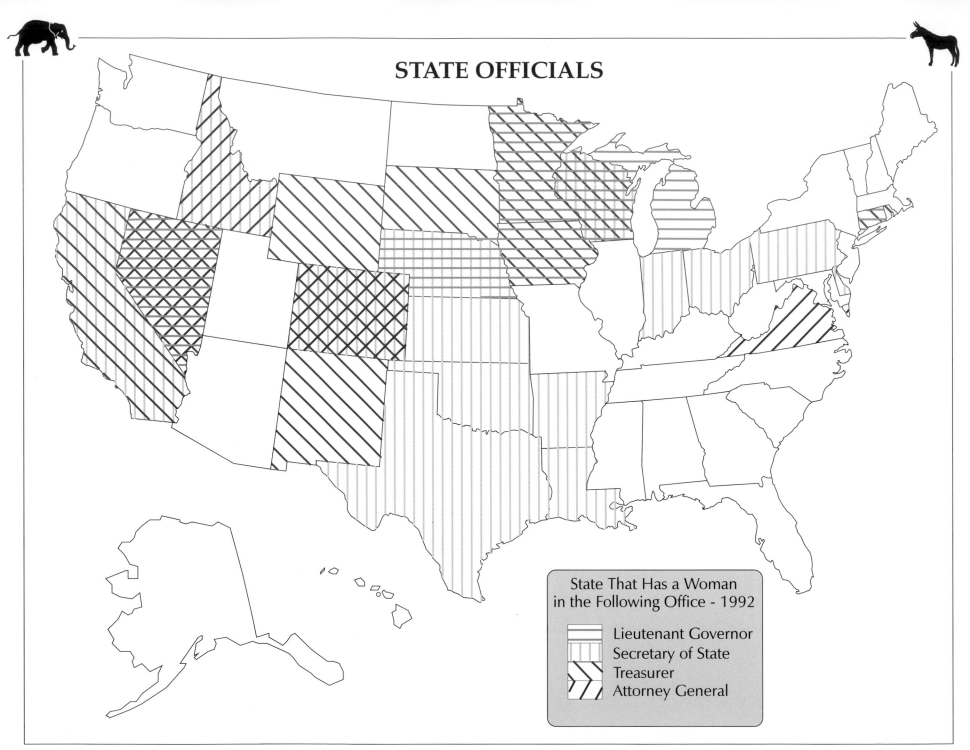

State That Has a Woman
in the Following Office - 1992

Lieutenant Governor
Secretary of State
Treasurer
Attorney General

WOMEN CABINET APPOINTEES

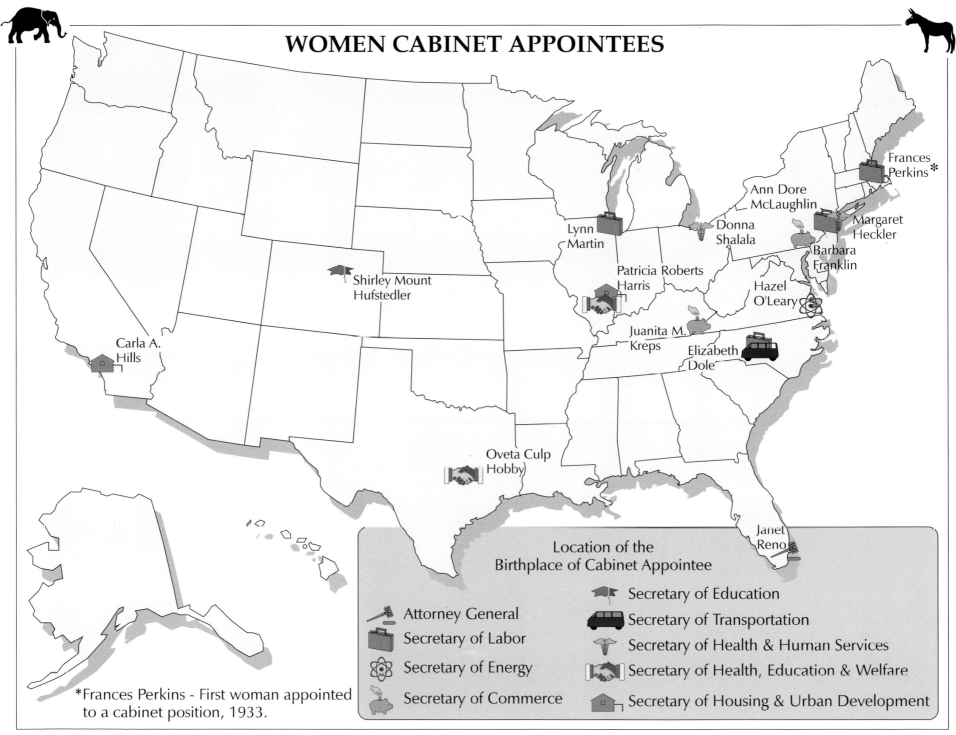

Frances Perkins*

Ann Dore McLaughlin

Lynn Martin

Donna Shalala

Margaret Heckler

Patricia Roberts Harris

Barbara Franklin

Shirley Mount Hufstedler

Hazel O'Leary

Carla A. Hills

Juanita M. Kreps

Elizabeth Dole

Oveta Culp Hobby

Janet Reno

Location of the
Birthplace of Cabinet Appointee

Attorney General

Secretary of Labor

Secretary of Energy

Secretary of Commerce

Secretary of Education

Secretary of Transportation

Secretary of Health & Human Services

Secretary of Health, Education & Welfare

Secretary of Housing & Urban Development

*Frances Perkins - First woman appointed to a cabinet position, 1933.

FIRST LADIES

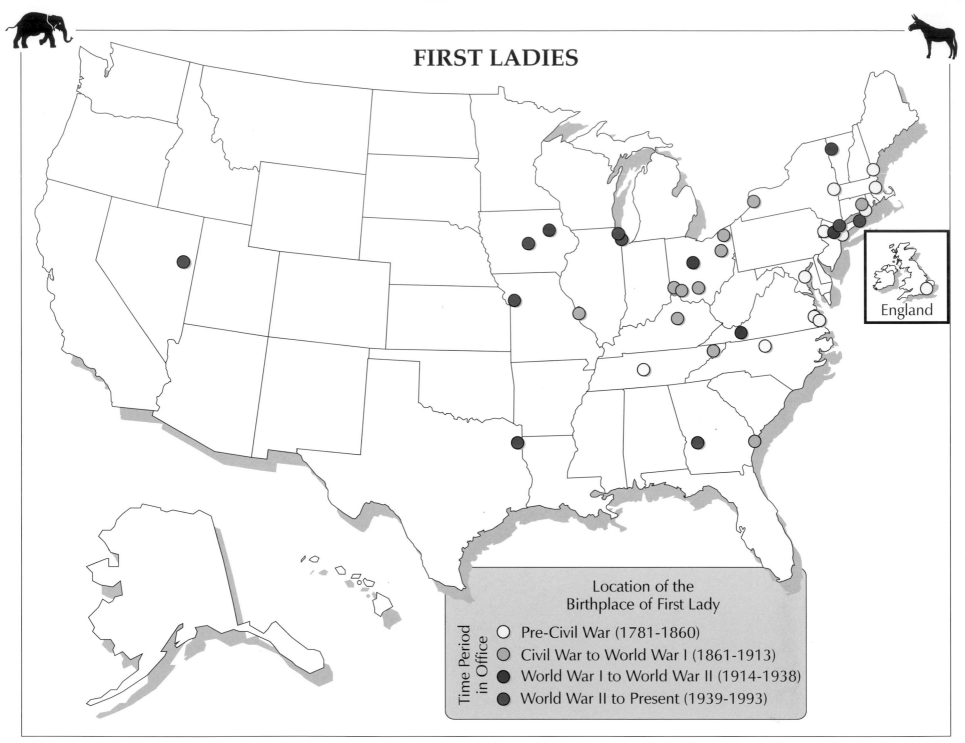

England

Location of the Birthplace of First Lady

Time Period in Office

○ Pre-Civil War (1781-1860)
◐ Civil War to World War I (1861-1913)
● World War I to World War II (1914-1938)
● World War II to Present (1939-1993)

APPENDIX

The following tables summarize the maps in the atlas. If a state has the highest rate or value for the country, a green square is indicated. Likewise if a state has the lowest rate or value for the country, a red square is plotted. For example, Alaska has the highest rates of working women, two-income families, and Native American women in poverty. It also has the highest median income and the greatest number of women-owned businesses while ranking the lowest in the country for women receiving social security.

In several cases there are ties among several states for ranking as the highest or lowest in the country. In each table the states have been grouped by geographic region so comparisons can be made with a state's neighbor or among regions.

DEMOGRAPHICS

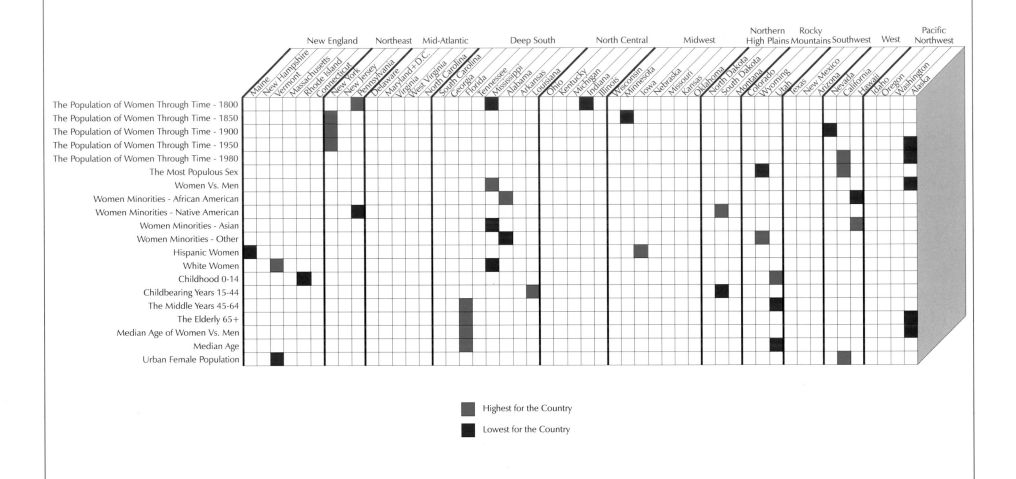

EDUCATION

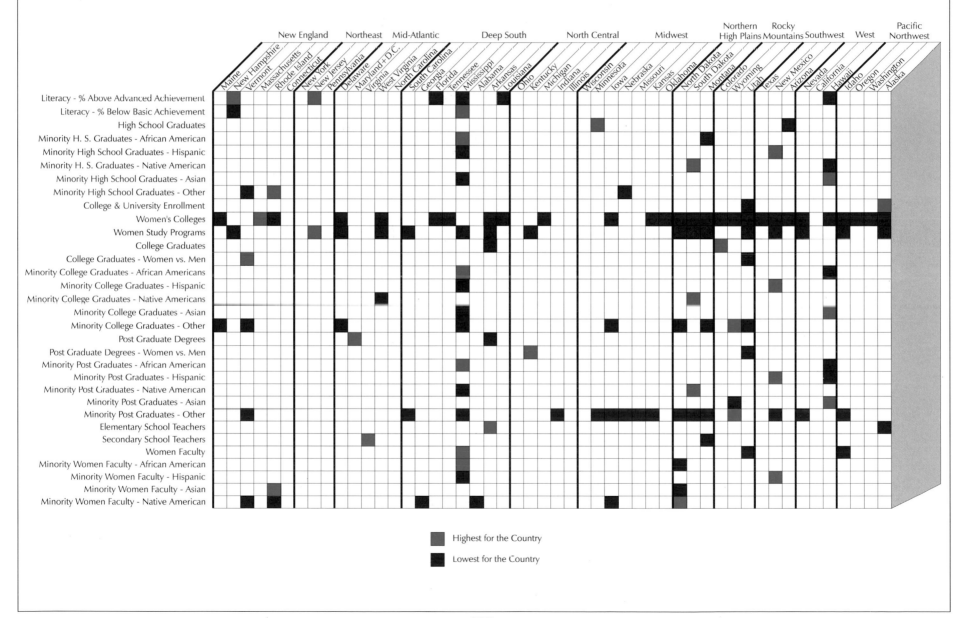

Highest for the Country

Lowest for the Country

EMPLOYMENT

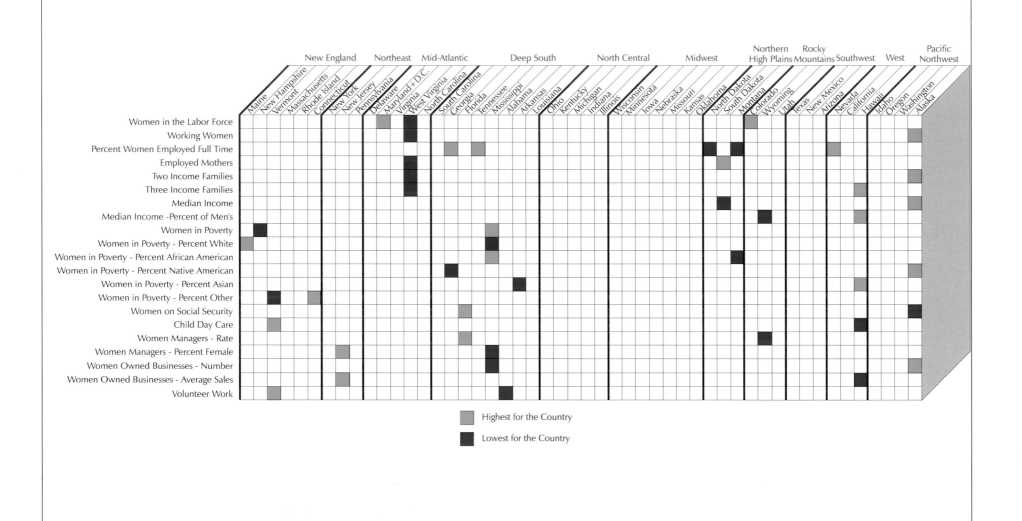

	New England	Northeast	Mid-Atlantic	Deep South	North Central	Midwest	Northern High Plains	Rocky Mountains	Southwest	West	Pacific Northwest

| | Highest for the Country |
| | Lowest for the Country |

226

FAMILY

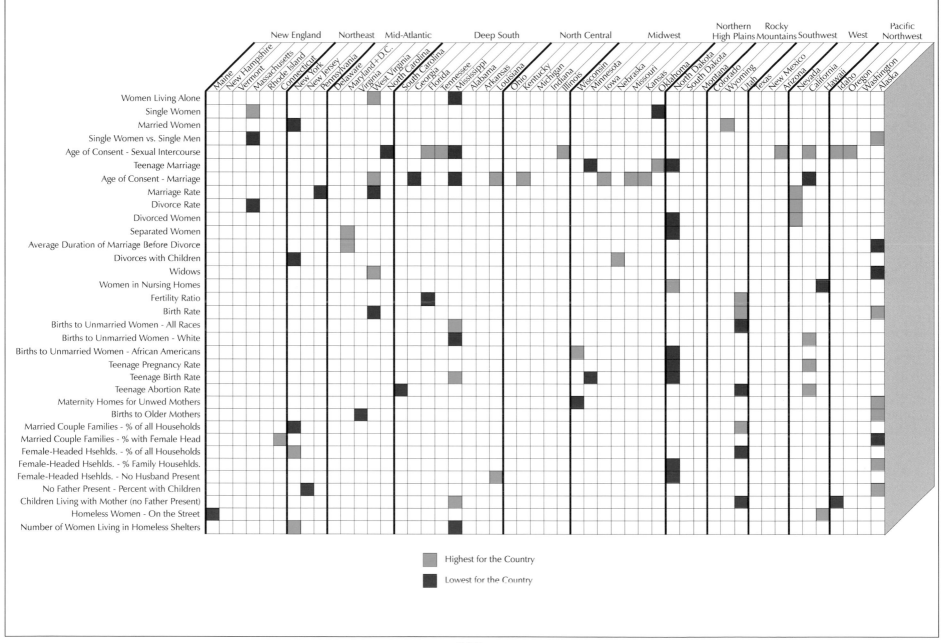

	New England			Northeast		Mid-Atlantic		Deep South		North Central		Midwest		Northern High Plains	Rocky Mountains	Southwest	West	Pacific Northwest

Legend:
- ▉ Highest for the Country
- ■ Lowest for the Country

HEALTH

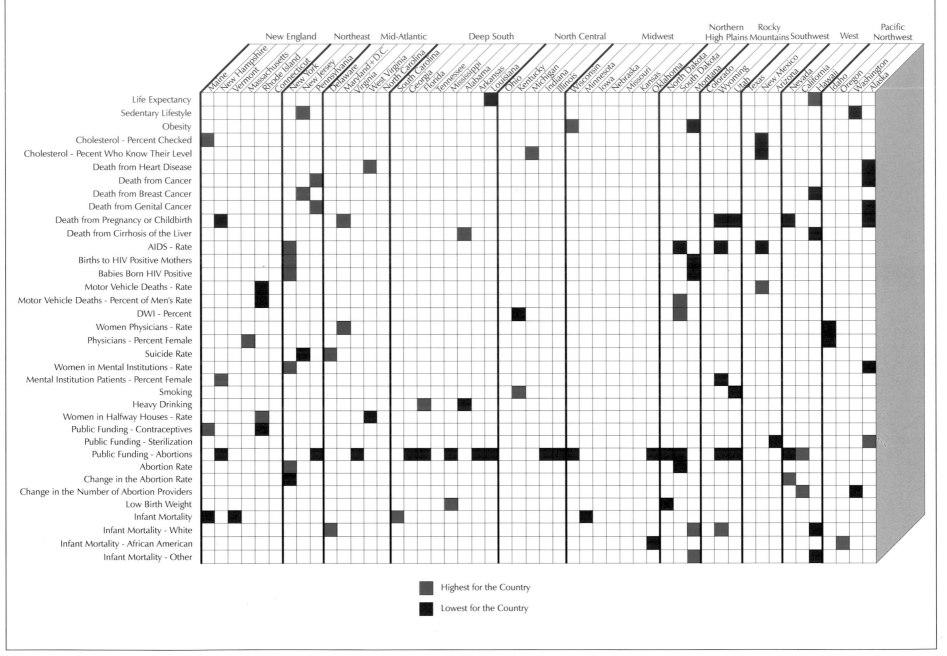

	New England						Northeast			Mid-Atlantic				Deep South							North Central				Midwest					Northern High Plains		Rocky Mountains		Southwest			West		Pacific Northwest	
	Maine	New Hampshire	Vermont	Massachusetts	Rhode Island	Connecticut	New York	New Jersey	Pennsylvania	Delaware	Maryland+D.C.	Virginia	West Virginia	North Carolina	South Carolina	Georgia	Florida	Tennessee	Mississippi	Alabama	Arkansas	Louisiana	Ohio	Kentucky	Michigan	Indiana	Illinois	Wisconsin	Minnesota	Iowa	Nebraska	Missouri	Kansas	Oklahoma	North Dakota	South Dakota	Montana	Colorado	Wyoming	Utah	Texas	New Mexico	Arizona	Nevada	California	Hawaii	Idaho	Oregon	Washington	Alaska

Figure content; individual cell markers represent "Highest for the Country" (gray) and "Lowest for the Country" (black).

■ Highest for the Country

■ Lowest for the Country

CRIME

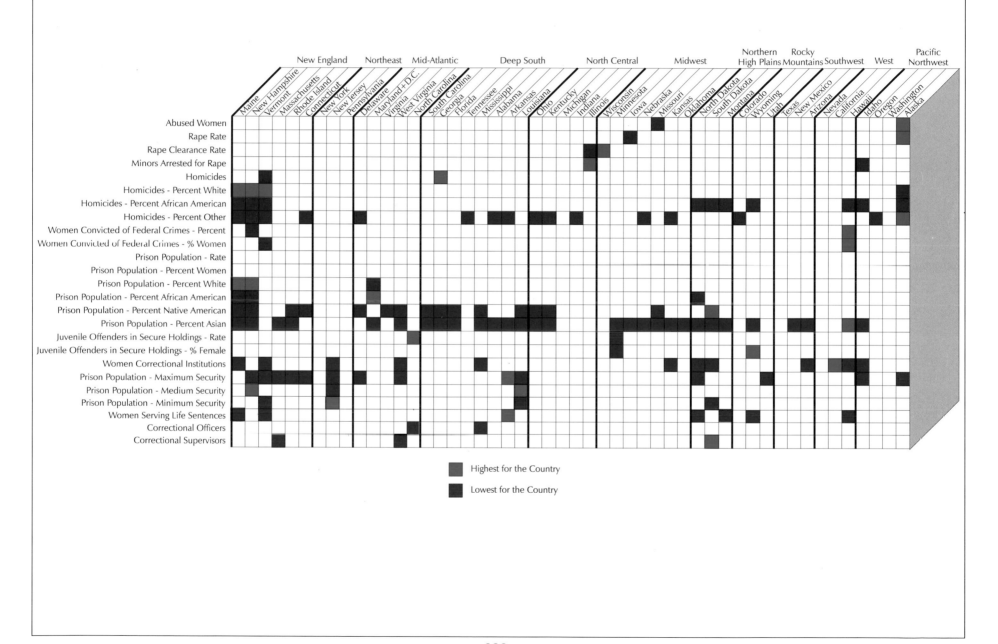

Highest for the Country

Lowest for the Country

POLITICS

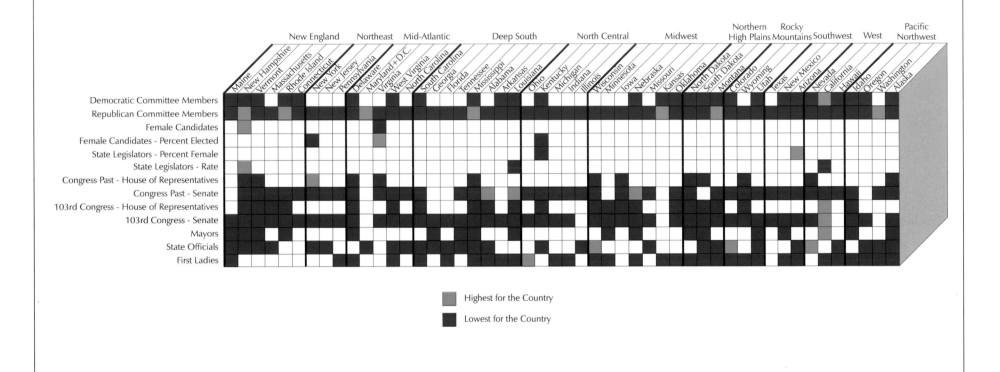

Highest for the Country

Lowest for the Country

NOTES

DEMOGRAPHICS

[1]Elaine Partnow, ed., *The Quotable Woman 1800–1981* (New York: Facts On File, 1982), 149.
[2]U.S. Department of Commerce, Bureau of the Census, *1990 Census of Population and Housing Summary* (Washington D.C.: U.S. Government Printing Office, 1990), A-11.
[3]*Ibid.*, A-12.

EDUCATION

[1]Elaine Partnow, ed., *The Quotable Woman 1800–1981* (New York: Facts On File, 1982), 125.
[2]"History of Education," *Encyclopaedia Britannica*, 1986, vol. 18, 61.
[3]Myra Sadker and David Sadker, "Sexism in the Classroom," *Psychology Today*, (March 1985).
[4]Jane Pauley, *Dateline*, Telecast: Feb. 8, 1994.
[5]I. V. S. Mullis, J. R. Campbell, and A. E. Farstrup, *Reading Report Card for the Nation and States* (Washington D.C.: Educational Testing Services, National Center for Education Statistics, 1993), Report 23-ST06, 53.
[6]*Encyclopaedia Britannica*, 1986, vol. 18 , 75.

EMPLOYMENT

[1]Joni Seager and Ann Olson, *Women in the World* (New York: Simon and Schuster, 1986), 43.
[2]Ruth Sidel, *Women and Children Last: The Plight of Poor Women in Affluent America* (New York: Viking, 1986), 49.
[3]Alice Kessler-Harris, *Out to Work: A History of Wage-Earning Women in the United States* (New York: Oxford University Press, 1982), 29.
[4]Sidel, 50.
[5]Bettina Berch, *The Endless Day: The Political Economy of Women and Work* (New York: Harcourt Brace Jovanovich, 1982), 41.
[6]Claudia Wallis, "Onward Women!", *Time* (Dec. 4, 1989): 85.
[7]Sidel, 55.
[8]*Ibid.*, 61.
[9]Diane Harris, "Does Your Pay Measure Up?" *Working Woman*, (January, 1994): 26.
[10]Seager, 107.
[11]*Ibid.*, 110.
[12]*Ibid.*, xvi.
[13]*Ibid.*, 107.
[14]U.S. Department of Commerce, Bureau of the Census, *1990 Census of the Population*, CD ROM Summary Tape File 3C.
[15]Donna Jackson, *How to Make the World a Better Place for Women in Five Minutes a Day* (New York: Hyperion, 1992), 38.
[16]*Ibid.*, 39.

[17]*Ibid.*, 4.
[18]*Ibid.*, 131.
[19]*Ibid.*, 35.
[20]*Ibid.*, 35.
[21]U.S. Department of Commerce, U.S. Bureau of the Census, *1987 Survey of Women-Owned Business Enterprises*, Series WB87-1, 527.

FAMILY

[1]Pat Schroeder, *Champion of the Great American Family* (New York: Random House, 1989), 10.
[2]*Ibid.*, 20.
[3]*Ibid.*, 59.
[4]U.S. Department of Commerce, Bureau of the Census, *1990 Census of Population and Housing, Summary Population and Housing Characteristics*, (Washington, D.C.: U.S. Government Printing Office) 117.
[5]"Cribonometry," *Sierra*, (May/June 1993), 38.
[6]Claudia Wallis, "Onward, Women!" *Time* (Dec. 4, 1989), 83.
[7]"Cribonometry," 36.
[8]S. K. Henshaw, "Teenage Abortion, Birth and Pregnancy Statistics, by State, 1988," *Family Planning Perspective*, 25, no.3, (May/June, 1993): 104–105.
[9]U.S. Department of Commerce, Bureau of the Census, *1990 Census of Population and Housing, Summary Population and Housing Characteristics* (Washington, D.C: U.S. Government Printing Office, 1990), 117.

HEALTH

[1]Elaine Partnow, ed., *The Quotable Woman 1800–1981* (New York: Facts On File, 1982), 213.
[2]*Journal of the American Medical Women's Association*, Nov./Dec. 1990 (quoted in Donna Jackson, *How to Make the World a Better Place for Women in Five Minutes a Day* [New York: Hyperion, 1992], 6).
[3]*Time*, Special Issue, Fall 1990 (quoted in Donna Jackson, *How to Make the World a Better Place for Women in Five Minutes a Day*, 6).
[4]Donna Jackson, *How to Make the World a Better Place for Women in Five Minutes a Day* (New York: Hyperion, 1992), 47.
[5]The Boston Women's Health Book Collective, *The New Our Bodies, Ourselves* (New York: Touchstone, 1992), 42.
[6]Jackson, 45–48.
[7]The Boston Women's Health Book Collective, 41.
[8]*Ibid.*, 101.
[9]U.S. Department of Commerce, Bureau of the Census, *Statistical Abstract of the United States, 1992*, Table No. 116.
[10]Mark S. Hoffman, ed., *The World Almanac and Book of Facts 1993* (New York: Pharos Books, 1993), 956.
[11]U.S. Department of Commerce, Bureau of the Census, *Statistical Abstract of the United States, 1992*, Table No. 116.
[12]The Boston Women's Health Book Collective, 60–61.
[13]Jackson, 14.
[14]The Boston Women's Health Book Collective, 55.
[15]Fact Sheet, "Family Planning and Reproductive Health Care: The Need for Clinical Services," Planned Parenthood Federation of America, Inc.
[16]The Boston Women's Health Book Collective, 370–371.
[17]Fact Sheet, "Family Planning in America," Planned Parenthood Federation of American, Inc.
[18]"Family Planning and Reproductive Health Care: The Need for Clinical Services."
[19]National Abortion Federation, Fact Sheet, "24 Hour Waiting Period for Abortion."
[20]*Facts in Brief*, The Alan Guttmacher Institute, "Contraceptive Services," Jan. 4, 1993.
[21]*The World Almanac and Book of Facts 1993*, 956.
[22]Metropolitan Life Insurance Company, *Statistical Bulletin*, vol. 67, No. 4, (Oct.–Dec. 1986), 12.
[23]*Ibid.*, 13–17.
[24]The Boston Women's Health Book Collective, 631.
[25]"Family Planning and Reproductive Health Care: The Need for Clinical Services."
[26]The Boston Women's Health Book Collective, 619.
[27]*Ibid.*, 627.
[28]Metropolitan Life Insurance Company, *Statistical Bulletin*.

[29]The Boston Women's Health Book Collective, 55–56.

[30]*Ibid.*, 327.

[31]"Family Planning and Reproductive Health Care: The Need for Clinical Services."

[32]The Boston Women's Health Book Collective, 336.

[33]"Suicide," *Encyclopaedia Britannica*, 1986, vol. 11, 359.

[34]The Boston Women's Health Book Collective, 101.

[35]U.S. Department of Commerce, Bureau of the Census, *Statistical Abstract of the United States, 1992*, Table No. 102.

[36]U.S. Department of Commerce, Bureau of the Census, *Statistical Abstract of the United States, 1988*, Table No. 104.

[37]U.S. Department of Commerce, Bureau of the Census, *Statistical Abstract of the United States, 1993*, Table No. 114.

[38]*Ibid.*, Table No. 112.

CRIME

[1]Georgette Bennett, *Crimewarps, The Future of Crime in America* (New York: Anchor Books, 1987), quote on book jacket.

[2]U.S. Department of Justice, *Uniform Crime Reports for the United States 1991* (Washington, D.C.), 16.

[3]Helen Tierney, ed., *Women's Studies Encyclopedia, Volume I, Views from the Sciences* (Westport, Conn.: Greenwood Press, 1989), 288.

[4]Bennett, 31.

[5]Frank Browning and John Gerassi, *The American Way of Crime* (New York: G. P. Putnam's Sons, 1989), 133.

[6]Timothy J. Flanagan and Kathleen Maguire, eds., *Bureau of Justice Statistics Sourcebook of Criminal Justice Statistics—1991* (Albany: State University of New York, 1992), Table 3.19.

[7]*Uniform Crime Reports for the United States 1991*, 16.

[8]Tierney, 35–37.

[9]*Ibid.*, 107.

[10]The Boston Women's Health Book Collective, 131–135.

[11]*Ibid.*, 137.

[12]Donna Jackson, *How to Make the World a Better Place for Women in Five Minutes a Day* (New York: Hyperion, 1992), 53–54.

[13]Neil Malamuth, "Rape Proclivity Among Men," *Journal of Social Issues*, 37 (1981): 138–157.

[14]Tierney, 315–317.

[15]Jackson, 59.

[16]Tierney, 82–83.

[17]*Uniform Crime Reports for the United States 1991*, 24.

POLITICS

[1]Linda Witt, Karen M. Paget, and Glenna Matthews, *Running As a Woman, Gender and Power in American Politics* (New York: The Free Press, 1994), xiii.

[2]Donna Jackson, *How to Make the World a Better Place for Women in Five Minutes a Day* (New York: Hyperion, 1992), 110.

[3]Witt, 4.

[4]*Ibid.*, 8.

[5]Dorothy W. Cantor and Toni Bernay, *Women in Power, The Secrets of Leadership* (Boston: Houghton Mifflin Company, 1992), 7.

[6]Witt, 31.

[7]National Women's Political Caucus, *National Directory of Women Elected Officials* (Washington D.C.), 18.

[8]Witt, 6.

[9]*Ibid.*, 88.

BIBLIOGRAPHY FOR MAPS

DEMOGRAPHICS

"The Population of Women Through Time"
U.S. Department of Commerce, Bureau of the Census. *Historical Statistics of the United States, Colonial Times to 1970*. Washington, D.C., 1975. Table A91-104.
U.S. Department of Commerce, Bureau of the Census. *1981 Census Population Profile of the United States*. Table 3.5.
"The Most Populous Sex"
U.S. Department of Commerce, Bureau of the Census. *1990 Census of Population General Population Characteristics United States*. CP-1-1. Table 282.
"Women vs. Men"
Ibid., Table 262.
"Women vs. Men in Major Cities"
U.S. Department of Commerce, Bureau of the Census. *1990 Census of Population General Population Characteristics Urbanized Areas*. CP-1-1C. Table 14.
"Women Minorities (Non-Hispanic)"
U.S. Department of Commerce, Bureau of the Census. *1990 Census of Population and Housing Summary*. CD-ROM 1C.
"Hispanic Women"
Ibid.
"White Women"
Ibid.
"Women Minorities in Major Cities (Non-Hispanic)"

U.S. Department of Commerce, Bureau of the Census. *1990 Census of Population General Population Characteristics Urbanized Areas*. CP-1-1C.
"Hispanic Women in Major Cities"
Ibid., Table 14.
U.S. Department of Commerce, Bureau of the Census. *Historical Statistics of the United States, Colonial Times to 1970*. 1975. Table A119-134.
"Population Pyramids Through Time"
U.S. Department of Commerce, Bureau of the Census. *Population Profile of the United States*. Population Characteristics Series P-20. no. 363. Table 4.
"Population Pyramid 1990"
U.S. Department of Commerce, Bureau of the Census. *1990 Census of Population General Population Characteristics United States*. CP-1-1. Table 262.
"Childhood"
U.S. Department of Commerce, Bureau of the Census. *1990 Census of Population and Housing Summary*. CD-ROM 1C.
"Childbearing Years"
Ibid.
"The Middle Years"
Ibid.
"The Elderly"
Ibid.
"Median Age Through Time"
U.S. Department of Commerce, Bureau of the Census. *Historical*

Statistics of the United States, Colonial Times to 1970. 1975. Table A143-157.

U.S. Department of Commerce, Bureau of the Census. *1990 Census of Population General Population Characteristics United States.* CP-1-1. Table 262.

"Median Age Women vs. Men"

U.S. Department of Commerce, Bureau of the Census. *1990 Census of Population General Population Characteristics United States.* CP-1-1. Table 262.

"Median Age"

Ibid., Table 262.

"Urban vs. Rural"

U.S. Department of Commerce, Bureau of the Census. *1990 Census of Population and Housing Summary.* CD-ROM 1C.

EDUCATION

"Literacy"

Mullis, Ina V. S. , J. R. Campbell, and A. E. Farstrup. *Reading Report Card for the Nation and States.* Washington, D.C.: Educational Testing Services, National Center for Educational Statistics, Report 23-ST06, 1993. Tables 3.5 and 3.6.

"High School Graduates"

U.S. Department of Commerce, Bureau of the Census. *1990 Equal Employment Opportunity.* CD-ROM EEO.

"Women Minorities High School Graduates"

Ibid.

"High School Dropouts 1987"

Center for Education Statistics, *Who Drops Out of High School? Findings from High School and Beyond.* Washington, D.C., 1987.

"Enrollment in Colleges and Universities"

U.S. Department of Commerce, Bureau of the Census. *Statistical Abstract of the United States.* Washington, D.C., 1993. Table 264.

"Women's Colleges"

College Entrance Examination Board. *The College Handbook, 1992.* New York, 1991.

"Women's Studies Programs, 1993"

College Entrance Examination Board. *Index of Majors, 1992.* New York, 1993.

"College Graduates"

U.S. Department of Commerce, Bureau of the Census. *1990 Equal Employment Opportunity.* CD-ROM EEO.

"Women Minorities With a Bachelor's Degree"

Ibid.

"Post-Graduate Degrees"

Ibid.

"Women Minorities With a Post-Graduate Degree"

Ibid.

"Distribution of Degree Specialization of Women and Men"

Commission on Professionals in Science and Technology. *Professional Women and Minorities.* Washington, D.C., 1989.

"Elementary School Teachers"

National Education Association. *1992–93 Estimates of School Statistics.* Washington, D.C., 1993.

"Secondary School Teachers"

Ibid.,Table 6.

"Women Faculty"

U.S. Equal Opportunity Employment Commission. *Job Patterns for Women in Higher Education 1993.* Washington, D.C., 1993.

"Women Minority Faculty in Colleges and Universities"

Ibid., Table 1.

EMPLOYMENT

"Labor Force Through Time"

U.S. Department of Commerce, Bureau of the Census. *Historical Statistics of the United States, Colonial Times to 1970.* Washington, D.C., 1975. Series D29-41.

"Women in the Labor Force"

U.S. Department of Labor, Bureau of Labor Statistics. *Geographic Profile of Employment and Unemployment 1990.* Washington, D.C., 1991. Bulletin 2381, Table 12.

"Working Women"

U.S. Department of Commerce, Bureau of the Census. *1990 Census of Population and Housing, Summary Social, Economic, and Housing Characteristics United States.* CPH-5-1, Table 3.

"Women in the Labor Force in Major Cities"
> U.S. Department of Labor, Bureau of Labor Statistics. *Geographic Profile of Employment and Unemployment 1990*. Washington, D.C., 1991. Bulletin 2381.

"Unemployment in Major Cities"
> *Ibid.*, Table 23.

"Full-Time vs. Part-Time Employment"
> *Ibid.*, Table 13.

"Working Mothers Through Time"
> *The 1992 Information Please Almanac*. Boston: Houghton Mifflin Co., 1992, p. 54.

"Employed Mothers"
> U.S. Department of Commerce, Bureau of the Census. *1990 Census of Population, Population Characteristics United States*. CD-ROM STF3C.

"Two-Income Families"
> *Ibid.*

"Two- & Three-Income Families"
> *Ibid.*

"Median Income"
> U.S. Department of Commerce, Bureau of the Census. *Social and Economic Characteristics*. CP-2-2 to CP-1-52, Alabama–Wyoming. Table 3.

"Median Earnings Through Time Women vs. Men"
> *The 1992 Information Please Almanac*. Boston: Houghton Mifflin Co., 1992, p. 57.

"Poverty Level"
> Hoffman, Mark, ed. *The World Almanac and Book of Facts*. New York: Pharos Books, 1993, p. 395.

"Consumer Price Index"
> *The 1992 Information Please Almanac*. Boston: Houghton Mifflin Co., 1992, p. 43.

"Minimum Wage"
> Hoffman, Mark, ed. *The World Almanac and Book of Facts*. New York: Pharos Books, 1993, p. 154.

"Women in Poverty"
> U.S. Department of Commerce, Bureau of the Census. *1990 Census of Population Characteristics United States*. CD-ROM STF3C.

"Racial Distribution of Women in Poverty"
> *Ibid.*

"Women on Social Security"
> U.S. Department of Health and Human Services. *Annual Statistical Supplement*. Social Security Bulletin, Washington, D.C., 1991. Table 5.J5.

"Child Day Care 1987"
> U.S. Department of Commerce, Bureau of the Census. *State and Metropolitan Area Data Book, 1992*. Washington, D.C., Table E.

"Selected State Laws Affecting Women in Private Industry, 1992"
> U.S. Department of Labor, Women's Bureau. *Times of Change: 1993 Handbook of Women Workers*. Washington, D.C., 1993. Table VII-2.

"Women in Management"
> U.S. Equal Opportunity Commission. *Job Patterns for Minorities and Women in Private Industry, 1990*. Washington, D.C., 1991. Table 2.

"Women-Owned Businesses"
> U.S. Department of Commerce, Bureau of the Census. *Statistical Abstract of the United States 1993*. Washington, D.C. Table 841.

"Volunteer Work"
> U.S. Department of Labor, Bureau of Labor Statistics. *Geographic Profile of Employment and Unemployment 1990*. Washington, D.C., 1991. Bulletin 2381, Table 13.

FAMILY

"Women Living Alone"
> U.S. Department of Commerce, Bureau of the Census. *1990 Census of Population General Population Characteristics United States*. CP-1-1.

"Single Women"
> *Ibid.*, Table 263.

"Married Women"
> *Ibid.*

"Single Women vs. Single Men"
> *Ibid.*

"Single Women vs. Single Men in Major Cities"
> U.S. Department of Commerce, Bureau of the Census. *1990 Census of Population General Population Characteristics Urbanized Areas*. CP-1-1C, Table 24.

"Common-Law Marriage and Cohabitation"

Council of State Governments. *Book of the States, 1992–3.* Lexington, Ky., 1993.

"Sexual Intercourse"
Guggenheim, M., and A. Sussman. *The Rights of Young People.* Toronto: Bantam Books, 1985.

"Teenage Marriage and Age of Consent"
U.S. Department of Commerce, Bureau of the Census. *1990 Census of Population General Population Characteristics.* CP-1-2 to CP-1-52, Alabama–Wyoming, Table 37.
Council of State Governments. *Book of the States, 1992–3.* Lexington, Ky., 1993.

"Marriage/Divorce Rates"
The 1992 Information Please Almanac. Boston: Houghton Mifflin, 1992. p. 806.

"Marriages"
Van Son, V. *CQ's State Fact Finder.* Washington, D.C.: Congressional Quarterly, Inc., 1992.
U.S. Department of Commerce, Bureau of the Census. *Statistical Abstract of the United States 1993.* Washington, D.C., 1993.

"Divorces"
Ibid., Table 147.

"Marriage vs. Divorce"
Ibid.

"Separated Women"
U.S. Department of Commerce, Bureau of the Census. *1990 Census of Population General Population Characteristics United States.* CP-1-1, Table 263.

"Divorced Women"
Ibid., Table 263.

"Average Duration of Marriage Before Divorce"
U.S. Department of Health and Human Services, Center for Disease Control. *Vital Statistics of the United States Marriage and Divorce.* 1987, vol. 3, Table 2-11.

"Divorces with Children"
Ibid.

"Laws Regulating Child Support and Custody"
"Family Law in Fifty States," *Family Law Quarterly.* vol. XXV, no. 4 (Winter 1992), Tables IX & X.

"Spousal Support"
Ibid., Tables IV, V & VII.

"Widows"
U.S. Department of Commerce, Bureau of the Census. *1990 Cen-*

sus of Population General Population Characteristics United States. CP-1-1, Table 263.

"Women in Nursing Homes"
U.S. Department of Commerce, Bureau of the Census. *1990 Census of Population General Population Characteristics.* CP-1-2 to CP-1-52, Alabama–Wyoming, Table 38.

"Fertility Ratio"
U.S. Department of Commerce, Bureau of the Census. *1990 Census of Population General Population Characteristics United States.* CP-1-1, Table 262.

"Birth Rate"
U.S. Department of Health and Human Services, Center for Disease Control. *Vital Statistics of the United States, Natality.* Washington, D.C., 1988, vol. 1, Table 1-47.

"Births to Unmarried Women"
Ibid., Table 1-36.

"Teenage Pregnancy/Birth/Abortion Rates"
"Family Planning Perspectives," *Teenage Abortion, Birth and Pregnancy Statistics by State, 1988*, vol. 25, no. 3, May/June, 1993.

"Maternity Homes for Unwed Mothers"
U.S. Department of Commerce, Bureau of the Census. *1990 Census of Population General Population Characteristics.* CP-1-2 to CP-1-52, Alabama–Wyoming, Table 38.

"Births to Older Mothers"
U.S. Department of Health and Human Services, Center for Disease Control. *Vital Statistics of the United States, Natality.* Washington, D.C., 1988, vol. 1, Table 1-60.

"Married-Couple Families"
U.S. Department of Commerce, Bureau of the Census. *1990 Census of Population General Population Characteristics United States.* CP-1-1, Table 275.

"Female-Headed Households"
Ibid., Table 263.

"Female-Headed Family Households (No Husband Present)"
Ibid.

"Children in Female-Headed Households (No Father Present)"
Ibid.
U.S. Department of Commerce, Bureau of the Census. *1990 Census of Population and Housing Summary.* CD-ROM 1C.

"Homeless Women"
U.S. Department of Commerce, Bureau of the Census. *1990 Cen-*

sus of Population General Population Characteristics. CP-1-2 to
CP-1-52, Alabama–Wyoming, Table 38.
"The Homeless in Major Cities"
    The Information Series on Current Topics. *Homeless in Amer-
ica: How It Could Happen Here.* Texas: Information Plus, 1991.

HEALTH

"Life Expectancy Through Time"
    Hoffman, Mark, ed. *The World Almanac and Book of Facts.* New
York: Pharos Books, 1993, p. 956.
"Life Expectancy 1979–1981"
    Metropolitan Life Insurance Company. *Statistical Bulletin,* vol.
67, no. 4, Oct–Dec. 1986, pp. 14–15.
"Sedentary Lifestyle"
    U.S. Department of Health and Human Services, Center for Dis-
ease Control Surveillance Summaries. *Morbidity and Mortality
Weekly Report,* vol. 39, no. SS-2, June, 1990, Table 2.
"Obesity"
    Ibid., Table 1.
"Cholesterol"
    U.S. Department of Health and Human Services, Center for Dis-
ease Control. *Morbidity and Mortality Weekly Report,* June 30,
1990, Tables 10 & 12.
"Death from Heart Disease"
    U.S. Department of Health and Human Services, Center for Dis-
ease Control. *Vital Statistics of the United States Morbidity,* vol.
2, Washington, D.C., 1988, Table 8-6.
"Death from Cancer"
    Ibid.
"Death from Breast Cancer"
    Ibid.
"Death from Cancer of the Genital Organs"
    Ibid.
"Death from Pregnancy and Childbirth"
    Ibid.
"Death from Chronic Liver Disease and Cirrhosis"
    Ibid.
"AIDS Through Time"

U.S. Department of Commerce, Bureau of the Census. *Statistical
Abstract of the United States 1993.* Washington, D.C., 1993.
Table 192.
"AIDS"
    Stine, G. J. *Acquired Immune Deficiency Syndrome.* Englewood
Cliffs, N.J.: Prentice Hall, 1993. Figs. 8-3A & 8-4A.
"Children Born with AIDS"
    Ibid., Table 8-8.
"Motor Vehicle Deaths"
    U.S. Department of Health and Human Services, Center for Dis-
ease Control. *Vital Statistics of the United States Morbidity.*
Washington, D.C., 1988, vol. 2. Table 8-6.
"Driving While Intoxicated"
    U.S. Department of Health and Human Services, Center for Dis-
ease Control. *Morbidity and Mortality Weekly Report.* Washing-
ton, D.C., June, 30 1990.
"Physicians"
    U.S. Department of Health and Human Services, Health Man-
power Bureau. *Characteristics of Physicians.* Washington, D.C.,
1993. Table C-3.
"Suicide"
    U.S. Department of Health and Human Services, Center for Dis-
ease Control. *Vital Statistics of the United States Morbidity.*
Washington, D.C., 1988, vol. 2. Table 8-6.
"Women in Mental Institutions"
    U.S. Department of Commerce, Bureau of the Census. *1990 Cen-
sus of Population General Population Characteristics.* CP-1-2 to
CP-1-52, Alabama–Wyoming. Table 38.
"Smoking"
    U.S. Department of Health and Human Services, Center for Dis-
ease Control Surveillance Summaries. *Morbidity and Mortality
Weekly Report.* Washington, D.C., vol. 39, no. SS-2, June, 1990.
Table 3.
"Heavy Drinking"
    Ibid., Table 7.
"Drug or Alcohol Halfway Houses"
    U.S. Department of Commerce, Bureau of the Census. *1990 Cen-
sus of Population General Population Characteristics.* CP-1-2 to
CP-1-52, Alabama–Wyoming. Table 38.
"Laws Regulating Abortions"
    The Naral Foundation. *Who Decides? A State-by-State Review of
Abortion Rights.* Washington, D.C., 1992.

"Public Funding"
"Family Planning Perspectives," *Public Funding of Contraceptive, Sterilization and Abortion Services, Fiscal Year 1990*, vol. 23, no. 5, Sept./Oct. 1991. Tables 1–3.
"Abortion Rate 1988"
U.S. Department of Commerce, Bureau of the Census. *Statistical Abstract of the United States 1993*. Washington, D.C., 1993. Table 102.
"Change in the Abortion Rate 1973–1988"
Ibid., Table 102.
U.S. Department of Commerce, Bureau of the Census. *Statistical Abstract of the United States 1992*. Washington, D.C., 1992. Table 104.
"Change in the Number of Abortion Providers from 1985 to 1988"
The Naral Foundation. *Who Decides? A State-by-State Review of Abortion Rights*. Washington, D.C., 1992.
"Place of Abortion vs. State of Residence"
Henshaw, S. K., L. M. Koonen, and J. C. Smith,"Characteristics of U.S. Women Having Abortions, 1987," *Family Planning Perspectives*, vol. 23, no. 2, March/April, 1991. Table 6.
"Low Birth Weight 1987–1989"
U.S. Department of Health and Human Services. *Health United States and Population Profile 1991*. Hyattsville, Md., 1992. Table 10.
"Infant Mortality"
U.S. Department of Health and Human Services, Center for Disease Control. *Vital Statistics of the United States: Morbidity*. Washington, D.C., 1989, vol. 2.
"Infant Mortality by Race"
Ibid., Table 8-2.

CRIME

"Abused Women"
U.S. Department of Commerce, Bureau of the Census. *1990 Census of Population General Population Characteristics*. CP-1-2 to CP-1-52, Alabama–Wyoming. Table 38.
"Rape Rate Through Time"
U.S. Department of Justice, Bureau of Justice Statistics. *Source-book of Criminal Justice Statistics, 1991*. Washington, D.C., Table 3.127.
"Rape Rate"
Ibid., Table 4.4.
"Rape Rate in Major Cities"
U.S. Department of Justice. *Crime in the United States, 1991*. Uniform Crime Reports, Washington, D.C.
"Rape Clearance Rate"
U.S. Department of Justice, Bureau of Justice Statistics. *Source-book of Criminal Justice Statistics, 1991*. Washington, D.C., Table 4.4.
"Minors Arrested for Rape"
Ibid.
"Marital Rape Laws 1985"
National Center on Women and Family Law. *Marital Rape Exemption Chart: State by State Analysis*. New York, 1985.
"Homicide"
U.S. Department of Health and Human Services, Center for Disease Control. *Vital Statistics of the United States: Morbidity*. Washington, D.C., 1988, vol. 2. Table 8-6.
"Women Convicted of Federal Crimes 1985"
Administrative Office of the U.S. Courts. *Federal Offenders in the U.S. Courts*. Washington, D.C., 1985. Table 3.
"Percentage of Homicides Committed by Women"
U.S. Department of Justice, Bureau of Justice Statistics. *Source-book of Criminal Justice Statistics, 1991*. Washington, D.C.
"Prison Population"
U.S. Department of Commerce, Bureau of the Census. *Statistical Abstract of the United States 1992*. Washington, D.C., 1992. Table 346.
U.S. Department of Justice, Bureau of Justice Statistics. *Correctional Populations in the United States*. Washington, D.C., 1990. Table 5.8.
"Racial Distribution of the Prison Population"
U.S. Department of Justice, Bureau of Justice Statistics. *Correctional Populations in the United States*. Washington, D.C., 1990. Table 5.8.
"Juvenile Offenders Under Supervision"
American Correctional Association. *Directory of Juvenile and Adult Correctional Departments, Institutions, Agencies and Paroling Authorities, 1993*. College Park, Md., 1993.
"Women's Correctional Institutions"

Ibid.
"Security Arrangements 1993"
   Ibid.
"Women on Death Row"
   The 1992 Information Please Almanac. Boston: Houghton Mifflin, 1992, p. 808.
   U.S. Department of Justice, Bureau of Justice Statistics. *Correctional Populations in the United States.* Washington, D.C., 1990. Table 7.3.
   U.S. Department of Justice, Bureau of Justice Statistics. *Sourcebook of Criminal Justice Statistics, 1991.* Washington, D.C. Table 6.91.
"Correctional Officers in Adult Systems"
   U.S. Department of Justice, Bureau of Justice Statistics. *Sourcebook of Criminal Justice Statistics, 1991.* Washington, D.C. Tables 1.104 & 1.106.

POLITICS

"The Right to Vote"
   Paulin, C. O., and J. K. Wright, eds. *Atlas of Historical Geography of the United States.* Washington, D.C.: The Carnegie Institution, 1932.
"Democratic and Republican Committees 1991"
   National Women's Political Caucus. *National Directory of Women Elected Officials.* Washington, D.C., 1992.
"Women in Politics"
   Ibid.
"Women as Candidates"
   Ibid.
"State Legislatures 1991"
   Ibid.
"Positions of Legislatures and Governors on Keeping Abortion Legal"
   The Naral Foundation. *Who Decides? A State-by-State Review of Abortion Rights.* Washington, D.C., 1992.

"Congress Past—The House of Representatives"
   National Women's Political Caucus. *National Directory of Women Elected Officials.* Washington, D.C., 1992.
"Congress Past—The Senate"
   Ibid.
"The 103rd Congress 1993"
   Ibid.
   Brownson, A. L., ed. *1993 Congressional Staff Directory/1.* Mt. Vernon, Va.: Staff Directories, Ltd., 1993.
"Mayors 1991"
   National Women's Political Caucus. *National Directory of Women Elected Officials.* Washington, D.C., 1992.
"Governors"
   Ibid.
   Barone, M., and G. Ujifusa. *The Almanac of American Politics, 1994.* Washington, D.C.: National Journal, 1993.
"State Officials"
   National Women's Political Caucus. *National Directory of Women Elected Officials.* Washington, D.C., 1992.
"Women Cabinet Appointees"
   The 1992 Information Please Almanac. Boston: Houghton Mifflin, 1992, pp. 641–645.
   Sicherman, B., and C. H. Greed, eds. *Notable American Women: The Modern Period.* Cambridge: Belknap Press of Harvard University Press, 1980.
   Who's Who of American Women, 1993–94. New Providence, N.J.: Reed Reference Publishing Co., 1993.
"First Ladies"
   Dictionary of American Biography. New York: Charles Scribner's Sons, 1933. S.V.
   National Cyclopedia of American Biography. Clifton, N.J.: James T. White & Company, 1984. S.V.
   1979 Hammond Almanac. Maplewood, N.J.: Hammond Almanac, Inc., 1978.
   Notable Names in American History: A Tabulated Register. Clifton, N.J.: James T. White & Company, 1973.
   The International Who's Who 1993–94. London: Europa Publications, 1993.

SUGGESTIONS FOR FURTHER READING

The Boston Women's Health Book Collective. *The New Our Bodies, Ourselves.* New York: Touchstone, 1992.

Cantor, Dorothy, and Toni Bernay. *Women in Power: The Secrets of Leadership.* Boston: Houghton Mifflin, 1992.

Gastril, Raymond D. *Cultural Regions of the United States.* Seattle: University of Washington Press, 1975.

Jackson, Donna. *How to Make the World a Better Place for Women in Five Minutes a Day.* New York: Hyperion, 1992.

Schroeder, Pat. *Champion of the Great American Family.* New York: Random House, 1989.

Sidel, Ruth. *Women and Children Last: The Plight of Poor Women in Affluent America.* New York: Viking, 1986.

Witt, Linda, Karen Paget, and Glenna Matthews. *Running As a Woman: Gender and Power in American Politics.* New York: The Free Press, 1994.

INDEX